EDITH WHARTON ABROAD

EDITH WHARTON ABROAD

Selected Travel Writings, 1888–1920

Edited by

Sarah Bird Wright

Chivers Press • Thorndike Press
Bath, Avon, England • Thorndike, Maine USA

This Large Print edition is published by Chivers Press, England, and by Thorndike Press, USA.

Published in 1996 in the U.K. by arrangement with Robert Hale Limited.

Published in 1996 in the U.S. by arrangement with St. Martin's Press, Inc.

U.K. Hardcover ISBN 0–7451–49073 (Chivers Large Print)
U.K. Softcover   ISBN 0–7451–49193 (Camden Large Print)
U.S. Softcover   ISBN 0–7862–06055 (General Series Edition)

The text of this Large Print edition is unabridged.

Other aspects of the book may vary from the original edition.

Set in 16pt. New Times Roman

Printed in Great Britain on acid-free paper.

British Library Cataloguing in Publication Data available

Library of Congress Cataloging-in-Publication Data

Wharton, Edith, 1862–1937
   Edith Wharton abroad : selected travel writings, 1888–1920 / Edith Wharton : edited by Sarah Bird Wright. 160
      p. cm.
   ISBN 0–7862–0605–5 (lg. print : sc)   ✓
  ✓1. Wharton, Edith. 1862–1937—Journeys.   2. Travelers' writings, American.   3. Voyages and travels.   I. Wright, Sarah Bird.   II. Title
[PS3545.H16A6   1996b]
818'.5203—dc20
                                                              95–47737

PERMISSIONS

The selections entitled 'North Africa,' 'Mount Athos,' and 'Chios and Smyrna,' from *The Cruise of the Vanadis*, are reprinted by permission of the author and the Watkins/Loomis Agency, and by courtesy of Claudine Lesage Sterne (Presses de L'UFR Clerc Université Picardie). The selections entitled 'Villas Near Rome' and 'Villas of Venetia,' from *Italian Villas and Their Gardens*; 'A Midsummer Week's Dream' and 'Picturesque Milan,' from *Italian Backgrounds*; 'From Rouen to Fontainebleau' and 'Paris to Poitiers,' from *A Motor-Flight Through France*; 'In Argonne' and 'In Lorraine and the Vosges,' from *Fighting France from Dunkerque to Belfort*; and 'Taste' and 'The New Frenchwoman' from *French Ways and Their Meaning* are reprinted by permission of the author's estate and the Watkins/Loomis Agency. The selection entitled 'Harems and Ceremonies' is reprinted with the permission of Scribner, an imprint of Simon & Schuster, from *In Morocco* by Edith Wharton, copyright 1920 Charles Scribner's Sons. It first appeared in the *Yale Review*, 1919.

The quotation from the Scribners/Edith Wharton correspondence at Princeton University Library is published with

For Mary Ann Caws

To whom writing is life and
'nothing is impracticable,' as Henry James
said of Edith Wharton

CONTENTS

LIST OF ILLUSTRATIONS

ACKNOWLEDGEMENTS

In compiling an anthology of Edith Wharton's travel writings, I have incurred debts to many people whose generous extension of time and knowledge has been invaluable. One of my more pleasant editorial tasks is to acknowledge their assistance.

In the course of doctoral work in the field of travel literature at the College of William and Mary, Williamsburg, Virginia, I discovered Wharton's works of travel. I believed them to have extraordinary charm and vitality, with a timeless quality allowing them to escape entirely the charge of being 'dated' that might legitimately be aimed at many travel books published between 1904 and 1920. Yet little scholarly attention had been paid to them and they were not widely known to the public. I chose her travel writings as the subject of my dissertation, now nearing completion, and came to believe an anthology of these texts would generate new interest in Wharton's work and in the genre of travel literature.

Richard S. Lowry of the English Department at William and Mary, has nurtured, reshaped, and consolidated my concepts of Wharton and has discussed many problems with me; the introduction and the notes have profited substantially from his

xi

suggestions. Robert A. Gross, Director of the American Studies program at William and Mary, has encouraged my work on Edith Wharton's travel writings, as have Scott Donaldson, Elsa Nettels, and Esther Lanigan of the William and Mary English Department.

Among those exerting particular influence upon this book is Mary Suzanne Schriber, the first critic to explore the implications of Wharton's travel writing. I am grateful not only for her inspiration and encouragement regarding Wharton, but also for her insights within the larger field of travel writing by American women during the nineteenth and twentieth centuries. I am also greatly indebted to Shari Benstock, whose *Women of the Left Bank* had already shed much light on the years of Wharton's expatriation, and whose recent biography of her has enlarged my knowledge of her friendships, writings, and life abroad.

Beverly Peterson and Nancy Parrish have extended, over several years, their sage counsel and bountiful help. My close friend Martha Edmonds has been infinitely sympathetic and supportive, always on the alert for Wharton exhibits, reviews, and publications. Joy Barnes has given generous help with Latin and classics in general. Estelle Crump and Robert Harden have been of great help in both large and small ways.

I am most grateful to Brewer Eddy of Technology Services of the College of William and Mary, who patiently tutored me in the intricacies and pitfalls of the laser scanner.

My abundant thanks are extended to Rebecca Cape of the Lilly Library, Indiana University, who assisted with the early photographs of Edith Wharton, and to Margaret Sherry of the Scribners Archive, Firestone Library, Princeton University, who, along with her staff, provided encouragement and guidance in Wharton research at Princeton. I am indebted also to the staff of the Beinecke Library, Yale University, for allowing me to use the resources of the library, particularly the Edith Wharton Collection. Scott Marshall of The Mount has assisted with research and been most supportive.

The selections from the works of Edith Wharton are included by kind permission of William Royall Tyler, owner of the Edith Wharton estate; my thanks go also to Gloria Loomis, literary agent of that estate, to Lily Oei of Watkins-Loomis, to Edith Golub of the Macmillan Publishing Company, and to the Rhoda Weyr Literary Agency.

In the course of the project, I came to know Claudine Lesage of the University of Amiens, France, who generously recounted the story of her discovery of the manuscript of *The Cruise of the Vanadis* and provided a *xerox* copy of it; I count this transatlantic friendship as one of the greatest rewards of my Wharton labors.

My quasi-immersion into the milieu of Edith

Wharton's travels as well as her texts was greatly enlivened by my long-time friends Margaret Crowe Hatcher, Mary Ann Caws, and Shirley Uber. Margaret and Mary Ann accompanied me in the summer of 1992 in retracing many of Wharton's footsteps in Paris, the Italian lakes, Florence, Venice, the Brenta Riviera, Parma, Provence, and Hyères. Mary Ann also rescued me from calamitous mis-translations and identified quotations from French, Italian, and German literature. Shirley and I traveled to Lenox, Massachusetts, in the summer of 1993, visiting The Mount and attending dramatizations of Wharton's work. Two other close friends from our 'salad days' in Boston have contributed greatly to the project: Carolyn Woznick has offered perceptive insights regarding permissions, and George Ursul has kept me posted for many months on New England and Wharton studies.

I am very pleased to thank Ilse Andrews, of the Goethe Institute, Boston, who, both promptly and astutely, identified a quotation from Goethe's *Venetian Epigrams*. Kelly Joyce and Randy Lakeman led me to the Goethe Institute and were, thus, instrumental in solving a long-standing puzzle.

The assistance and support of my agent, Susan Urstadt, who was enthusiastic about the idea from the beginning, have been invaluable. And I take particular pleasure in thanking my editor, Jennifer Farthing of St Martin's, for her tactful editing, informed assistance, and resourcefulness.

My son, Alexander Grant Wright, has shared his expertise in Internet research (of special value was his downloading of the Index of the Edith Wharton Collection at Yale, which saved many hours there) and generously devoted Cambridge lunch hours to verifying sources in the Harvard libraries. Gratitude of many years duration is owed my husband, Lewis Wright, who has been unfailingly supportive of my work on the anthology, who searched out rare copies of Wharton's travel works, and who exhibited great forbearance about my many domestic shortcomings.

GLOSSARY OF FOREIGN WORDS AND PHRASES
(as they appear in Edith Wharton's texts)

à cordon	Fr., balustrade made of thick, twisted rope
'à coups de crosse'	Fr., with blows from rifle butt-ends
babouches	Ar., Oriental slippers of a type without heels
barocchismo	It., spirit of the Baroque
basse-cour	Fr., poultry-yard
batterie de cuisine	Fr., complete set of kitchen utensils
berrichonnes	Fr., natives of the Berry region
bled	Ar., rural area (hinterland behind a fertile populated area)
bonne	Fr., servant
bosco	It., wood, forest
boschi	It., groves, thickets
bosquets	Fr., groves, thickets
bottegha	It., shop
bravi	It., bullies, cut-throats
Caïd	Ar., leader, commander of a region
campanili	It., bell-towers
carriole	Fr., small covered carriage
carte du Tendre	Fr., map of sentimental love (as used in French seventeenth-century highly polished and cultivated circles)

canvasses	Turk., police officers
Certosa	It., Carthusian monastery
chasseurs-à-pied	Fr., light infantry
château d'eau	Fr., reservoir, water tower
château-fort	Fr., medieval citadel
chemin de ronde	Fr., walkway around the ramparts of a fortress
cinque-cento	It., sixteenth-century
clocheton	Fr., bell-turret
comme une bête	Fr., as an animal, a dumb creature
commedia dell'arte	It., improvisatory comedy of skill, based on a pre-arranged theme, with stock characters such as Harlequin, Pierrot, and Columbine; originated at Bergamo, Italy, in the sixteenth century (see introduction)
corps de bâtiment	Fr., main building
cour d'honneur	Fr., main quadrangle
È stupendo! È stupendo!	It., marvelous, wonderful
en berceau	Fr., arbor, bower
estafettes	Fr., couriers, express messengers
ferronnière	Fr., ornamental headdress (iron chain with jewel)
galbe	Fr., graceful shape or outline (slightly swelling)
gandourah	Ar., sleeveless shirtlike garment
gens du pays	Fr., people of the region

grande coquette	Fr., leading coquette (great flirt)
grande salle	Fr., large room, gallery
grisailles	Fr., decorative paintings in gray monochrome
'Haute Mère-Dieu'	Fr., 'Noble Mother of God'
haute ville	Fr., upper town
hauteur	Fr., haughty demeanor
infirmière major	Fr., chief hospital attendant
jardin anglais	Fr., English garden
jeu de tarots	Fr., game of tarots
laissez-passer	Fr., permit
maison de plaisance	Fr., country seat
manoirs	Fr., manor houses
marchande des quatre saisons	Fr., peddler, street merchant (of fruits and vegetables)
marmitons	Fr., cook's boys
médecin-chef	Fr., chief physician
mellah	Ar., Jewish quarter
mirador	Sp., enclosed balcony
mise en scène	Fr., stage set
mitrailleuse	Fr., machine-gun
'Monuments Funèbres'	Fr., tombstones
nargilehs	Turk., hookas, or small standing appliances for smoking tobacco
obus	Fr., artillery shell
odalisques	Fr., Turkish female slaves
paesi	It., villages, little towns
parterres de broderie	Fr., intricately patterned flower-beds

xix

'permis de séjour'	Fr., permission to reside
pfennig	Ger., one-hundredth part of a mark; i.e., less than a penny
piano nobile	It., main floor
Pickelhaube	Ger., spiked helmet
place	Fr., square, public area
pratique	Fr., 'get pratique' get out of quarantine
presepii	It., manger scenes
putti	It., cherubs
quattro-cento	It., fifteenth-century
rahat-loukoum	Turk., Turkish sweet-meat; one type is jelly-like or gummy candy cubes or rectangles with powdered sugar [Turkish delight]
rampe douce	Fr., gentle ramp
rilievi	It., reliefs
rispetti	It., respectful sentiments
ronds-points	Fr., traffic circles
'ces satanés Allemands'	Fr., 'these devilish Germans'
scudi	It., pl. of scudo, silver coin used from 17th to 19th century; value roughly equivalent to one dollar.
sloughis	Ar., hounds, Persian greyhounds
sous-officiers	Fr., non-commissioned officers
stucchi	It., plaster figures
table d'hôte	Fr., guests sitting around the table
tapis vert	Fr., green carpet (metaphor for grass)

Taube	Ger., bird [here a metaphor for airplane]
théâtre d'eau	Fr., 'water theater' (ornamental fountains)
'tisanes'	Fr., herb tea
villeggiatura	It., country holidays, vacation season
villa suburbana	It., country house
ville de province	Fr., provincial town
villini	It., small country houses
voitures-de-place	Fr., hackney-carriages, carriages for hire
yataghans	Turk., long knives or short sabers, double-curved with no crosspiece

PREFACE

Edith Wharton's life of travel began in 1866 when at age four she accompanied her parents on a six-year tour of Europe that included extended residence in Rome and Paris. Her childhood experience in these beautiful cities—walks with her mother on the Palatine slopes above Rome and games with friends in the Tuileries of Paris—laid the groundwork for her lifelong love of Europe. But it was her father's desire to see the Moorish courtyards and fountains of Granada's ancient palace that made 'travel' synonymous with 'adventure.' Under the spell of Washington Irving's *Alhambra*, George Frederic Jones took his family on an arduous (and potentially dangerous) trip by horse-drawn carriage across Spain—a 'wild early pilgrimage' that gave his five-year-old daughter 'an incurable passion for the road' and left her with a jumble of sensations—jingling diligence bells, cracking whips and yelling muleteers, jabbering beggars, squalid posadas, a breakdown on a windswept sierra, and a taste for chocolate and olives.

Writing her memoirs almost seventy years later, Edith recalled that her father's copy of Washington Irving's *Alhambra,* spurred her desire to tell stories. Its closely printed pages, heavy black type, narrow margins, and rough-edged yellow sheets set her off 'full sail on the sea of dreams.' She paced the floor of hotel rooms, book in hand (often upside down, as she did not yet know how to read), 'making up' stories and turning the book's pages in rhythm to her own voice. Parents and nurses spied on her activities through keyholes, her mother trying to copy down the rush of words that spilled from the little redhaired girl.

Her 'passion' for travel and the 'obsession' to tell stories joined together to form the primary springboard of Edith Wharton's creativity. These activities often proceeded apace—travel providing the occasion (and the necessary leisure) to write. She crossed the Atlantic some sixty times, using the long days at sea to outline new writing projects or complete works-in-progress. Crossing Europe by carriage, train, or automobile, she wrote on a portable lapboard. The freshness and spontaneity of her travel writing owes much to this practice of writing en route.

Travel was never merely a pastime in Edith Wharton's life. With reading, it served as her primary means of education, enlarging the narrow circumference of Old New York to which she returned with her parents in 1872. Born with a quick eye, Edith experienced the world visually. Just as learning to read and write developed her natural inclination to the cadences of language, so did the varieties of landscape, gardens, and architecture she saw on her early travels educate her eye to the nuances of line, proportion, and balance. Edith Wharton's genius as novelist and travel writer lay in seeing her subject clearly and having at hand the words to express what she saw. She took the same care in finding the mot juste to render psychological states in her characters as she did to describe architecture and landscape.

Travel expanded Edith's horizons but it also tempered her responses. She did not 'ooh' and 'ah' at majestic mountains glimpsed from a train carriage in Switzerland or moonlit Aegean isles seen from a steam yacht. Instead, she translated these scenes into words, her discriminating eye testing the accuracy of each adjective and adverb and her ear measuring the rise and fall of syllables. Starting from Paris on her spring 1907 'motor-flight' into the French countryside with Henry James, she writes that it was the 'blandest of late March mornings, all April in the air, and the Seine fringing itself with a mist of yellowish willows.' She has captured in words that subtle, almost indescribable shift in Ile de France weather from March to April.

Later in the day, as her chauffeured motor-car sweeps through villages and passes Loire valley vineyards, she observes subtle changes in landscape and architecture and draws conclusions about French character from the physiognomy of faces glimpsed in doorways. If her eye is a camera, her voice—so high and clear in her writing—blends storytelling with cultural criticism. She sets scenes, provides historical background, offers opinions on everything from politics to cuisine, catalogs delays caused by bad weather and illness, and speculates on the private lives of the locals. As readers, we are not left behind as armchair observers to this motor-flight; we are participants in its adventure. She speaks to us as if we were seated next to her in the Panhard or at her side in the old walled garden 'full of spring flowers and clipped yews' in Montrejeau where the travellers enjoyed a 'gay repast.'

*　　　*　　　*

Edith Wharton's travel writing, always graced with literary and theatrical effects, carries with it the rich history of her reading. In *Italian Backgrounds* she enlivened the landscape with characters and costumes from the commedia dell'arte tradition; *In Morocco* echoes themes of Scheherazade in *Arabian nights*. In *A Motor-Flight Through France*, she recreates the camaraderie and adventure of a medieval pilgrimage. We hear echoes of Chaucer's *Canterbury Tales*, for example, when Edith pictures a rotund and quizzical Henry James gazing at the windows of Nohant, home of George Sand. Curious about the amorous adventures of this latter-day Wife of Bath, he muses: 'And in which of those rooms, I wonder, did George herself sleep?' Turning to Edith with a twinkling side glance, he asks: 'Though in which, indeed, in which indeed, my dear, did she not?'

The center of emotional gravity for the 1907 motor-flight (and for two other visits Edith made to the Berry region of France) was George Sand. Edith had packed in her book box several volumes of Sand's memoirs, *Histoire de ma vie*, and her Panhard motor (which James called a 'Vehicle of Passion') was christened 'George' in Sand's honor. For this trip especially, the 'motor-car ... restored the romance of travel,' as Edith claimed in the opening sentence of *A Motor-Flight*. Like George Sand, whose travels provided an escape route from an oppressive marriage, Edith Wharton measured her independence as a woman by travelling wherever and whenever she pleased.

From her first voyage to the Greek isles at age twenty-six, Edith visited terrains that Western women had rarely, if ever, entered. She prided herself on these unique experiences: a close-up view from the shoreline of Mount Athos (recounted in *The Cruise of the Vanadis*; a visit to a sultan's harem (*In Morocco*); an Allied officer's quarters, where she spent a winter night while delivering supplies to the Western front (*Fighting France*). On occasion, as in North Africa in 1914 when an intruder broke into her room during the night, her travels brought her close to danger. At other times, as when her car had to be lowered by ropes down a mountain pass in Italy, her travel adventures struck a comic note. At all times, however, travel was for Edith Wharton a means of pushing outward the boundaries of her universe. She travelled farther, faster, and in greater luxury than most women (or men) of her generation.

Luxurious accommodations and personal comforts were not always essential to Edith Wharton's mode of travel, however. When the pull of curiosity was strong enough she would endure any hardship to reach her goal. In spring 1894, at work on *Italian Backgrounds*, she undertook an arduous trip over mountainous back roads in an 'archaic little carriage' to see a group of terra-cotta religious figures at the Franciscan monastery of San Vivaldo. The trip was well worth its discomforts. On the basis of her research, Edith refuted the provenance of the figures and established that they were the work of Giovanni della Robbia—an attribution that still holds today. Even in the final years of her life, when her travels were often interrupted by bouts of illness and fatigue, she twice braved foul weather, bad roads, and questionable food and lodging to follow the route of St James to Santiago de Compostela.

Whatever its risks to Edith's health or the promise of rewards in new writing subjects, travel brought with it the lure of romance. Every trip followed a trajectory of desire for expanding horizons and experiences that she could not resist. This was never more the case than in the summer of 1909, when she and the American journalist William Morton Fullerton took a three-day car trip across Essex, accompanied by Henry James. Earlier that summer, and after more than a year of hesitation and self-scrutiny, she had consummated her love for Fullerton in a room at the Charing Cross Hotel in London. A grimy, noisy train station hotel was not the setting she would have chosen for this momentous event. She had hoped that their long-delayed tryst would take place in a country hotel in a 'green wood' somewhere in France. The Charing Cross Hotel had for Fullerton certain advantages—it was inexpensive and convenient (he was leaving on a trip to the United States the next day).

When Fullerton returned to England in mid-July, he surprised Edith at Lamb House, where she was visiting James. He proposed a motor trip—an unexpected request, since Fullerton, son of a poor family, felt uncomfortable in the luxurious accommodations of her car. But car travel allowed them to discover the hidden beauties of the Essex countryside and to stay at small inns. Bucolic scenes, filled with sunshine, birds, and roses by day and 'singing stars' by night, fueled the lovers' passion. If Henry James suspected Edith was playing George Sand to Fullerton's Frederic Chopin, he said nothing of it. Recognizing Edith's dissatisfaction in her marriage and knowing that Teddy Wharton was slipping into madness, James hoped Edith could find some brief measure of happiness.

Her joy in Fullerton was shortlived and not to be repeated. Among the 'parentheses of travel' that Edith sought out at every turn of the road, those three days and nights in summer 1909 were perhaps the most elusive—combining seduction, secrecy, and adventure. She could not record these special pleasures in travel essays, but seven years later she transposed the scene of her passion from the pale green woods of the English countryside to a sun-drenched July in New England. The scent of wild thyme wafts across the Berkshire hills in *Summer* as the young lovers discover their trysting place along a country road that Edith had often seen on afternoon 'motor-flights' from The Mount, her summer home in Lenox, Massachusetts. Written as a counter to the frozen starkness of *Ethan Frome, Summer* is the most lyrical of her novels. Seductive and evocative, its setting serves not as mere background but comes alive as character—a palpable presence in the story which conditions its events. Edith Wharton's ability to draw setting as 'character' in *Summer* derives as much from her experience as a travel writer as it does from her work as a novelist. Indeed, for her, the two roles are indistinguishable.

—SHARI BENSTOCK

[Shari Benstock is professor of English and Women's Studies at the University of Miami (Florida). She is the author and editor of nine books, including *Women of the Left Bank: Paris, 1900-1940* (University of Texas Press, 1986) and *No Gifts from Chance: A Biography of Edith Wharton* (Scribner's, 1994).]

INTRODUCTION

When Henry James observed in 1902 that Edith Wharton 'must be tethered in native pastures, even if it reduces her to a back-yard in New York' he clearly did not foresee publication of the seven travel books that constitute a vital and enduring segment of her work. They validate her role as an experienced cicerone, well able to enlighten her countrymen about the subtleties of taste and aesthetic achievements of the Old World.

Edith Wharton's upbringing in an elite and wealthy New York family, her extensive reading, and her wide-ranging early travels endowed her with a substantial capital of what Pierre Bourdieu calls 'the competence of the "connoisseur"'. This 'competence' cannot be transmitted solely by precept or prescription, but derives from long contact with cultured persons and places. It is what distinguishes Wharton's travel books from many contemporary accounts and justifies Blake Nevius's characterization of them as 'brilliantly written and permanently interesting'. They manifest a thorough knowledge of art and architecture as well as an ability to juxtapose them against a complex background of theology, classical mythology, history, and literature. Her cultural

1

competence, or taste, allows her to integrate the scholarly and imaginative approaches to travel, a quality much desired by her audience. This audience consisted not only of affluent Americans who went regularly to Europe, as their parents and grandparents had done, but also of literate middle-class travellers who were able, before World War I, to travel to Europe on a more modest level—or who, at least, could travel vicariously by purchasing her books.

Few writers have been better equipped, beginning in childhood, for such a task. 'Perhaps, after all, it is not a bad thing to begin one's travels at four', Wharton reflected at the age of seventy-one. In 1866, her parents, Frederic and Lucretia Jones, who had suffered reverses in New York real estate during the Civil War, went to live in Europe, taking along Edith, then four. During the ensuing six years, she absorbed the landscape, art, and architecture of France, Italy, Germany, and other European countries. The experience permanently shaped her outlook, giving her, for the rest of her life, a 'background of beauty and old-established order,' as she expressed it in her memoir. As an adult she recalled 'the lost Rome' of her 'infancy,' the 'warm scent of the box hedges on the Pincian, and the texture of weather-worn sun-gilt stone.' From an arduous trip to Spain during the second year of their European residence, she 'brought back an incurable passion for the road.'

On the Joneses' return to New York in 1872, Edith entered the 'kingdom' of her father's library and continued to internalize her European experience, reading widely in literature, history, and philosophy. Her works of travel are, as a result of her reading, marked by erudition. As Mary Suzanne Schriber observes,[1] in her travel books she 'displays a formidable knowledge of political, literary, and art history. She understands Correggio in relation to Zucchero and the town of La Châtre in the light of the novels of George Sand.' She was fluent in French, German, and Italian as well as English, and conversant with literature in all four languages.

In 1880, when Edith Wharton was eighteen, the Joneses returned to Europe for two years because of her father's bad health; he died at Cannes in 1882. The second visit confirmed her attachment to Europe; she 'felt the stir of old associations,' especially when she and her father followed 'step by step Ruskin's arbitrary itineraries' in Florence and Venice. Shari Benstock gives a full account of Edith Wharton's ancestors, upbringing, and early years of travel in her biography of Wharton, *No Gifts from Chance*. Her love for travel was lifelong and shared by her husband, Edward Wharton, whom she married in 1885. For a number of years, they spent four months abroad each year, principally in Italy. Her biographer R. W. B. Lewis has said that Italy was 'the first European love of Edith Wharton's maturity ... a recurring act of discovery.' They were accompanied by their close friend Egerton Winthrop on most of their journeys in Italy, as well as by Catharine Gross, their housekeeper (who had been Edith's personal attendant since 1884), and probably by a maid as well. The Wharton's travels continued each year for nearly two decades, not only in Italy but also in France, England and other countries. In 1888 they took an Aegean cruise on a chartered steam yacht, the *Vanadis* (discussed in the section on *The Cruise of the Vanadis*). In 1897, Wharton published her first book-length prose work, *The Decoration of Houses*, written with the architect Ogden Codman. Although not a travel book in the usual sense, it contains an elaborate codification of European principles of harmony and design that can be imported, on a domestic scale, by Americans in their house planning. Many of its principles, such as 'proportion is the good breeding of architecture,' were formulated during Wharton's early years in Europe, and, to some degree, it may be regarded as an archive for much of her travel writing.

By 1902, the Whartons had sold their house at Newport and built The Mount in Lenox, Massachusetts, where they spent part of each year. Excellent accounts of the building of The

Mount, as well as the Whartons' early years there, when they entertained Henry James, Gaillard Lapsley, Howard Sturgis, and others, are given by Benstock and also by Lewis. It was in Lenox that Wharton wrote her first full-length novel, *The Valley of Decision*, compiled *Italian Villas and Their Gardens* and *Italian Backgrounds* from earlier essays, together with new ones, and wrote *The House of Mirth*. Soon after they moved into The Mount, however, Teddy suffered a nervous collapse, followed by another in 1903. His condition hampered her work on *The House of Mirth*, but, during trips to Newport, he seemed to improve. The same year, they were able to visit Italy, where she embarked on extensive visits to villas and gardens, collecting materials for the articles compiled as *Italian Villas and Their Gardens* (they began appearing in *The Century* in 1903; the book was published in 1904).

The year 1904 brought a significant shift in the Whartons' travels; they gave up their annual pilgrimage to Italy, preferring explorations in France. This change heralded Edith's later expatriation. They drove through France toward the Spanish border, visiting Pau and travelling back to Paris through Périgueux, Limoges, Bourges, and Blois. Just as the Whartons' travels in 1904 brought a fundamental abandonment of Italy for France, the end of the year 1905 began the final period of Edith Wharton's relinquishment of

America for Europe, specifically France. The preceding two decades had led almost inexorably to her decision, though in some respects it was an enigmatic one, made just at the peak of her achievement in two literary genres: fiction and travel writing. Her bicontinental habitation between 1885 and 1905 had, it may be argued, reinforced her concepts of both native and foreign pastures, the disadvantages of each highlighting the positive aspects of the other. Even in the midst of her annual journeys abroad, Wharton seems to have exhibited a strong affinity to Homer's Odysseus, who, in the midst of his foreign travels, found 'his native home deep imag'd in his soul' (*The Odyssey*, Bk. 13, 1.38).

As early as 1904 the Whartons had acquired their first motor-car (a Panhard-Levassor), and their automobile trips, especially through France, were, from all indications, one of the chief pleasures of the remaining years of their marriage. Teddy closed in their automobile and, as he put it, 'added every known accessorie [*sic*] and comfort'. Edith wrote several articles for *The Atlantic* about three separate trips through France, which were later collected as *A Motor-Flight Through France*, published by Scribner's in 1908. Europe—particularly France—was an increasing attraction to Wharton. Schriber argues that in the process of writing (for serial publication) and rewriting (in book form)

6

about her travels in Italy and France, Edith 'became convinced as never before that the geographical balance of her life must change, that it must correspond to her own psychological and intellectual balance, that Europe was in fact her home and America an alien land'.

The years 1906–1907 are regarded by both Benstock and Lewis as the decisive time of Wharton's final expatriation. Her physical residence in the Faubourg began in 1907, when she and her husband sublet the apartment of the George Vanderbilts in a stately town house at 58 Rue de Varenne, in the Faubourg Saint-Germain. In January 1910, the Whartons moved into another apartment at 53 Rue de Varenne. She was to live there until 1919, when she moved into the Pavillon Colombe just outside Paris in Saint-Brice-sous-Forêt.

Teddy's nervous decline, which had begun several years earlier, intensified in France. His resistance to living permanently in Paris was abetted, according to Lewis, by his ineptitude at speaking French and conversing on a literary level with Edith's friends. He was more at home at The Mount, where he could indulge in hunting and other outdoor pursuits. Until 1902, when he was 53, he had been 'robust physically and mentally alert.' But he began to experience alternate episodes of mania and depression as early as 1904; by 1908, when the Whartons returned to Paris, they had

7

intensified. In December 1908, he confessed that he had embezzled some of his wife's funds, purchased an apartment in Boston, and established a mistress there; it was later revealed that he had spent at least $50,000. The funds were restored from his mother's legacy, which he had just inherited, but he was prohibited from managing Edith's financial affairs and later was asked to resign as trustee. Lewis attributes his behavior to the exaction of 'financial and sexual revenge'. Benstock emphasizes the strain of hereditary insanity in the Wharton family. He became increasingly agitated at The Mount during the summer of 1911, and Edith suggested separation. She decided to move permanently to France and did so in the fall of 1911. The Mount was sold in November 1911 and Teddy arrived back in Paris in February 1912. By January 1913, his erratic behavior had finally convinced Edith that divorce was the only solution, despite the American social repercussions she feared. Because of Teddy's excesses and the lessening stigma of divorce, however, she actually received considerable support from friends and family.

After leaving The Mount in 1911, Edith Wharton lived in France until her death in 1937, only returning to the United States twice: In late 1913 for the wedding of her niece, and in 1923 to accept an honorary degree from Yale University, the first bestowed on a woman by a major university. In the years preceding and following her divorce, she made many trips with such close friends as Mary and Bernard Berenson, Walter Berry, Henry James, Howard Sturgis, Gaillard Lapsley, Minnie and Paul Bourget, and others. Her zest for travel was frequently alarming, especially to James. As Lewis observes, he was 'disturbed by the rush and movement' of her life and characterized her visits to him at Rye, Sussex: 'General eagle-pounces and eagle-flights of her deranging and desolating, ravaging, burning and destroying energy ... the Angel of Devastation was the mildest name we knew her by'.

When she was not travelling, Edith led a fulfilling life in Paris, where she had friends 'from worlds as widely different as the University, the literary and Academic *milieux*, and the old and aloof society of the Faubourg Saint-Germain'; in fact, she had an advantage as a 'stranger and a newcomer,' since she was not expected to fit into the 'old social pigeon-holes'. At the time, she wrote later, 'the core of my life was under my own roof, among my books and my intimate friends.' Her chief satisfaction, however, was her work, 'which was growing and spreading and absorbing more and more of my time and my imagination'.

The onset of World War I brought an end to Wharton's travels and the harmonious balance of her pre-war life in the Faubourg, which was divided among social life, travel, and disciplined writing. At the end of July, 1914, returning from a journey to Spain, she spent the night at Poitiers. She recalled that the atmosphere had seemed 'strange, ominous and unreal, like the yellow glare that precedes a storm. There were moments when I felt as if I had died, and waked up in an unknown world'. Two days later, when war was declared, she found she had done just that. Her attitude at the beginning of the war, as reflected in her letters, seems a curious blend of horror and fatalism. On August 22, she wrote Bernard Berenson that Paris 'never looked so appealingly humanly beautiful as now—poor Andromeda!—with the monster careering up to her'. Looking back on the eve of war, she extolled France and, especially, Paris, 'so made for peace and art and all humanest graces'.

She began at once to participate in war work and established four separate relief projects: American Hostels for Refugees, to assist French and Belgian refugees swarming into Paris; a workroom for seamstresses; the Children of Flanders Rescue Committee, caring for 750 Flemish children; and a cure program for soldiers afflicted with tuberculosis. In early 1915, she was asked by the French Red Cross to visit military hospitals at the front and report on their needs; her first was at Châlons-sur-Marne. She asked permission to make other trips to the front and write magazine articles about her experiences with the hope of alerting her 'rich and generous compatriots' to the desperate needs of hospitals, and to 'bring home to American readers some of the dreadful realities of war.' The articles were compiled into *Fighting France: From Dunkerque to Belfort.* She also edited *The Book of the Homeless*, soliciting contributions from well-known writers and artists; it was published in early 1916, earning about $10,000 for war relief; it is now a valuable collectors' item. In April 1916, she was made a Chevalier of the Legion of Honor, France's highest accolade, and two years later received the Medal of Queen Elizabeth from King Albert of Belgium. After America's entry into the war, Wharton was asked to write a series of articles making 'France and things French intelligible to the American soldier'. These were collected as *French Ways and Their Meaning* (1919). In 1917, she was invited to Morocco as the special guest of the Resident-General, Hubert Lyautey. She wrote a series of articles about her experiences, which were compiled as *In Morocco* (1920), her last travel book.

After the war, Wharton's fealty to France was confirmed, on a domestic scale, by the purchase of two French properties. In 1917, she had begun searching for a house near Paris to serve as a spring and autumn home; as Lewis puts it, she was looking 'beyond the war's end to a life of tranquillity and literary dedication'. Elisina Tyler, a close friend, discovered an old villa with a walled garden, Jean-Marie, in the village of Saint Brice-sous-Forêt, about ten miles north of Paris. She purchased it in 1918, began renovations, and moved in in the summer of 1919, restoring its original name, Pavillon Colombe. She would spend summers and autumns here until her death in 1937. In 1919, she obtained, on a long lease, a second estate high above the Mediterranean on the French Riviera at Hyères. This was a convent built within a château, Sainte Claire du Vieux Château. It was to be her winter and spring home for the remainder of her life.

* * *

'I was a traveler long before I was a noveler ... I am not yet sure which branch of the art I prefer,' wrote William Dean Howells.[2] Edith Wharton too was first a traveller, developing, in her travel texts, the persona of the connoisseur and, arguably, sharing Howells's ambivalence as to which genre she preferred. In *A Backward Glance,* she is reticent about her achievements in this field. Her fiction, of course, sold far better than her travel books, and, as she wrote her memoir in 1934, may have seemed to constitute a finer and more memorable body of work. Yet, taken as a whole, her travel works embody a connoisseurship that may well have provided considerable cultural 'capital' for her fiction. Lewis has stated that Edith Wharton was one of the most accomplished practitioners in American literary history in the genre 'unsatisfactorily known as "travel writing."' His dissatisfaction with the generic definition of travel literature suggests that, from the beginning, travel writing was more or less a hybrid genre. During the eighteenth and nineteenth centuries, particularly, much travel literature grew out of the belles lettres tradition of essay writing, a product of upper class gentility, a badge of 'culture.' At the same time, travel writing participated in a number of other discourses, such as art history, ethnography, history, and sociology, each of which was 'professionalizing' during the era in which Wharton wrote. Yet travel writing at this time seemed to resist the new tendency toward expertise and insisted upon the older paradigm of the educated amateur—the amateur whose qualifications were not formalized and whose journeys were free of the constraints of a narrow academic focus. Wharton was in some respects an untrained 'amateur,' but one with certain intellectual credentials, particularly a command of several languages and an erudite background derived from many years of reading history, mythology, art criticism, and philosophy. But even as she strove for

13

acknowledgment as an art historian, she was aware that her special gifts of observation and able descriptive powers might be better suited to a less exacting and more flexible genre, that is, fiction. This paradox endures throughout Wharton's travel writing.

A second ambiguity is also relevant to her accomplishments in the field of travel writing. Amy Kaplan situates Wharton's writing 'at the complex intersection of class and gender'. By her own admission, she felt constricted by class as much as by gender. She considered writing an antidote to the idleness of her class, which viewed authorship as, in her words, 'something between a black art and a form of manual labor'. Kaplan writes of her construction of a separate 'personality' in the mind of the public and her effort 'to write herself out of the private domestic sphere and to inscribe a public identity in the marketplace'. The very class that had provided the economic means for her intellectual nourishment in the form of leisure, foreign travel, and richly stocked personal libraries espoused frivolous social pursuits and denigrated public literary endeavor, especially on the part of women. Moreover, to enter the realm of professional authorship, Wharton had to 'grapple with the precedent of women novelists who ventured into the market only to reinforce their place at home'. She thus had to distance herself from the legacy of popular and commercially

14

successful domestic or sentimental women novelists, such as Fanny Fern, Catharine Maria Sedgwick, and Harriet Beecher Stowe.[3]

Wharton protested, in her fiction, against the patriarchal social and economic authority, the matrix of both gender and class, within which she was enmeshed by the circumstances of birth. In her actual travels, however, she implicitly assented to both forms of authority. The early journeys she took, in the company of her husband and servants, were made possible by the antebellum mercantile fortunes assembled by her ancestors; those fortunes, and the more substantial ones of the postbellum Gilded Age, brought into existence the idle society against which she inveighed in her fiction. In her travel writing, however, adroitly sidestepping the issues of gender and economic privilege, she 'flew at nobler game,' to use Locke's phrase, and contended for stature as a scholar and connoisseur.

Throughout her travel works, Wharton displays a certain ambivalence toward the profession of art history. In *A Backward Glance*, she recalls her enthusiasm for the travel books of the 1870s and 1880s of the 'cultured dilettante' type, written by 'gifted amateurs' such as the British writers Vernon Lee [Violet Paget], Walter Pater, and John Addington Symonds. Bernard Berenson, whose volumes on Italian painting combined 'sternest scientific accuracy' with aesthetic sensibility, began, according to Wharton, to clear away the 'sentimental undergrowth' left by the gifted amateur. In the light of the new scholarly standards, Wharton is, as she expresses it, on the verge of expressing shame at having added the 'facile vibrations' of her own travel books [*Italian Villas and Their Gardens and Italian Backgrounds*] to this canon. However, she stops short of doing so, insisting that even the amateur may perceive the soul of a work, an 'imponderable something,' and that a lover of beauty may still enlighten 'receptive' travellers. Wharton consents, conditionally, to the status of 'gifted amateur' even as, particularly in her early travel works, she strives for recognition as a scholar and connoisseur of art.[4] She becomes, in the words of Henry James, 'one of the people on whom nothing is lost.'

Four tenets give shape to Wharton's travel accounts and underlie much of her argument: A dislike of architectural restoration, a preference for 'parentheses' of travel instead of the 'catalogued riches of guidebooks'; an attachment to the previously neglected period of the Baroque; and, as a corollary to the latter, an enduring interest in what might be termed its verbal analogue, the commedia dell'arte, the improvisatory strolling theater that began in Italy during the sixteenth century.

Wharton follows John Ruskin in abhorring restoration and preferring structures that are enduring testaments to the ages in which they were constructed. In 'The Lamp of Memory,' Ruskin calls restoration 'a Lie from beginning to end,' arguing that it destroys 'that spirit which is given only by the hand and eye of the workman.' Restoring even a half-inch of lost finish can only be conjectural, since the 'brute hardness of the new carving' effaces the 'sweetness in the gentle lines which rain and sun had wrought'. There can be no real fidelity to the original building. Even in the 1888 diary of the cruise aboard the *Vanadis*, Wharton reveals a dislike of restoration. She comments ironically on the fortress of Euryalus at Syracuse in Sicily: 'Luckily it has escaped the distinction of being restored'. Too many 'venerable architectural relics,' she says, writing of her motor trips through France, have had to 'sacrifice their bloom of *vétusté* [decay, decrepitude]'. It is only in remote monuments untouched by the 'arch-restorer' that one gets 'the sense of undisguised antiquity, or a long stolid existence exposed to every elemental influence.' She prefers a protofictional authentic ruin so that she can reconstruct her own cultural fiction around it; that is, perform her own 'restoration,' which may take the form of imaginative historical or fictional vignettes. Even Wharton, however, cannot admire buildings that have completely crumbled. Her visit to Morocco points up the necessity for a *via media* in the matter of

17

conservation versus restoration; she describes it as a country built by 'nomads' and mourns the absence of even the most basic preservation. Wharton concludes, on visiting Morocco, that 'the passion for building seems allied, in this country of inconsequences, to the supine indifference that lets existing constructions crumble back to clay. "Dust to dust" should have been the motto of the Moroccan palace-builders'.

Wharton's abhorrence of the restored structure may also be a by-product of her wish to deflect mass tourism even as she caters to an elite and affluent audience. She is zealous about seeking out and describing little-known 'by-ways' of travel (generating, paradoxically, attention that might invoke the dreaded Baedeker star and attract more visitors).[5] Her travel writing is rooted not only in her esteem for discriminating taste, but also in a passion for authenticity. She abhors guidebooks, which seek out that authenticity to legitimate the tourist attraction. She produces and validates a collateral 'abroad,' not represented in guidebooks, with historical gaps filled in and amplified and byways inviting exploration. Should this 'abroad' attract large numbers of visitors, however, then the privileged, quasi-solitary wandering may be eradicated by mass tourism. One of the 'rarest and most delicate pleasures of the continental tourist' is actually to 'circumvent the compiler of his guide-book.' The only refuge left from his 'omniscience' is to approach 'the places he describes by a route which he has not taken'. She argues that 'it is rather in the intervals between such systematized study of the past, in the parentheses of travel, that one obtains those more intimate glimpses which help to compose the image of each city, to preserve its personality in the traveller's mind'.

Although Wharton agrees with Ruskin about restoration, she counters his conviction that the Baroque, a period he termed the 'Grotesque Renaissance,' is decadent when compared with Medieval and Renaissance art and architecture. He wrote that the architects of such churches as the Jesuiti, San Clemente, and the Scalzi in Venice took liberties with marble 'from mere love of juggling and falsehood for their own sake,' and possessed only 'such powers of imitation as are devoted in England to the manufacture of peaches and eggs out of Derbyshire spar'. Wharton, in contrast, sees the Baroque as the 'spectacular and external life which had developed from the more secluded civilization of the Renaissance as some blossom of immense size and dazzling colour may develop in the atmosphere of the forcing-house from a smaller and more delicate flower'. She cherishes the intricate friezes of dancing angels and wistful putti in

Baroque churches; the 'mossy urns,' the elaborate fountains, and grottoes in the gardens of Italian villas; and the revels of 'demi-gods' in the paintings and frescoes of Tiepolo, Luini, and Michelozzo. In reifying the Baroque, Wharton offers a corrective to its devaluation by the 'submissive generation of art critics' taught by Ruskin and re-educates her readers. In the final chapter of *Italian Backgrounds*, she enumerates over two dozen of the many majestic structures that would disappear if Baroque Rome were removed, including the Spanish Steps, Bernini's fountain of the Triton, Borromini's church of San Carlo ('a kaleidoscope of whirling line and ornament'), the Fountain of Trevi, and the 'Angels of Passion' on the bridge of Sant' Angelo.

A fourth motif found in Wharton's fiction as well as her travel writing is her preoccupation with the commedia dell'arte, the 'comedy of skill,' the peripatetic Italian theater of the sixteenth, seventeenth, and eighteenth centuries, which was based in part on improvisation and incorporated famous stock characters such as Arlecchino (or Harlequin), Arlecchina, Pulcinella, Corallina, Brighella, Pantalone, and Captain Spavento. Performances were given at all social levels, from the street to the halls of villas. Actors and actresses sometimes played a single role their entire lives. Although Wharton's interest in the commedia dell'arte is most evident in her travel writing about Italy, it is also present in *A Motor-Flight Through France* and her historical novel *The Valley of Decision*. Wharton often imagines the players on stage, the 'airy superstructure of their wit' rounding out her depiction of physical scenes, such as the Lake of Iseo or the decrepit Farnese Theater at Parma.

*   *   *

Choosing the selections for the present anthology was exceedingly difficult; each chapter omitted offered a pressing claim for inclusion. Although the principal criterion was literary appeal, the final decisions were shaped by varied considerations. For example, 'Africa,' from *The Cruise of the Vanadis*, took priority as the first known example of Wharton's travel writing, and 'Harems and Ceremonies,' from *In Morocco*, as her final published travel article; moreover, the latter contains accounts of her privileged visits to five harems and is revealing of certain gender-based pre-occupations. It is hoped that the extracts chosen will tempt the reader to search out her complete travel books, since most have been reprinted or are available in libraries.

21

The Cruise of the Vanadis
[1888; published 1992]

It is now known that Wharton's travel writing, at least in private, had almost as early a genesis as her fiction and poetry. In 1991, a French scholar, Claudine Lesage of the University of Amiens, discovered in the public library in Hyères a bound, typed transcription of the diary Wharton had kept of the 1888 Mediterranean cruise she and her husband, along with James Van Alen, took aboard the chartered steam yacht *Vanadis*; she was twenty-six at the time. Lesage states, in her introductory note, that the reasons Wharton did not publish the diary are unknown, but that the responsibility for doing so had clearly devolved on her, since she had discovered it. She observes that the diary counters the widely held notion that Wharton's 'beginnings as a writer were a mere accident, an occupation for an idle rich woman.' Instead, she argues, it is clear that 'just as a violinist diligently practises her scales before appearing in front of an audience she had been writing extensively though privately'. She calls the diary Wharton's 'maiden *Odyssey* into literature'. It is unlikely that Wharton ever intended the diary to be published, since in later years she denied, or failed to recall, having written it at all. She declares in *A Backward Glance*, 'until 1918 I never kept even the briefest of diaries'.

22

Wharton's profound craving for travel is suggested by her choice of the epigraph to *The Cruise of the Vanadis*, from Goethe's *Faust*:

[*Faust*]. Ja wär nur ein Zaubermantel
  mein!
Und trüg er mich in fremde Länder,
mir soll ter um die köstlichsten Gewänder
Nicht feil um einen Königsmantel sein.

[*Faust*]. Oh, if only some magic cloak were
  mine,
A cloak to waft me into unknown lands!
I'd not exchange it for the costliest robes—
No, not for the crown and mantle of a king!
(*Faust*, I, 'Outside the City Gate,' 11. 1122–25, p. 55)

The lines are from a scene between the sedentary, pedantic Wagner and Faust, who is beset by conflicting desires for repose and exertion. He appeals to the 'spirits of the air' to enable him to escape a stagnant, quiescent existence and convey him to 'some new rainbow life.' The epigraph from Goethe imparts a motive of impetuous and romantic escapism, of freedom from earthbound concerns, which agrees with her later characterization of the cruise in *A Backward Glance* as having been undertaken improvidently and enthusiastically. The *Vanadis* diary and its epigraph suggest that

23

travel not only met a deeply felt inner need on the part of Edith Wharton, but also offered a means of escape from what had turned out to be a disappointing marriage.

The Cruise of the Vanadis is evidence of Wharton's practice of recording her observations and ordering them within the rich literary context provided by her early reading. Although she also mentions various guidebooks and previous accounts, Homer and Shelley figure in the diary as much as 'The Mediterranean Handbook' that was evidently on hand. It is known that even when travelling by carriage the Whartons took along a carton of books, so it is not unlikely that they had a number of books on board the *Vanadis*.[6]

In the diary, Wharton is essentially a novice, continually testing her experiences against those of others and against her literary background. She offers no apologies for disagreeing with 'authorities' about the sights she records, foreshadowing the day in her later works of travel when she will discount them altogether. She is, for example, disappointed in the Cathedral of Monreale, but states: 'Of course I know that in saying this I am running counter to the opinion of the highest authorities; but this Journal is written not to record other people's opinions, but to note as exactly as possible the impression which I myself received'. This is the credo she follows throughout the diary: To record her own exact impressions. Here we have an interesting example of how she struggled to define her bias against (but nevertheless in response to) critics of whom she is aware.

'Africa'

The first essay in *The Cruise of the Vanadis*, this is, so far as is known, Wharton's earliest travel text. It embodies many of the themes that persist throughout her works of travel: Interest in landscape and gardens, art and architecture, the pageant of local life, and the historical, mythological, and aesthetic context of places visited. She is eager to visit the Jardin d'Essai, and compares the mountains in the Gulf of Tunis to Shelley's *'peaked isles.'* One aspect of 'Africa,' as well as the remainder of *The Cruise of the Vanadis*, that differs from her later travel texts is the precise description of her surroundings. She gives full particulars of ports of call on the voyage, incidental details that are frequently suppressed in her later travel writing. The furnishings of the *Vanadis* are described in detail, and the crew members listed. In much of her later travel writing, such information is omitted, imparting a timeless quality to her writing but, at the same time, causing many readers to long for her reactions to the circumstances of travel. This chapter contains a poignant glimpse of Wharton as a beginning writer: 'Hard as it is to write of these things vividly, it is harder still to forget a first sight of the Bazaars of Tunis.'

'Chios and Smyrna'

In most of *The Cruise of the Vanadis*, Wharton's observations are secular, encompassing the lives and homes of the local inhabitants, their gardens, the sites of classical temples and citadels, and hotels (rarely mentioned in detail in her later works). In this chapter, she is less the religious pilgrim of 'Mount Athos' than a voracious intellectual wanderer, open to all experiences and eager to convey the flavor of the towns and bazaars. Smyrna, for example, has a 'medley of different types' Wharton has never seen equalled, and she offers full descriptions of the people and sights, especially in the bazaars.

'Mount Athos'

Wharton's account of Mount Athos is thought to be the first by an American. Mount Athos, also known as the Holy Mountain, is the Greek peninsula that is home to more than twenty Orthodox (Greek, Russian, Rumanian) monasteries, some dating from as early as the tenth century. She may have hoped to invade the male sanctuary of Mount Athos and record a rare look at the site from a woman's point of view, or at least to moor the *Vanadis* launch at one of the landings and inspect the terrain closely. (No female, human or animal, is admitted, as it is considered to be the Garden of the Virgin.) The men in Wharton's party were allowed to land, and she directed the

26

launch to approach the boat-house of Stavroniketa, frankly 'determined to go as near the forbidden shores' as possible. She was prevented from landing by monks who rushed down to fend off her approach. She was clearly frustrated at having to rely on the secondhand reports of her husband and their friend James Van Alen in order to describe the icons, frescoes, and other treasures of the Byzantine monasteries. Her account, however, is supported by references to the studies of the antiquarian H. F. Tozer and Lord Curzon.[7] She discusses the history of the Holy Mountain, and describes the architecture and foliage visible from the sea with meticulous detail. Throughout the chapter, she evinces the meticulous concern with scholarship that will be the hallmark of her later travel writing.

The chapter about Mount Athos provides an early look at Wharton as pilgrim, a role that is much in evidence in her later travel texts, such as *Italian Backgrounds* and *A Motor-Flight Through France*, where she emphasizes the architecture, painting, and sculpture of shrines, churches, and cathedrals.

Italian Villas and Their Gardens [1904]

Usually considered Wharton's first published travel book, this work is marked by a high level of scholarship. The volume was actually commissioned to accompany the watercolors

27

of Maxfield Parrish, and also includes drawings, from photographs, of some of the gardens and villas, as well as black and white sketches. Other artists who contributed were C. A. Vanderhoof, Malcolm Fraser, and Ella Denison. The book is primarily a learned survey of garden architecture and ornamentation rather than a study of the villas. We may imagine Wharton visiting the gardens in 1903 with a scholar's eye, detecting, beneath the palimpsest of eighteenth-century horticulturists bent on transforming every garden into an English park, the original garden outlines and plantings. She sketches the history of the villas, most of which were built during the Renaissance and Baroque periods. Her mission is to evoke, for the reader, the original tripartite relationship between villa, garden, and surrounding landscape. Wharton was disappointed that the publisher (the Century Company) refused to include detailed plans of each garden, a defect noted by early reviewers, which would have undoubtedly clarified much of the text. The book contains descriptions of more than seventy-five villas and their gardens; Wharton is careful to point out that *villa*, in Italian, connotes both house and pleasure-grounds rather than the house alone. The volume has a bibliography of reference works in four languages, capsule biographies of fifty-five architects and landscape gardeners of the fifteenth through

28

the eighteenth centuries, and a detailed index. As was the case with most of Wharton's travel books, serial publication preceded compilation of the book.

'Villas Near Rome'

In this chapter, Wharton describes many villas outside Rome, including the Villa Farnese at Caprarola, the Villa d'Este at Tivoli, and several at Frascati. Many were built by cardinals. Some date from the Renaissance; others were built in the sixteenth century, during the period of transition between the Renaissance and the Baroque. Wharton admires the classicism of the Renaissance villas, but, throughout the chapter, her interest in the Baroque is quite evident. The Villa Farnese at Caprarola, dating from the late sixteenth century, with its 'huge sylvan figures half emerging from their stone sheaths,' seems *'born, not built,'* a phrase used by the architectural historian Vasari. The best example of a *théâtre d'eau*, or water theater, is at the Villa Conti (now Torlonia). She praises water theaters, not only in this chapter but throughout *Italian Villas and Their Gardens*, as the pinnacle of the garden architect's art during the sixteenth and seventeenth centuries, combining natural topography and hydraulic engineering in a brilliant spectacle. She believes the water theater at the Villa Aldobrandini, however, though praised by critics, has too 'heavy' a touch of the Baroque, with an 'Atlas spouting' and a cascade of water from the hilltop. The Villa Lante offers a more pleasing example of 'what the Germans call "water-art,"' with an inner fountain surrounded by an outer basin crossed by four small bridges. At the Villa Conti (now Torlonia) at Frascati, Wharton approves of the fountain, a 'baroque pile of rock-work' with basins receiving both the recirculated fountain spray and cascading water from the hillside. Here the suggestion of tautness, of controlled energy, is a key element in Wharton's admiration of the sculpture and architecture of the Baroque period. She also admires the 'mossy urns,' mythical sea-gods, grottoes, and interplay of light, water, and shadow that characterize other villas of the period. Among those open to the public today are the Villa Farnese at Caprarola, the Villa d'Este at Tivoli, the Villa Aldobrandini at Frascati (park only), and the Villa Lante at Bagnaia.

'Villas of Venetia'

Wharton focuses in this chapter on examples of the Venetian *maison de plaisance*, or pleasure house, in the environs of Venice, on the Brenta Riviera, in Padua, Battaglia, and Treviso, and in the Euganean hills. Within Venice, of course, there are no large-scale gardens or hillsides, no beech-alleys or rustic grottoes. Her charge from *The Century* magazine had been to write the text for the planned series of water colors and paintings already commissioned from Maxfield Parrish, covering villas with extensive gardens. (In *Italian Backgrounds*, where she has a clear field, Wharton pays considerable attention to palaces in Venice itself, such as the Palazzo Grassi and the Palazzo Querini-Stampaglia, which have noted frescoes.)

The villas on the Brenta Riviera, the canal/river running from Venice to Padua (about thirty miles), are of particular interest. About seventy villas were built along the Brenta, beginning in the fifteenth century. The Venetian nobility spent the *villeggiatura*, or vacation season, here (and many owners still follow suit). Architectural styles range from the austerity of the sixteenth century to the more fanciful Baroque of the seventeenth and the restrained classicism of the eighteenth. The commedia dell'arte is significant in this chapter, since some villas have garden statuary based on the stock characters. In *The Valley of Decision* Wharton describes life in an imaginary villa on the Brenta and causes a travelling troupe of actors to give a performance of the commedia dell'arte, another instance of her enduring interest in this theatrical genre. The Brenta was well known to Dante, who mentions it in the 'Inferno' and 'Paradiso' sections of the *Divine Comedy*, and it was painted by Canaletto. Goethe travelled its length on a canopied barge in 1786 and described it in his *Italian Journey*; other famous visitors included Carlo Goldoni, Voltaire, Byron, and George Sand.

Among the villas and gardens described in this chapter are several that can be visited today, including Malcontenta, La Mira, and Strà, all on the Brenta, as well as the Villa Valmarana near Vicenza (with frescoes by Tiepolo). This chapter contains the only plan in the book, of the Botanic Garden at Padua, which is open to the public.

Italian Backgrounds [1905]

In this volume Wharton seemingly builds, chronologically, on the foundation of *Italian Villas and Their Gardens* in assessing the art and landscape of Italy on a broad scale. Most of the book, however, had been published in serial form before *Italian Villas* appeared, and was based on travels undertaken before her visits to the specific villas and gardens described in that volume. To some extent, both works represent a synthesis of her travels in Italy, which spanned two decades. *Italian Backgrounds*, unlike *Italian Villas and Their Gardens*, focuses on the landscape of the countryside and on the civic and ecclesiastical architecture of towns and regions, including Parma, Milan, the northern Italian lakes, the

Pennine Alps, Venice, Sicily, Rome and other regions.

'A Midsummer Week's Dream: August in Italy'

At the opening of 'A Midsummer Week's Dream,' Wharton and her party have fled to a posting-inn below the Splügen Pass from the valley below, seeking a refuge from the stylish 'crowd of the Vorderrheinthal.' They find, however, that they seem to be 'living in the landscape of a sanatorium prospectus'; the healthy walks and climbs are insufficient. Splügen, though charming, is painfully non-Italian. They board the diligence to Chiavenna and traverse the 'savage landscape' of the Splügen pass. The remainder of the chapter is devoted to their visits to the towns and lakes of northern Italy: Lake Como, Sondrio, Tirano, the Valtelline, Edolo, the Val Camonica, Lake Iseo, Cerveno, Breno, Lovere, and Brescia.

The commedia dell'arte figures in the chapter epigraph, the first two lines of Paul Verlaine's poem 'Clair de Lune.' He compares the soul of the poet's loved one to a *paysage choisi*,' or 'chosen landscape,' that has been charmed by the strolling players, or maskers, in their disguises. The metaphor provides the framework for Wharton's description of the Lake of Iseo: She imagines the villages on the shore as a backdrop for the performances of comedies 'in the Bergamasque dialect, with

33

Harlequin in striped cloak, and Brighella in conical hat and wide green and white trousers strutting up and down before the shuttered house in which Dr Graziano hides his pretty ward.' The lake reflects the 'eighteenth century of Longhi, of Tiepolo and Goldoni ... as in some magic crystal,' to be discovered beneath the waves by 'some later traveller ... if ever the boundaries between fact and fancy waver, it may well be under the spell of the Italian midsummer madness.' The spontaneity and imaginative outreach that are the most distinctive features of the commedia dell'arte are the dramatic equivalent of the Baroque flowering in architecture, sculpture and painting which, for Wharton, eclipsed the pale formality of the Renaissance.

Wharton charms the reader by turning herself into a reluctant tourist. After cataloguing the aesthetic treasures of Brescia, she reflects that 'in summer there is a strong temptation to sit and think of these things rather than to go and see them,' and, in a rare depiction of her actual surroundings, mentions the comfort of her hotel courtyard, with its tinkling fountain and electric fans.

'Picturesque Milan'
In this essay, Wharton defends the art and architecture of the Baroque against the 'submissive generation of art critics' taught by

Ruskin to develop a fanatical preference for the Gothic. Much of the chapter focuses on the architecture and sculpture of Milan that have been largely overlooked, rather than the 'catalogued riches' of the city. Near Milan, the pilgrimage church of the Madonna of Saronno has a cupola with seventeenth-century frescoes painted by Guadenzio Ferrari, with a 'circle of choiring angels' so joyous that 'form seems to pass into sound,' recalling the angel-choruses of 'Faust' or the last lines of the 'Paradiso.'[8] Here the viewer is called upon to *hear* the painting, envisioning 'celestial pastures.' Sensations of sound, color, sight, and memory are inextricably mixed. By valuing the fusion of associations that may be aroused by a work of art, and that may have combined in its inception on the part of the artist, Wharton is, in this passage, more amateur than art historian. At the same time, such flights of fancy are one of the 'facile vibrations' that she feels might enlighten 'receptive' travellers more effectively than scholarly discourse.

The chapter also confirms Wharton's suspicion of restoration and her defense of ruins. She describes the Certosa [monastery] of Chiaravalle, with its 'noble colonnaded cupola,' as one of the 'conspicuous objects' in the landscape near Milan. Its appeal, however, lies in the fact that the interior is 'falling to ruin ... one feels the melancholy charm of a

35

beautiful building which has been allowed to decay as naturally as a tree. The disintegrating touch of nature is less cruel than the restoring touch of man.' Wharton dismisses the more famous fourteenth-century Carthusian Certosa of Pavia, nearby, because it is 'catalogued' and 'railed off from the sight-seer'; it has, in other words, attracted the dreaded Baedeker star.

A Motor-Flight Through France [1908]

The 'abroad' that Wharton evokes in her first two published works of travel, *Italian Villas and Their Gardens* and *Italian Backgrounds*, largely predates the automotive era, and partakes far more of the nineteenth century than the twentieth. She and her party traverse little-known Italian routes at a leisurely pace, by horse-drawn carriage and stagecoach, lingering in the aura of the commedia dell'arte, Goethe, Hester Piozzi, Lady Mary Wortley Montagu, and Stendhal. Between *Italian Backgrounds* (1905) and *A Motor-Flight Through France* (1908), Wharton crosses a Rubicon; henceforth, leisurely exploration gives way to rapid visitation and Italy succumbs to France. Her travel writing becomes less a compilation of heuristic essays than a chronicle of sites and routes.

The three separate journeys chronicled in *A*

Motor-Flight Through France represent, in the words of Schriber, 'a record of the twilight of the long-standing American romance with Europe that World War I was destined to alter forever'. Wharton's first work of travel based on motor travel and her first about France, is, with its brisk pace, in many ways in dialogue with *In Morocco*. For the first time, constraints of time affect the itinerary, as in *In Morocco*. *Motor-Flight* appears to be uncharacteristically concerned with routes and speed and villages sighted but ruled out for lack of time. She is, in fact, accommodating herself to the new realities of the age. The motor-car that had been a stunning innovation in 1903, when she visited many of the villas that were to figure in *Italian Villas and Their Gardens*, is now a staple of transport. The freedom of the motor-car delights the Wharton's travelling companion, Henry James, who accompanied Wharton and her husband on several of their journeys in different provinces of France.

A Motor-Flight Through France embodies new perspectives and new values. Wharton still seeks 'by-ways,' in the sense of little-known places, but her journeys are more rapid and free of the 'bondage to fixed hours and the beaten track' that have characterized railway travel in the past. The motor-car has, as she puts it, restored the 'adventure and the novelty

37

which enlivened the way of our posting grandparents.' In one sense it has allowed her to reenact and redefine the European pilgrimages of Irving, Hawthorne, Cooper, and Emerson that had charmed the 'artless travellers' of her parents' day.[9] But twentieth-century mobility has also eroded leisure: She is forced to overlook many tempting 'by-ways' and, agonizingly, 'take as a mere parenthesis' towns that once would have merited a lengthy stay.

'From Rouen to Fontainebleau'
This chapter is the third in the first part of *A Motor-Flight Through France*, based on a two-week automobile trip made in May 1906 by the Whartons, accompanied by Edith's brother, Harry Jones. As they wander past the small towns of the Seine, en route from Rouen to Les Andelys (Great and Little Andelys, 'two of the quaintest towns of France'), Wharton returns to her defense of ruins. She praises the twelfth-century Norman Château Gaillard, erected by Richard Coeur de Lion in Le Petit Andely, in a bend of the river. It is a 'poor fluttering rag of a ruin,' yet, in a 'hoarse, cracked whisper' it speaks more eloquently and plaintively of feudalism than such restored castles as Pierrefonds, from which the 'growths of time' have been 'stripped.' They stop for an outdoor meal in the courtyard of an old inn of the type

38

that the 'demands of the motorist' is making obsolete, one where 'Manon and des Grieux' might have dined on their way to Paris.[10]

'Paris to Poitiers'
This chapter is the first in the second part of *A Motor-Flight Through France*, based on the Whartons' second 'motor-flight,' in March 1907, when Henry James was their companion. As usual, Wharton does not indicate the identities of her companions. She perceives, as in Italy, little-recognized aspects of 'show towns' such as Chartres and Blois. Chartres has 'Balzacian gables,' and, in the Cathedral, 'waves of unearthly red and blue' flow in rivers from the famous rose window until they are 'gathered up at last into the mystical heart of the apse.' At Blois she sees the 'poetry of old roofs.'

They visit George Sand's home at Nohant, where Wharton is particularly fascinated by the small theater, which includes two stages. One has life-size scenery for actors and actresses, and the other is a marionette theater recalling the commedia dell'arte as it was incorporated by Goethe in *Wilhelm Meister*. Goethe and George Sand were among the writers Wharton most admired; their acknowledgement of the imaginative power of this form of theater must have validated her own attachment to it.

39

Fighting France:
From Dunkerque to Belfort [1915]

By 1913, Edith Wharton had divorced her husband and moved permanently to France; the era of the Belle Epoque was drawing to a close. In the light of the horrifying events of World War I, the aesthetic exposition that had characterized her earlier works of travel is supplanted by the polemical discourse of *Fighting France: From Dunkerque to Belfort* (1915). This book is based on her wartime experiences in Paris and on humanitarian visits to the front lines. She is both reporter and outspoken advocate of America's entry into the war, evoking the horrors of World War I more movingly than many seasoned journalists. Wharton did not immediately perceive, according to Lewis, that the war had ended the Belle Epoque, the era that had nurtured her work and shaped her outlook, but at first considered the war to be its 'grandest hour'. As it continued, and she was confronted by the human tragedy on every side, she dedicated herself to relief work. This volume offers a wrenching account of the first year of World War I, omitting all mention of her own prodigious efforts. In addition to long days spent in war work, she wrote several articles for *Scribner's Magazine*. The first, 'The Look of Paris,' was a moving account of the general mobilization. Charles Scribner wrote her, 'I have heard more comment on the first article "The Look of Paris" than anything we have published in a long time.'[11] In connection with her war work, Wharton was able to obtain permission to visit the front several times and, as soon as she could, dispatched articles to *Scribner's* about each tour. *Fighting France* is also eloquent testimony to Wharton's stance as a recorder and interpreter of the national cultural heritage. Her conclusion makes clear her opinion of the glory of the French spirit. She writes that the war has been 'a calamity unheard of,' but insists that France has never 'been afraid of the unheard of. No race has ever yet so audaciously dispensed with old precedents; as none has ever so revered their relics'.

'In Argonne'
In the second chapter of the book, Wharton describes a journey made in February 1915 to the region of the Forest of Argonne, east of Paris, which includes such towns as Montmirail, Châlons, Sainte Menehould, Blercourt, Bar-le-Duc, and Verdun. Her tour is, of course, radically different from the carefree days of the journeys described in *A Motor-Flight Through France*, yet there is the same attachment to the countryside and empathy with the French people. The deep-seated distrust and hatred of Germany that had smoldered in French hearts since the War

of 1870 made a profound impression on Wharton. She returns to it again in her 1923 novel *A Son at the Front*, depicting an elderly veteran of that war attempting to join the army during World War I. She makes clear the indomitable spirit of the French people, even as she discusses the tragic loss of domestic and religious treasures, such as the ruined church of Clermont-en-Argonne with its 'torn traceries.'

'In Lorraine and the Vosges'
In May 1915, Edith Wharton again received permission to visit the front, going east once more from Paris, this time toward Lorraine and the Vosges. She and her escorts pass numerous 'murdered houses,' but before the 'black holes' that once were homes there are flowers and vegetables in 'freshly raked and watered gardens,' which she regards as a symbol of 'human energy coming back to replant and rebuild the wilderness.' Beyond Commercy, they come to the village of Gerbéviller, the 'martyr town,' where the Germans built fires on every hearth and tossed in explosives simultaneously. Wharton observes drily that 'as a sensational image of havoc' it seems unlikely any town can surpass it. In Ménil, they discover a curé who has found his 'gratified vocation' in creating a war museum within his chapel commemorating the battles of the region. He zealously tends the

42

fallen, fencing and marking their graves.

In the village of Crévic, only one house has been destroyed, that of the Resident-General of Morocco, Hubert Lyautey. The Germans had made a bonfire of all his family portraits, papers, and furniture. (It was at his invitation that Wharton visited Morocco in 1917.) Two miles from the German frontier, and within sight of it, they visit a tenaciously held corner of France containing an underground hospital and 'cheery catacombs' with 'neat rows of bunks, mess-tables,' and 'sizzling sauce-pans over kitchen-fires.' Wharton praises the 'single-mindedness' of the French soldiers and sees the frontier as a dividing-line: On the German side are the 'men who made the war' and on the French 'the men who had been made by it.'

French Ways and Their Meaning [1919]

Wharton's next book attempts to define the 'national ideal' to which she refers in the conclusion of *Fighting France*. It is not a travel book in the conventional sense, as she does not discuss the many aesthetic treasures of the country that had once existed (the subject of *A Motor-Flight Through France*) and been lost (as detailed in Fighting France: From Dunkerque to Belfort). Instead, she examines the enduring mores and philosophical outlook of the French from a post-war perspective. She

43

considers four salient qualities of the Gallic spirit: reverence, taste, continuity, and intellectual honesty.

Wharton concludes *French Ways* and *Their Meaning* by declaring passionately that one can answer all criticisms of French shortcomings by crying, '*Look at the results*! Read her history, study her art, follow up the current of her ideas; then look about you, and you will see that the whole world is full of her spilt glory.' It is a glory she believed would become apparent to all Americans after the Armistice. In one way, she is answering the superficial misunderstandings that were the result of her compatriots' experiences in the trenches and villages of France. Perhaps, at the same time, she means to defend and justify her decision to make her home permanently in France by bisecting 'patria'—the country of her birth has many shortcomings but, being young, may change and cannot be wholly relinquished; the country of her maturity so nurtures her, despite its foibles, that it secures her full canonical allegiance up to the point of assuming citizenship. *French Ways and Their Meaning* was ordered to be placed in all ships' libraries by the U.S. Department of the Navy.

'Taste'
In this chapter Wharton asserts that French people '"have taste" as naturally as they breathe: It is not regarded as an
44

accomplishment, like playing the flute.' She does not focus on individual manifestations of taste, but rather on civic attainments: Stone quays along rivers, carefully planned prospects, and, above all, 'suitability,' or proportion, in colonnades, cupolas, and sculpture, to give three examples. Americans, she suggests, are not trained to have the 'seeing eye' possessed by French people, who are inherently a 'race of artists.' Deference to the past should not be rigid and indiscriminate, but tempered by taste, which she defines as the 'atmosphere in which art lives, and outside of which it cannot live.' Taste regulates and preserves 'reverence'; everything must be in scale, well proportioned, and 'suitable.' Here there is an echo of the precept of *The Decoration of Houses*, 'proportion is the good breeding of architecture.' A corollary is that perfect proportion implies suitability, both evidence of 'taste.' Suitability is 'fitness.' It 'expresses the mysterious demand of eye and mind for symmetry, harmony and order.' It is the quality that makes well-designed quays and orderly avenues of trees pleasing. It is also the essence of the Collège des Quatre Nations in Paris, 'a certain building with curved wings and a small central dome' that is the home of the French Academy. What begins here as a seemingly idle architectural comment is then developed into her principal argument: The French Academy is the linchpin of French

45

taste and culture, with no equivalent in America.

The chapter also contains a discourse on education. Wharton disagrees with the 'bottled' education in America, 'abridged into summaries and short courses.' The French approach learning with the 'patience, deliberateness, and reverence' that are the elements of 'taste.' America must learn that there are no shortcuts to its acquisition. Wharton indicts the myth of 'college education,' which led one woman graduate to claim she had learned 'art' one year, 'music' another, and 'languages' another. In this chapter, Wharton implies that it ought to be feasible to learn 'taste' if enough patience and effort are applied, along with the honoring of precedent, but it is arguable whether that is possible in a new country, such as America, just beginning to value its past.

'The New Frenchwoman'

'The New Frenchwoman' suggests that constrictions of gender preoccupy Wharton in her nonfiction as well as her fiction and presage her interest in the conditions of women in Morocco. She visited Morocco in 1917, the same year the article was published in the *Ladies Home Journal*. She accuses American women of not being 'grown up' as French women are. Although they may dress well and even cook, they are still in 'kindergarten,' in a

'Montessori-method baby-school.' American women may have more legal rights, but they actually enjoy only a 'semblance of freedom.' The Frenchwoman, in contrast, 'rules French life' and does so 'under a triple crown, as a business woman, as a mother, and above all as an artist.' The middle-class Frenchwoman is always her husband's business partner, for no one else can have such a vested interest in the success of the business. France has attained the ideal of 'frank and free social relations between men and women,' which has been retarded in America because of the hypocritical belief transmitted to the New World from Puritan England that such relations are dangerous to the position of women. Therefore, the American woman in her prime, who has advanced from the freedom of girlhood to the responsibilities of marriage, motherhood, and her household, is suddenly 'withdrawn from circulation.' The 'liberation' and 'progress' of American women are but a mirage, for their economic and social security depends on marriage. In 'standing by' marriage, American culture undermines freedom, because the American woman loses stature upon marriage and withers away in the company of her children and the wives of other men. The Frenchwoman is a free spirit and her position improves after marriage. Young girls are protected and sheltered, for the woman 'does not count till she is married,' at which time she enjoys 'extraordinary social freedom.' It is axiomatic, however, that she must 'know what's being said about things,' as her friend Madame de Trézac explains to the hapless Undine Spragg, American wife of the Marquis de Chelles in *The Custom of the Country*.

'To know what's being said about things' is the mandate of both native and foreign-born women if they hope to participate in French social life to the extent of interesting French men. As Wharton notes, 'Men and women equally, when they have the range of interests that real cultivation gives, need the stimulus of different points of view, the refreshment of new ideas as well as of new faces,' so they will always seek the company of those in other households.

In her own practice, for the remaining twenty years of her life, Wharton clearly enacted the role of a Frenchwoman far more than that of an American. She was an 'artist' in a dual sense: Not only did she write every morning (winning the Pulitzer Prize for Literature in 1921 for *The Age of Innocence*), but she also excelled in the social and practical arts: Deftly arranging dinner parties, corresponding with close French friends (both men and women), negotiating with publishers on her behalf and that of friends, entertaining houseguests, gardening, travelling, and participating fully in the literary and social life of Paris and Hyères.

In Morocco [1920]

In her last travel book, *In Morocco*, Wharton undertakes to provide material for a guidebook to a country without one, at least in English. The year 1917, the worst of the war years, also brought a welcome change in the form of a visit to Morocco. She explains in *A Backward Glance* that she visited the French colony in 1917 in order to see one of the annual industrial exhibitions that a friend, General Hubert Lyautey, Resident-General of French Morocco, had been organizing since 1914 in order to impress on French subjects that World War I 'in no way affected her normal activities.'[12] General Lyautey had been encouraged to invite guests from allied and neutral countries. Morocco at that time was 'untouched by foreign travel,' and he sent Wharton, accompanied by her close friend Walter Berry, on a three-week motor tour of the colony.

When writing of Morocco, Wharton's perspective is both American and French, to the extent that she was by that time a resident of France and had endured the war there. Her Western, Christian heritage is alien to that of a North African Islamic colony governed by her adopted country. She is, moreover, a visitor under the protection of the Resident-General, and a professional woman, a connoisseur of art and a celebrated novelist. Her viewpoint is, therefore, triply foreign. In the acknowledgments, she insists that she is not addressing those who wish 'authoritative utterances,' which are principally available in French, but the 'happy wanderers' who may be planning to visit Morocco. She supplies what she terms a 'slight sketch of the history and art of the country' (actually, the chapter called 'A Sketch of Moroccan History' is a detailed and scholarly exploration of her subject). She claims the chief merit of the sketch is its 'absence of originality' and makes a point of thanking various 'cultivated and cordial French officials,' such as the director of the French School of Fine Arts in Morocco and the historian of the Portuguese Mazagan. Such disclaimers cannot mask the achievement of *In Morocco*, which is one of the most finely wrought of her travel books. It contains the traveller's frank interest in the daily spectacle of costumes, bazaars, and festivals that marks *The Cruise of the Vanadis*, the scholar's sensitivity to art (and mourning of its loss) that characterizes *Italian Backgrounds*, the connoisseur's assessment of the inhabitants' domestic settings, interior and exterior, that is evident in *Italian Villas and Their Gardens*, and the amateur's fascination with the relations between the sexes that is one of the hallmarks of *French Ways and Their Meaning*.

'Something veil'd and abstracted is often a part of the manners of these beings'—a quotation from Walt Whitman—serves as the epigraph for Wharton's novel *A Son at the Front*. It might have served equally well as the epigraph for *In Morocco*. The country is both distant and largely forbidden to Western European visitors; it is a 'riddle' with persistent paradoxes: 'perpetual flux' yet 'immovable stability,' and 'barbarous customs' along with 'sensuous refinements.' The material culture is puzzling; there is an 'absence of artistic originality' which co-exists with a 'gift for regrouping borrowed motives.' The 'patient and exquisite workmanship' is then negated by 'immediate neglect and degradation of the thing once made'. Many of her observations evoke *The Cruise of the Vanadis*: Both accounts manifest an interest in the colorful street life, the bazaars, the various types of people, and the unwritten mores of the country. In Morocco, of course, Wharton is more privileged; it is a rare visitor who is permitted to witness traditional ceremonies such as the Sacrifice of the Sheep (the Aïd-el-Kebir) or to enter the various harems (the rigidly restricted women's quarters).

In Morocco is also imbued with Wharton's appreciation of French contributions to that country. Her journey confirms the value of French expertise, brought benevolently to bear in promoting the country's traditional crafts and in conserving the country's aesthetic treasures. From the acknowledgments, it is

51

evident that she spoke and read French throughout the journey, and relied on more French than English sources to round out and substantiate her facts. In a larger sense, however, she represents democratic Christendom as opposed to patriarchal, autocratic Islam, although she is very respectful in describing Muslim feasts and processions.

'Harems and Ceremonies'
This chapter describes visits made by Wharton and Mme. Lyautey to several different harems (or women's quarters), in Rabat, Fez, and Marrakech. In each harem, the ladies are hospitably received and offered refreshments by servants, but conversation is, for the most part, stilted. Wharton sees the status of women as far worse than that of their American or French counterparts. Throughout the chapter, she is critical of the deleterious effects produced in women by lives spent within harems and the 'shadowy evils of the social system that hangs like a millstone about the neck of Islam.' In the harem at Marrakech, she finds a stifling atmosphere in which the young female inhabitants are idle and without curiosity.

One of her sharpest criticisms of the women in the various harems is that they are languid; they 'toil not, nor do they spin,' but leave all labor to servants. Wharton herself, despite having servants, was accustomed both to 'toil' and to 'spin'; the indolence of the women is, for her, far worse than the 'performance of leisure' (to use Thorstein Veblen's term) she criticized in many of her novels, the meaningless social calls and observance of various amenities. It is as though Morocco, unlike France, is not 'grown-up' (a term she uses to describe American women compared with their French counterparts in *French Ways and Their Meaning*), but dominated by talented adolescents who have an attitude of carpe diem. In Morocco as a whole, she concludes that both sexes 'live till old age in an atmosphere of sensuality without seduction.'

*   *   *

In viewing the sequence of Wharton's travel texts, it is clear that what is at stake is the rhetorical construction of an independent or autonomous stance of connoisseurship imaged in terms of class and gender that makes legitimate a peculiarly Whartonian artistry. This construction is shaped by, and in turn, shapes Wharton's engagement with cultural nationalism and her final expatriation. The events of World War I ratify her deepest childhood attachment to France, which, in *The Marne*, she calls the 'Naomi-country that had but to beckon, and their children rose and came'. Wharton's travel accounts may be

53

divided into the three that have an American texture and perspective underlying a European nap, written before her expatriation, and the four whose background formations are quintessentially French, though with a certain reserve of tough American fiber, written after she settled in France. During the twenty-nine years between keeping the 1888 journal later published as *The Cruise of the Vanadis* and her visit to Morocco in 1917, Wharton's voice was modulated by her circumstances and her aesthetic, professional, and political posture. In *The Cruise of the Vanadis*, she is essentially a youthful 'apprentice' (to use Lesage's phrase), unfettered by obligations to parents or publishers, but only to herself, to make the best possible use of her lifetime of reading and self-education, and conceivably to counter the objections the Wharton and Jones families had made to the extravagance of their cruise. Although she writes as an adept observer and intrepid tourist, it is probable that her journal was kept entirely in private and meant more as an exercise than a public offering. In *Italian Villas and Their Gardens*, she is an earnest scholar, deciphering the patterns and plantings of ancient gardens at the same time she is constructing an argument about how the spirit, rather than the letter, of Italian horticulture might best be followed in America. Her orientation is still firmly toward America. In *Italian Backgrounds*, she is part pilgrim reenacting the Grand Tour taken by her ancestors and part scholar and archaeologist, excavating unknown by-ways and works of art. Her mission is not assimilation to a foreign country, but the revelation, to her countrymen, of an Italy previously unknown to them. Before her next work of travel, Wharton's background becomes less firmly American; there are strong elements of Francophilia in *A Motor-Flight Through France*. Here she is an authoritative guide to the country that, as a nation, is in the ascendant in her psyche. In *Fighting France: From Dunkerque to Belfort*, she assumes an almost sacerdotal role in persuading America to assist in the defense of France; she has been transformed into a compassionate humanitarian. The ravaged country speaks in a humble voice; she is no longer the privileged traveller of *Italian Backgrounds*, whimsically posting in a diligence from Switzerland to Italy because in August her party can have 'the best part of the country' to themselves. She has, instead, become a forceful executive and anguished beggar, writing articles and letters addressed to America at large from one who is assisting France at large. In *French Ways and Their Meaning* she becomes a partisan of French mores, history, and culture, re-creating a Utopia she had never found in America. In her final travel book, *In Morocco*, she is the consummate connoisseur, synthesizing the

55

history, religious and social institutions, domestic patterns, and political conditions of Morocco, aided by her own acute perceptions, French scholarly studies, museum officials, and government interpreters. As Wharton becomes more preoccupied with the care of her two French homes and with the writing of fiction, rather than travel accounts, her prodigious achievements as a connoisseur recede, although they are still visible as nuggets within her novels and short stories. She possesses, in full measure, the 'seeing eye' she ascribes to the French, but it is not again employed in dissecting the *habitus*, to use Bourdieu's term, of a foreign country: Its aesthetic glories, quixotic customs, national sorrows, and primordial lineaments.

REFERENCES
1 'Edith Wharton and Travel Writing as Self-Discovery,' 257–267. The Jones library, as Wharton described it in *A Backward Glance*, was rich in works by Plutarch, Lamartine, Milton, Corneille, Racine, Thierry, Schliemnann, Macaulay, Gaskell, Hugo, and Coleridge. She read Tennyson, Browning, and *Innocents Abroad*. Ruskin, she wrote, 'fed me with visions of the Italy for which I had never ceased to pine.' She also devoured poets, literary critics, Kugler's *Handbook of Italian Painting*, Hamilton's *History of Philosophy*, and

other books. The list of writers whose works she explored also included Carlyle, Evelyn, de Sévigné, Burney, Dante, Herbert, Pope, Wordsworth, Campbell, Addison, the Elizabethan dramatists, Keats, Shelley, Lacroix (author of works on art), the 'amiable' Mrs Jameson (the British author of several volumes of art history), and for travel, the Arctic explorations that her father loved. Wharton recalls her inner life as a young girl in *A Backward Glance*: 'though living authors were so remote, the dead were my most living companions'.

2 Joseph Henry Harper, *The House of Harper: A Century of Publishing in Franklin Square* (New York: Harper, 1912), 326.

3 There was also a tradition of popular women travel writers. Harriet Beecher Stowe, for instance, had a ready audience for her *Sunny Memories of Foreign Lands* (1854). The following decades brought travel accounts by dozens of women: Mary Blake (on Mexico and Europe); Anna Dodd (on France and England); Julia Dorr (on England); Susan Hale (on Spain); Adelaide Hall (on Europe and the Mediterranean); and Eliza Skidmore (on Alaska, Malaya, and Japan). These women writers did not, however, bring to there travel narratives the unique aesthetic perception and connoisseurship that were the hallmarks of Wharton's travel writing. Mary Sue

57

Schriber presents a penetrating discussion of the correlation between increasing tourism during the late nineteenth century and the broadening market for travel works by women ('Introduction,' *A Motor-Flight Through France*, ed. Schriber, xxxvii-xl).

4 Her first success in the field of art history came with the re-attribution in 1893 of the groups of terra cotta statues on the Via Crucis at the monastery of San Vivaldo, Italy. They had long been attributed to Giovanni Gonnelli, a seventeenth-century artist, but she was convinced that they were created much earlier, and Florentine authorities re-attributed them to Giovanni della Robbia. She published an account of her discovery in 'A Tuscan Shrine' (*Scribner's Magazine*, 17 [Jan. 1895], 23–32), which later became a chapter in *Italian Backgrounds*.

5 Karl Baedeker, a German printer, published a series of guidebooks, which are still published today. The first, about the Rhine from Mainz to Cologne, was published in 1828. Though the era of mass tourism was still far away, he was quick to capitalize on the rising popularity of travel. Wharton was increasingly dismissive of all guidebooks.

6 'The Mediterranean Handbook,' which she often calls 'untrustworthy,' might have been W. H. D. Adams, *The Mediterranean Illustrated* (London, 1877). The *Catalogue*

of the British Library does not list any volume called *The Mediterranean Handbook* in the years prior to her cruise, nor does the *Catalogue* of the Bibliothèque Nationale. It is possible, though, that such a guidebook was on the market at the time, or that Wharton is translating a French or German title, though her usual practice is to use the original language.

7 Henry Fanshawe Tozer, *The Monks of Mount Athos*, 1862 [n.p.] and the Hon. Robert Curzon, *A Visit to Monasteries in the Levant* (New York: Putnam), 1852.

8 A reference to Gounod's opera *Faust* (1859).

9 In *A Backward Glance*, Wharton describes their taste for 'scenery, ruins and historic sites; places about which some sentimental legend hung, and to which Scott, Byron, Hans Andersen, Bulwer, Washington Irving or Hawthorne gently led the timid sight-seer.' To them 'water-falls—especially water-falls—were endlessly enjoyable' (*BG* 62–63).

10 Manon Lescaut and the young Chevalier des Grieux are characters in the eighteenth-century novel *L'Histoire du Chevalier des Grieux et de Manon Lescaut* by Abbé Prévost; the opera *Manon* (1884) by Massenet and Manon Lescaut (1893) by Puccini were based on the novel.

11 Letter from Charles Scribner to Edith

Wharton, July 13, 1915; Scribners Archives, Firestone Library, Princeton University. Quoted by permission.

12 The story of the French protectorate in Morocco, to which the Germans had agreed in 1911 in exchange for French territory in Africa is a complex one, fully explained in the final chapter of *In Morocco*, 'General Lyautey's Work in Morocco.' The previous August, he had saved Morocco for France when war broke out by refusing to send all of his troops home and by refusing to relinquish the territory that he had gained. In 1956 Morocco became independent and a member of the United Nations.

THE CRUISE OF THE VANADIS

Africa

ALGIERS; THE VANADIS; DESCRIPTION OF
THE YACHT; DEPARTURE FOR TUNIS; STOP
AT BONE; RUINS OF HIPPONE, THE BISHOPRIC
OF ST. AUGUSTINE; ARRIVAL AT LA CALLE
ON THE *VILLE D'ORAN*; THE GULF OF TUNIS;
ITS BEAUTY; GOLETTA DEPARTURE FROM
TUNIS FOR MALTA.

On the seventeenth of February after two weeks of icy fog in Paris, we left Marseilles for Algiers, in the steamer *Ville de Madrid*. The Gulf of Lions was in its usual disturbed condition, and it was after a very rough passage that we reached Algiers on the following night. The steam-yacht Vanadis, which we had chartered in England for our Mediterranean cruise, lay awaiting us in the harbour, and the gig came alongside the steamer as soon as we anchored.

We had to row ashore first, to pass through the Custom House, in common with all the other passengers; and on setting foot in the sea of mud which covered the landing-place, we were surrounded by the first Arabs we had ever seen—startlingly picturesque in the flashes of lantern light, with their white burnouses and

61

long white cloaks. A few minutes later we were again in the gig, being rapidly rowed across the wide harbour, under a sky glittering with stars, and our first view of Algiers, stretching its illuminated curve high above the dark waters of the bay, was extremely fine. We were soon alongside the yacht, and presently found ourselves peacefully seated at supper in the brightly lighted saloon, which had been filled with roses and violets in honour of our coming.

As soon as we had supped, we proceeded to inspect our yacht, little thinking, as we found our way from one room to another, with what a home-like feeling she would soon be invested. The Vanadis is a steam-yacht of 333 tons, with a length of 167 feet over all, and 21 feet beam. On deck there is a comfortable deck-house, with seats along the sides, a table, and racks over-head. Below there is a large saloon, plainly panelled in maple, with two long swinging tables, a small stove, and a shelf for books running the whole length of both sides of the saloon, above the sofas. One of the two tables we used to dine at, the other was soon covered with a varied collection of inkstands, blotting-books, maps and vases of flowers. Aft of the saloon were our two state-rooms, occupying the full width of the yacht, and comfortably fitted with shelves, drawers, hanging-closets and large bath-tubs. Forward were our fellow-traveller's room, two rooms for the maid and valet, and a fourth in which they took their meals. The engines and the men's quarters were of course aft. The crew numbered sixteen, and consisted of the captain and mate, two engineers, two firemen, the boatswain, five able seamen, two stewards and two cooks.

We spent three days and a half in Algiers, but as I was ill and passed the greater part of my time on the yacht, my recollections of it are much less clear than of many other places where we only stayed for a few hours. Never was town more nobly placed. Backed by the green slopes of the Sahel, the tiers of white houses follow the long curve of the bay, above which they are raised by the high arches of the terrace-like Boulevard de la République, and over the denser roofs of the city lie the scattered villas of Mustapha Supérieur, their horse-shoe windows glancing seaward through groves of orange and palm, their white walls tapestried with crimson bougainvillea. The harbour, crowded with shipping, is bounded on one side by a mole of modern construction, on the other by the jetty which thirty thousand Christian captives toiled to build less than four hundred years ago. But the reality of Christian slavery in Africa is brought much closer to us by Goethe's description of Prince Palagonia whom he saw, hardly more than a hundred years ago, clad in black small-clothes, with silk stockings and silver buckles, begging in the streets of Palermo for money to ransom the

Christian captives of Algeria. Even in 1816 three thousand still remained to be released by Lord Exmouth when he destroyed the fleet of the Algerine pirates.

It seems incredible that such things should have been within the memory of living man, when one walks today through the streets of the French quarter, crowded with carriages and tourists, and lined with shops as inviting as those of Nice.

To see the Arab side of Algiers one must go to the market or the mosques, or better still, climb the steep lanes which lead upward from the Parisian arcades of the Rue Bab-Azoun. In these narrow streets, we saw veiled women hurrying along with the peculiar shuffling gait due to the loose slippers of the East, their painted eyes shining through the thin white yashmak; then there were dark doorways in which old Arabs sat squatting over their tailoring or shoe-making; and groups of stalking Bedouins in ragged garments which had once been white, and negroes and Jews and half-clothed children, and all the other fantastic figures which go to make up the pageantry of an Eastern street scene. We hired a little phaeton one day, and drove out to Mustapha Supérieur, catching charming glimpses of walled gardens and Mauresque villas, and meeting omnibuses crowded with wild-looking figures, and driven at a headlong pace down the muddy suburban roads.

Mustapha, though quite as pretty as any of the suburbs near Cannes or Nice, lacks the neatness and garden-like look which we associate with the Riviera; but perhaps the general air of slovenliness is atoned for, to many eyes, by the picturesque populace filling the untidy streets. And nowhere in Europe could one see anything so Oriental as the little arcaded café at Mustapha, where white-robed Algerines sit crouched on the terrace, drinking their coffee under a group of plane-trees. We passed the summer palace of the Governor, getting a glimpse of well-kept gardens through the gateways, and then drove through the *Vallon de la Femme Sauvage* ... This wild little ravine led us to the quarter called Mustapha Inférieur, lying near the sea on the lower slope of the Sahel; and here we found the Jardin d'Essai, which I was particularly anxious to see. We walked under avenues of India-rubber trees as large as oaks, and between trellises of tea-roses in bloom, and high clumps of Arundo donax, but a cold wind sweeping through the long alleys made the scene cheerless in spite of this southern vegetation. It was, however, a bad time to visit the Jardin d'Essai, for it had been very cold for some days in Europe, and we heard afterwards that there was snow at Avignon and skating near Marseilles, while we were shivering under the India-rubber trees of Algiers. Perhaps it may have been owing to the exceptional weather that all the more delicate palms, such as Latana Borbonica, Phoenix, Cycas revoluta, &c., were sheltered by tents of matting.

On the 22nd of February, at about 3 P.M., we started for Tunis, but the wind was so high and the sea so rough, that on the following afternoon we put in at Bone. Never was tranquil harbour more welcome, and as soon as we could get pratique we were set ashore and took a walk through the town. It is charmingly situated on a bay surrounded by mountains, and close by lie the ruins of Hippone, the Bishopric of St Augustine. The town itself is clean and pretty, with an arcaded French quarter, as usual, and a square planted with palms, and beds of roses and violets. At the head of this square stands the modern Catholic cathedral, and a little further on a gate in the wall of the town leads into the country. In the Arab quarter we saw many striking figures—children in bright frocks, with broad gold bracelets, women in white burnouses, with black silk yashmaks over their faces, and strangest of all, the Jewesses with silk turbans over their plaited hair (like 17th century pictures of Judith or Herodias) loose flowing sleeves of embroidered gauze or muslin, and flowered silk dresses with jackets braided with gold.

The afternoon of our arrival we went ashore in the steam-launch, and drove to Hippone. The road lies through a lane overshadowed by high hedges of prickly pear and aloes, behind which we caught glimpses of orange and lemon groves full of fruit. The ruins stand on a hill overgrown with olives and consist of the piers and vaulting of a very old church, covered with a climbing mass of green. Whether it is the church destroyed in the 7th century or a later one, I do not know. Higher up the hill, Catholic ardour is raising the walls and columns of a new Cathedral, the crypt of which is already finished and used as a church. Here we met some Sisters of Charity, who showed us the French Orphanage near by, and after lingering for some time to look at the beautiful view of mountains, plain and sea, we drove back to Bone. This time our road led through the valley behind the town, skirting a stream overhung with cactuses and blooming mimosa. All the trees were in full leaf, and the land was a blaze of young spring green.

I was still so unwell that on February 24th we decided to take the large steamer *Ville d'Oran* to Malta, stopping at Tunis on the way, while the yacht went straight to Malta as Tunis roadstead is a very bad place to lie in. Of course, no sooner had we decided on this plan, than the wind fell, and we steamed out over a calm sea, followed by the Vanadis, and deeply regretting that we had left her. As it turned out, however, I had a lucky escape, for she met bad weather in the Malta channel; and besides we should have been very sorry not to see Tunis.

The afternoon was overcast, but the clouds broke away and when we reached the village of La Calle at 7 in the evening the moon shone out over the smooth sea and the fantastic outline of the African mountains. We lay some time at La Calle, a coral-fishing village principally populated by Italians, and the evening was so warm that we sat on deck until late, watching the unloading of a cargo of rails which were to go towards the building of a projected railway, and listening to the strange outbursts of Italian patois from the boats which swarmed about our sides.

The next morning we awoke in the Gulf of Tunis, and I never looked out on a lovelier sight than when I went on deck. To our left lay a clump of mountains, ethereal as Shelley's *peaked isles*; to our right, across the water, the cliff of Cape Carthage, with a white village clinging to its side, and the ruins of Carthage on the bay below; and beyond this again, on the water's edge, the long line of Goletta with its flat roofs and domes, and boats with gaily-coloured lateen sails putting out from its crowded wharves. The company's steam-launch took us off to Goletta, the Piraeus of Tunis, and a short walk through the little town brought us to the railway station. While we waited for the train to start we were much amused by watching the strangely-dressed Tunisian women walking in the streets. They wear short blouses to their hips, and their legs, from their feet up, are tightly wound in bands of white linen. To add to the grotesqueness of their appearance, they wear a kind of horned headdress of gold, bound about the temples with a fold of black silk, and nothing can be conceived more ludicrous than the fat, elderly women thus arrayed, who were walking unconcernedly through the cosmopolitan crowd about the railway station.

Presently the archaic little train started on its leisurely progress, skirting the shores of the *El-Bahira* or Salt Lake to the north-east of Tunis, past marshy flats where Arabs were guarding their sheep and cows, with here and there a flat-roofed villa and a cluster of palms, until we reached Tunis station. The Boulevard de la Marine, provincially French as its name implies, led us in a few minutes from the station to the hotel, where we had a moderately good breakfast in a not over-clean dining-room. A short distance beyond the hotel, the Boulevard ends at the Bab-el-Bahr or sea gate, which leads at once into the Arab quarter. Passing through that arch, one leaves behind in a moment the recent civilization which has created the hotel and the Boulevard de la Marine. If certain parts of Tunis have been greatly changed since it passed under the French protectorate, it is hard to believe that others have been in any way affected by it; for nothing can be conceived more purely Oriental than the Bazaars of Tunis. We plunged at once into a steep street, which proved to be the provision-bazaar or market, and which, like all the others, leads up to the Kasbah (the Citadel) on the hill-top. It was thronged with a brightly-tinted crowd, composed of Arabs, veiled women, Jews in richly embroidered garments, water-carriers, sweet-meats sellers carrying trays of dates and candies on their heads, negroes in gaudy robes, donkeys laden with branches of dates, and a hundred other fanciful figures, multi-coloured as a carnival procession. Soon we reached a roofed bazaar where white-robed Tunisians sat in matted niches making yellow shoes. Each bazaar is dedicated almost entirely to one trade, and in the cobbler's bazaar hundreds of yellow shoes line the walls of the dark little shops, and every cobbler seems to have a pair in hand. Overhead, streaks of sunshine filtered through between the roofing of planks, and here and there a tuft of green foliage stood out against the blue sky, while in the shops all was in cool shadow. Another turn, and we found ourselves in a vaulted bazaar, where the saddlers were embroidering harnesses and bridles in gold and silver thread, or lazy merchants, reclining on carpets, drank their coffee, and watched over their bales of silks and gauzes. But who shall describe the cool, greenish light of this whitewashed tunnel, or the picturesque groups crouched in each doorway, or the doorways themselves, with their twisted fret-work painted in bright colours; not forgetting the occasional glimpse of a vaulted courtyard, with a palm against the sky; the gleaming marble columns of the fore-court of a mosque, on whose steps an Arab kneels in prayer; the veiled women shuffling to and fro, the negroes, the dogs, the donkeys, the coffee-shops where coffee is brewed at a blue and white tiled stove for the group of Tunisians who sit in the doorway around tables inlaid with mother-of-pearl? Hard as it is to write of these things vividly, it is harder still to forget a first sight of the Bazaars of Tunis.

As no Christians are allowed to enter the mosques in the Regency of Tunis, we continued our ramble until we reached the whitewashed Kasbah on the top of the hill (now turned into a barrack) and then went back to the hotel. We met few Christians in the bazaars, and the step through the Bab-el-Bahr to the Boulevard de la Marine brought us back to civilization as abruptly as we had left it. We hired a carriage, and drove out to the Bardo, the Bey's Summer Palace. The way leads through a squalid modern suburb, a wilderness of whitewashed walls and mud and misery; then out into the country between hedges of prickly pear, along a road which is only enlivened by an occasional procession of camels, or a party of veiled women on donkeys. The scenery about Tunis is flat and uninteresting; and though the fortified exterior of the Bardo is fine, it is hardly worth taking the drive for.

Inside, we were led through one or two tiled courts, with remnants of Moorish work about the doorways, to what the attendant evidently thought the only thing worth showing: a suite of state apartments, furnished in the worst European taste of forty years ago, and adorned with the usual number of clocks with which Eastern potentates love to surround themselves.

We returned to Tunis and took the afternoon train back to Goletta, where we found that the steam-launch had already left the wharf, and for some time it seemed unlikely that we should get back to the *Ville d'Oran* before she sailed, as there was not a boat to be found anywhere. At last some of the sailors of the English schooner yacht *Ione* took pity on us and rowed us to the steamer in the yacht's dingy.

The next morning, Feb. 26th, we left Tunis at 10 A.M. It was a glorious morning, and the rocky island of Zembra rose up boldly from the blue waves at the head of the gulf as we steamed out to sea.

A little later, we passed the larger island of Pantellaria, with its white village nestling in thickets of olive-trees and backed by wooden hills. Pantellaria is very little visited, and is said to be a primitive and curious place, but unluckily it has no harbours, and the Malta

Channel is a bad place to lie in.

Chios and Smyrna

THE HARBORS OF CHIOS; INJURY TO THE
TOWN BY EARTHQUAKES; GULF OF SMYRNA;
THE BAZAARS OF SMYRNA; BRIDGANDAGE.

On the morning of April 9th we left Patmos for
Chios, passing close to the island of Samos,
where we lay to for a moment off the port of
Tigani. Although we heard tempting accounts
of ancient ruins to be seen near Tigani we were
afraid to land, as there was said to be fever in
the island, and we did not like to risk the loss of
our clean bill of health; so we took a look at the
high, mountainous shores, and then steamed
on to Chios. We reached Chios at about 5 P.M..
and as we approached the harbour in the
afternoon light we thought it the most
beautiful island we had yet seen. The white
town lies outspread along the bay, guarded by
a ruined Genoese fortress on the water's
edge—for Chios belonged to Genoa for nearly
two hundred and fifty years—and behind it,
stretching up to the enfolding mountains, is a
veritable Conca d'Oro, a forest of orange-
trees, cypresses, olives and figs. Here and there
white country houses peep out through the
verdure of delicious gardens, and even where
we lay in the harbour the air was sweet with the
smell of orange-blossoms.

We went ashore, and found the town a busy and dirty place. It has been entirely rebuilt since the great earthquake of 1881, and the dirty streets with tall houses and a pretentious French *Halle* are a poor substitute for the shady bazaars which they probably replace. In spite of its loveliness a blight seems to hang over Chios, as if it had not recovered from the awful Turkish massacre which Canaris avenged by the destruction of the Turkish fleet, and which was followed in less than sixty years by the fresh disaster of the earthquake in which nearly six thousand perished. Chios has had more than her share of calamities, and the hopeless, degraded look of the place seems to say that the people are tired of fighting adversity. We wandered through the streets, looked at the stalls filled with queer, barbaric Chian pottery, and tried to see the fortress, but were stopped by a sentinel. It is curious that the Turks should imagine that strangers would take the trouble to carry off plans of their tumble-down forts, but we met with the same opposition everywhere in Turkish dominions. There must be beautiful rides all about Chios, but as the earthquake demolished every town and monastery in the island, there is no objective point to go to, and we were so much impressed with the desolation of the place that we were glad to start for Smyrna the next morning.

The 10th was a beautiful day with a cool

breeze blowing, and when I came on deck rather late we were steaming up the wide Gulf of Smyrna with our awnings set fore and aft. As we approached the head of the gulf the scenery grew very fine. The mountains rise boldly on every side, with a fringe of trees and meadows along the shore, and above the splendid harbour lies Smyrna, her white houses outspread upon the cypress-covered hills. As we entered the port crowded with shipping we thought that the quay with tall white houses and a tramway looked strangely European; and we were struck, as we had been at Chios, with the gabled, red-tiled roofs of the houses, which give a very un-Oriental look to the town, compared with the flat house-tops we had seen all through the Egean.

The Vanadis was moored to the quay, and at 3 P.M. we went ashore, and went to the Ottoman Bank to call on Mr Reade, one of the directors, to whom we brought letters. Mr Reade kindly offered to take us through the bazaars, and we started down Frank Street, the principal street of Smyrna. It runs through the whole length of the Frank quarter, parallel with the quay, and is filled with European shops where everything is to be found which the civilized heart can desire. Connecting it with the other parallel streets and with the quay are long narrow passages with gates at either end, called *Frank passages*, lined with houses, which were built and occupied by the

Europeans at a time when the persecutions of the Turks made it necessary for them to have the means of shutting themselves in during any disturbance. These passages are now chiefly taken up with shops, restaurants, and wholesale warehouses, but here and there the blossoming pergola of an old garden shows above a high wall.

Frank Street ends at the bazaars which, though less Oriental than those of Tunis, are bright and picturesque, and offer pretty pictures at every turn. The shops, however, are really small shops, with windows in the back, not mere niches as at Tunis, and the shop-keepers wear European dress and although they offer lemonade and coffee [they] would probably be surprised if one accepted it. To make up for these disappointments, there are the trains of loaded camels, the donkeys with necklaces of large blue beads to protect them from the evil eye, the stalls hung with silks from Aleppo, the open spaces planted with blossoming acacias, the latticed fountains, the mosques with their fore-courts and minarets for the bazaars are a city in themselves, with khans, mosques, cafés, squares and fountains. Then there are the picturesque people; the Turkish women in brightly striped garments like dominos, with yellow shoes, and black veils over their faces; the Jewesses wearing long, loose robes of silk, with little caps embroidered in gold on their plaited hair, the gorgeous cavasses of the foreign consulates, in embroidered dresses, with sashes full of jewelled pistols and yataghans, the old Turks in flowing robes and white turbans, the lemonade-sellers in bright yellow coats, the negresses in gaudy colours, the gypsies, the Greek priests, all forming a medley of different types which I have never seen equalled anywhere.

Nothing, in fact, can be more curious than the mixture of Orientalism and European civilization which meets one at every turn in Smyrna. I could not get used to seeing the tramways blocked by trains of loaded camels, the voitures-de-place filled with veiled Turkish women, and the savage-looking Turks and Albanians with weapons in their belts, side by side with fashionably-dressed Levantines and Europeans. In Frank Street one can buy Zola's last novel, a ready-made dress, or a batterie de cuisine, while in the bazaars close by are sold narghilehs, clogs from Bagdad, rahat-loukoum, and other Eastern products. We stayed a long time in the bazaars, and on our return to the yacht we had a visit from Mr Charles Biliotti (brother to our Rhodian friend) and his wife.

The next day was a very busy one, as coal and water were being put in, the boat's bottom scrubbed, and the men all fitted with straw hats. In the morning I went to call on Mme Biliotti, and she took us all through the bazaars and showed us many things which we had failed to see the day before—such as the provision booths where bits of roasted meat are stuck on skewers all ready to be bought and eaten, the interior of the Khans, and the very curious iron-mongers' bazaar. We had a late luncheon on the yacht, and our fellow-traveller went for a drive in the suburbs, but we declined to peril our necks after the tales of brigandage which everyone in Smyrna had poured into our ears.

Mr and Mrs Emmett (the American Consul and his wife) came to dine with us, and although they lived not far from the quay and were escorted by an armed cavass, they thought it unsafe to drive or walk, and therefore came from their house by boat. They told us the most appalling things about the state of Smyrna. It was considered unsafe to drive out in a carriage as far as the suburban villages of Bournabat and Boujah, where many of the Europeans have their summer villas, and within a month twenty one murders had been committed in the streets of Smyrna. Several rich merchants had received letters signed *One of the Seven*, and threatening them with death if they refused to pay some thousands of francs. The first man who received such a letter disregarded it, and was murdered in the open day at his own door; consequently the next victims selected paid their tribute without a murmur. This state of affairs was said to be caused by the dishonesty of the governor of Smyrna, who had for some time past pocketed the salaries of the police, and left them no resource but to connive at the murders and robberies and take a share of the booty as their payment. As to the murderers themselves, the Turks all said they were Greeks, but in a cosmopolitan place like Smyrna it seems more likely that they were made up of the dregs of different nations.

Two years ago some of these brigands seized a young man, a cousin of Mme Biliotti's, in the neighbourhood of Smyrna, and kept him captive for several weeks, ill-treating him cruelly. The sum they asked for his ransom was so large that his father, who was a poor man, could not pay it, and not until a collection was taken up throughout the city could the needed money be obtained. Shortly afterwards the police, who had probably received their salaries that month, caught the brigands, cut off their heads and carried them back to Smyrna, where they were impaled on the gates of the Governor's Palace.

Mount Athos

PORT IERO; HISTORY OF MOUNT ATHOS; TWO KINDS OF MONASTERIES; THE ANCHORITES; LEGENDS CONCERNING THE PEAK OF ATHOS; THE AUTHOR STARTS ON A VOYAGE OF DISCOVERY AND ALARMS THE

CALOYERS; STAVRONIKETA; THIS VOYAGE
ENDS AT PANTACROTORAS; THE TURKISH
GOVERNOR WEARIED OF *RIEN QUE DES
MASCULINS ET PAS DE THÉÂTRE*;
MARVELLOUS EIKONS AND FAMOUS
TREASURES OF THE MONASTERIES;
XEROPOTAMU; XENOPHU, DOGHEIREIU,
COSTAMUNITO AND RUSSICO; ARRIVAL AT
EURIPO; ADMIRAL MANSELL.

We had intended to leave Mitylene at midnight
on the 13th of April, but the weather changed
in the night and by morning it was blowing a
gale. The Captain thought that we could start,
but the weather was so bad that we had to put
back, and finally after some hesitation we
decided to run around into Port Iero, but as I
was not up I unluckily did not see the entrance
to the port, which is said to be very fine, and is
called I believe *the Little Bosphorus*.

We anchored off a small cove with a group
of villages on the hillside above it, but it was
too rough to land, so we steamed to another
anchorage on the opposite side of the bay,
where the water was quieter. Here we went
ashore, and walked through shady olive-
groves to a village on a hill about a mile and a
half from the shore. This village, though
prettily situated, is dirty and unattractive, and,
after picking our way through its muddy
streets followed by the sullen stares of the
inhabitants, we walked back to the yacht.

The wind fell that night and the next morning we started at 5 A.M. for Mount Athos. Although it was still cold the weather was beautiful and in spite of the recent gale the waves had subsided into a long soothing roll. We ran between the islands of Shati and Lemnos, and as we coasted along the western side of Lemnos, we caught sight of the peak of Athos rising faint and blue from the sea ahead of us. The nearer we drew the more beautiful it became, until at last its mighty wall was close before us, dark against the brilliant sky as the sun set in a yellow blaze behind the low hills of the Sithonian promontory.

It was ticklish work groping along in the dusk to find an anchorage on the east coast of the Sacred Mountain, but fortunately the night was calm, and the new moon helped us, as well as the fishing beacons which the monks had lighted along the water's edge, and by 8:30 P.M. we had anchored in a shallow bay about ten miles from the peak of Athos.

So little seems to be known about Mount Athos that a few words about its history may not be amiss. Tradition ascribes the founding of some of the monasteries to the time of Constantine, and it is likely that hermitages and colonies of monks existed there from an early time. Tozer, however, calls St Athanasius of Trebizond the *originator of the present conventual system* on Mount Athos. He founded the Lavra in the tenth century. This

81

name of course signifies *the street*, and owes its origin to the street of cells which was the earliest form of monastery; and this goes to show that the Lavra when built, was the chief, if not the only monastery on the promontory. Others were soon built, and there are now about twenty on the sacred mountain, in addition to the central village of Karyes and the numerous outlying retreats and communities of farming monks. Tozer calls these monasteries *with the sole exception of Pompeii, the most ancient existing specimens of domestic architecture*, and the fact that they are still used for the purpose for which they were originally intended, adds, of course, not a little to their interest.[1]

The monasteries are all governed by a Superior called the *First Man of Athos*; but although Turkey allows great privileges to this ancient settlement of the Greek Church, a Turkish Governor lives at Karyes, who nominally represents the Sultan's suzerainty although his actual authority is of the slenderest.

The monasteries are of two kinds, the Coenobite, under the general rule of one Hegumenos, where the caloyers have *all things in common*, and the Idiorrhythmic, where the caloyers, although living together, preserve a great measure of independence, take their meals apart, and even maintain their private servants if they choose.

It need hardly be added that the rule in the latter monasteries is much less strict, and more popular among the richer monks. The caloyers are nearly all laymen, as they have too many services to perform if they take holy orders. They are a rough and illiterate set, about three thousand in number, not including the *seculars* who are employed as servants or farm-labourers without taking monastic vows. The monasteries are full of treasures in the shape of reliquaries, crosses, eikons and frescoes; in fact the churches of Mount Athos are said to contain the finest collection of mediæval jewelry in Europe.

In some of the monasteries all the monks are Greek, in others Slavonic and Russian; and Russico, the Russian monastery, is said to be in the present day a hot-bed of Russian political spies. This possibility, and the telegraph-wire which has recently been carried to the village of Karyes, are the only discordant elements in the curiously preserved mediævalism of the Sacred Mountain. Otherwise the life there is as archaic as the frescoes on the chapel walls.

Besides the monasteries there are the hermitages, built in the clefts of the peak of Athos, where anchorites live in seclusion as complete as that of the Thebaid; to say nothing of the *Sketes*, or villages of farming monks gathered around a central church.

The early established rule that no female, human or animal, is to set foot on the

83

promontory, is maintained as strictly as ever; and as hens fall under this ban, the eggs for the monastic tables have to be brought all the way from Lemnos.

As to the Sacred Mountain itself it is a narrow mountainous promontory about forty miles long, projecting into the sea from the coast-line of European Turkey. At the isthmus, where the ground is low, it is about a mile and a half wide; from this point it widens slightly and swells into a high ridge with variously broken slopes, rising as it runs seaward to a height of four thousand feet; then, after a slight drop in the land, the peak of Athos springs up suddenly almost seven thousand feet high, its summit crowned by the chapel of the Transfiguration, its base plunged in the Mediterranean waves.

Various legends are connected with the peak of Athos. It is said to have been the mountain on which Satan tempted Christ; and certainly from its peak one may well behold the riches and the glory of this world. Another story tells that St Athanasius found a heathen image (probably a statue of Zeus) where the chapel now stands; and that the Devil punished him for throwing the idol into the sea by pulling down each night the rising walls of the Lavra.

On the 6th of August the festival of the Transfiguration is celebrated on the summit of the peak. The service goes on all night, at dawn the Eucharist is celebrated; and then the monks, marching in companies and chanting psalms, go down from the mountain to the monasteries below.

The next morning we looked out on a scene of exquisite beauty. I can only compare the promontory of the Sacred Mountain to one of the wooded mountain-spurs on the Italian side of a Swiss pass, torn up from its roots and plunged into the Mediterranean. We lay just off the monastery of Iveron, which stands on the water's edge, backed by hills covered from top to base with spring foliage, in which the brilliant pink of the blossoming Judas-trees was mingled with a hundred tints of green. Southward, the wooded slopes trend away towards the peak of Athos, its grey sides streaked with snowy marble, while to the north the indented shore line carries the eye onward to the monasteries of Stavroniketa and Pantacrotoras on successive ledges of rock overhanging the sea. Iveron itself is a large building with mighty walls surmounted by a range of balconied wooden structures with steep tiled roofs, which produce the effect of a line of Swiss chalets perched on the top of a mediæval fortress. A square gate-tower guards it at the water's edge, and above the gabled roofs rises a medley of cupolas and towers, backed by a mass of verdure.

High up the hillside the white walls of farm-houses and *retreats* sparkle through thickets of larch, chestnut and plane-tree, and a few miles away, below the central ridge of the promontory, the roofs and steeples of the village of Karyes rise from a sea of bright foliage mixed with dark clumps of cypress.

At 9 A.M.. the two men went ashore, taking the cook as interpreter, and set out for Karyes, where our books told us that the *First Man* lived. They had their walk for nothing, however, for when they got to Karyes they were told that to find the *First Man* they must go to the monastery of Vatopedi.

In the meantime I ordered steam up in the launch, and started out on a voyage of discovery, determined to go as near the forbidden shores as I could. I ran in close to Iveron and tried to photograph it, but the launch rolled so that I could not steady the camera. I then ran close in under the shore in the direction of Stavroniketa, passing a picturesque square tower used as a boat-house, with a fishing-boat drawn up under its dark archway. This tower is connected with the hillside by a wooden bridge close to which, in a bower of green, is perched a balconied cottage where a group of caloyers sat in the sunshine watching me with evident curiosity. We went in so close to the shore that they clambered hurriedly down the hill to prevent my landing, and with their shocks of black hair and long woollen robes flying behind them they were a wild enough looking set to frighten any intruder away.

Stavroniketa is a small but picturesque building on top of a rock which projects boldly into the sea. It is guarded by a gate-tower with an embattled parapet, and the stone arches of an aqueduct connect it with the hill behind. As we came close to it, I noticed that the rock on which it is built was thickly tufted with crimson snapdragon, white iris, and a sort of dwarf white-yellow laburnum.

As we steamed on the scene increased in beauty. Here a white chapel with a cross above its tiled cupola gleams through the trees; there a boat-house guarded by a tower stands close upon the shore; while scattered along the higher ridges of the promontory clusters of quaint houses with a minaret-like spire rising in their midst show the position of some *Skete* or independent community of farming monks. Where the slopes are not covered with foliage, they are terraced and planted with olives, vines and vegetables, and this careful tilth, combined with the trains of fat mules with packsaddles grazing near the monasteries, gives a look of rural prosperity to the scene which is more suggestive of Switzerland or Tyrol than of the East.

We ran on to Pantacrotoras, which is placed close to the sea, like the others, and has a boat-harbour guarded by a rock on the top of which a large wooden cross has been fixed. A soft and fertile valley opens behind it in folds of richest green. From Pantacrotoras I turned and went back to the yacht, where the two men did not arrive until 3 P.M.

They brought with them the Turkish Governor of Mount Athos, who lives at Karyes, a stout old gentleman in frock-coat, fez and Rhodian boots, accompanied by a bristling little aide-de-camp. The Governor had brought me two old Turkish water jars of brown glazed pottery, which he called *des antiques*. He was very jolly, and told me in the strangest possible French that he had been pining for two years on Mount Athos *avec rien que des masculins et pas de théâtre*.

I think, however, that the motion of the yacht disturbed him, for he and his aide took leave rather hurriedly, becoming terribly involved with their large swords as they climbed down the side ladder to the gig.

As soon as they had left we got under weigh and steamed northward along the coast to the monastery of Vatopedi, the wealthiest of the Sacred Mountain, and the largest except the Lavra. Its situation is less fine than that of the others, as Athos itself is out of sight, but it lies on a pretty bay enclosed in wooded hills, and forms in itself the finest group of buildings that we saw on the promontory.

A kind of terrace planted with olives and cypresses slopes gradually up from the beach to the base of the monastery-wall, and above this wall rises a fantastic line of balconies, towers, cupolas, tiled roofs and chimneys, interspersed here and there with slender bright green poplars. All these broken and irregular groups of buildings are painted in various colours, the châlets red, blue and green, and the towers white, while the roofs are covered with a lichenous growth like gold; and nothing can be conceived more brilliant and fairy-like than this combination of colours, lit up, as we saw it, by the setting sun, and framed in thickets of green.

Everything at Vatopedi is kept in perfect repair, and as all restorations at Mount Athos are made scrupulously like the original, one can admire the neatness and brightness of this great group of buildings without feeling that it involves the loss of anything that might have been better worth seeing.

Along the shore is a row of boat-houses (boat-towers would be more correct) each surmounted by its white châlet with black wooden balconies, and there are one or two stone outbuildings among the olives on the terraces.

I stayed on deck while the two men went ashore to visit the First Man, and no sooner had we anchored than the numberless balconies above the monastery-wall were crowded with caloyers gazing eagerly out at the yacht.

As I looked at this scene, it seemed hard to realize that many of the monasteries on the promontory have existed as we now see them since the tenth century, if not earlier, and that within their walls the same life has been going on unbrokenly—a life unaffected by modern inventions, discoveries and revolutions, a life as primly mediæval as when the hermit Athanasius laid the first stone of the Lavra.

The two men were received with great courtesy wherever they went, and saw all the marvellous eikons set with uncut rubies, sapphires and emeralds, and the other famous treasures which the monasteries contain. In one of the monasteries they saw a monk frescoing a wall, and on going close to him they found that he was referring as he painted to the book of rules which was written for the artists of the Greek Church in the very beginning of Byzantine art by Dionysius of Agrapha. When they returned from Vatopedi they brought a picture of the monastery, which the First Man had given them, and also a boat-load of fresh vegetables contributed by the kindly monks.

No wonder that Xerxes cut a canal through the promontory of the Sacred Mountain, if the sea around it in his days was as lumpy and disagreeable as it was the next morning when we left Vatopedi.

There was a breeze from the eastward, and the strong current, racing against it, kicked up such a swell that even the flower vases on the swinging tables were upset, and everything around them drenched and damaged by the overflow.

We left Vatopedi at 9 A.M. and as there was too much sea on to stop at the Lavra we ran straight around Mount Athos to get in the lee of the west coast. When I came on deck we had just rounded the great peak, and were running close under it. On the western side it plunges down into the sea with splendid abruptness, its grey marble sides clothed far up with pine-trees *fledging the wild-ridged mountain steep by steep.*[2]

The water here is so deep that we ran in almost close enough, it seemed, to touch the cliffs, and as we drew near we saw that here and there, among the inaccessible ledges high overhead, hermitages clung like birds' nests to the rocks. In some cases they are no more than little wooden sheds, with balconies which literally overhang the precipitous cliffs; in others a tiny patch of ground has been reclaimed and a white hut peeps out through olives and Judas-trees.

How these places were ever reached, or how the hermits ever carried enough materials down the perpendicular face of the rock to build even such tiny hovels, is incomprehensible; but there they are, in every crack and cranny, and as we blew our whistle in passing a hermit appeared on each balcony with the promptitude of cuckoos in Swiss clocks when the hour strikes.

As we advanced the cliffs, though still four thousand feet high and very steep, were clothed in a thick scrub of cytisus, heather, Judas-trees and evergreen shrubs, mingled with olive and cypress, and to the sides of this green precipice clung two *Sketes*, more like Swiss villages than Greek monastic settlements. Their white houses, with the inevitable black balconies, showed pleasantly through the masses of Spring foliage, presided over by the guardian spire of the central church, and I have never seen a lovelier picture of sunny peacefulness than they presented as we looked up at them from the deck of the yacht.

On we steamed, and rounding a projecting point came suddenly upon the monastery of St Paul, which Curzon well compares to a Gothic castle.[3] With its towers backed by a crenellated wall it stands in bold picturesqueness at the foot of a mountain-chasm down which a torrent pours, as it seems, from the very peak of Athos. This stream had not yet begun to flow when we saw it, and masses of snow choked the upper part of its bed, contrasting strangely with the verdure below.

Nothing can be conceived finer than the scenery on this side of Athos. Two other monasteries follow in succession along the shore, each guarded in the rear by an embrasured wall, each with diversely grouped balconies, domes and towers, and a setting of many-tinted green. These are the monasteries of St Dionysios and St Gregory.

A little further on, perched on a splinter of

rock which rises up hundreds of feet from the sea, stands the monastery of Simopetra, perhaps more grandly placed than any of the others. Seven tiers of balconies overhang its walls and an aqueduct with a double row of arches connects it with the face of the cliff behind.

Beyond this another bend of the coast took us out of sight of Athos, and the cliffs here become lower and less wild in aspect.

We passed Xeropotamu on a high cornice of rock, with its boat-house on a beach of white pebbles far below; then came Russico close to the water's edge, a large and ugly mass of buildings surmounted by bubble-like pale green domes on every one of which glitters a gilded cross.

After Russico comes the smaller and prettier Xenophu, also close to the water, with its square tower crowned by a peaked green roof, and close to this Dogheiareiu, a group of castellated walls and towers, with red domes and a clump of velvety cypresses.

We ran on a little further, catching sight of Constamunito high up the mountain side further to the north; then we turned, and steamed back to Russico, which owing to Tozer's bad map we had mistaken for Xeropotamu. At Russico an occasional steamer touches, and we tied up to a buoy while the two men went ashore.

They found a caloyer who spoke English

and took them all over the monastery, but there was not much to be seen except the cross-shaped refectory frescoed with scenes from the life of Christ, where the monks sat eating while one of their number read aloud to them from a lectern in the wall. Each monk had a plate of soup, a lump of coarse bread and a handful of raw onions, and at every second plate there was a bottle of wine.

From Russico we steamed to Xeropotamu, which the men also wished to visit, and then back again to Russico, where we tied up to the buoy until it should be time to get under weigh for Euboea, as we did not wish to make the island of Skiathos before daylight.

We had a beautiful sunset, and a calm night flooded with moonlight which idealized the pale green domes of Russico; and at 10 P.M. we got under weigh, sadly remembering that henceforward we were homeward bound, and that each day would leave the *purple East* further in our wake.

At 4:30 the next morning we passed Skiathos, and entered the narrow channel between Greece and Euboea. It was very pretty winding down the quiet waters with the barren hills of Greece on one side, on the other those of Euboea, covered near the base with a low growth of light green conifers (probably the Isthmian pine) while the snow still lay thick upon the higher peaks.

During the day we passed an English steam-yacht of our own size, the first we had seen in a month, so far off the beaten track had our wanderings taken us.

As we advanced the hills seemed to close in around us, until at last it appeared as though we were sailing over a glassy inland lake, with the walled town of Euripo lying at its head. As we approached we saw the drawbridge and fortress which connect Euripo with the mainland, and the narrow channel between them did not look wide enough to let a row-boat pass. The extraordinary current which runs here had set the wrong way just before we arrived, and we could not pass the bridge and run along, as we had hoped to do, as far as Armyra bay or Marathon. Our time was growing short, and we were realizing its value more and more each day, so that the delay was disappointing; but there was nothing to do but anchor, and spend the afternoon in exploring Euripo.

We rowed ashore expecting to land in five minutes as we usually did, but the officials were very disagreeable and kept us waiting a full hour for pratique. The inhabitants of Euripo are a sullen, ill-favoured lot, and as for the town, a short walk sufficed to convince us that it has nothing to recommend it but its fine double girdle of walls and the fortress in the middle of the channel. We walked across the drawbridge, and under the arched gate of the fortress, which Mark guards; then over

95

another small bridge to the mainland, where we took our first steps on the soil of Greece.

From thence the view over the town is pretty, although disfigured by factory chimneys; but when we walked through the streets we were much disappointed. I suppose that the frequent earthquakes are the cause of the shabby, tumble-down look of the houses, which are forlorn without being picturesque. We strolled about for a little while, and then hurried back to the drawbridge to see the yacht pass through with the change of the current. She looked like a picture as she shot through the narrow passage just beneath us, her awning set, her brasses shining in the sun, and rounded up to anchor in the bay beyond the bridge where we were to lie that night.

We were still loitering there, and I had just remarked that I could not understand what had induced the Englishman Captain Mansell, of whom Lady Brassey speaks, to fix upon Euripo as his place of abode, when a little old gentleman with a white beard came up to us and introduced himself as Admiral Mansell![4]

The ten or twelve years elapsing since Lady Brassey wrote, although they had brought him promotion, had apparently not shaken his allegiance to Euripo, for there he was, as ready as ever to take us to his house and offer us a bouquet from his garden, just as he is described as doing in *Sunshine and Storm*. He told us that at one time the hills of Attica on the further side of the drawbridge were so full of brigands that for eight months at a time he did not venture off the island; and on one occasion forty brigands marched into the town, surrounded the house of a Greek gentleman and carried him and his wife off for a six weeks' retreat among the mountains, from which they were only released by the payment of £2000. Since the murder of Messers Herbert and Vyner, however, there has been no brigandage in Greece, and except on the orders of Turkey or Albania the traveller is as safe as in Switzerland or Italy.

Admiral Mansell took us to his house, and showed us his garden full of orange and lemon trees, and the little one-story cottage in one corner where he and his wife sleep every night for fear of earthquakes. We asked him to dine with us but his wife was too ill for him to leave her, and so we wished him goodbye and returned to the yacht.

REFERENCES
1 Henry Fanshawe Tozer, *The Monks of Mount Athos*, 1862 [no publisher].
2 Wharton misquotes Keats's 'Ode to Psyche.' The line actually reads '[those dark-cluster'd trees]/Fledge the wild-ridged mountains steep by steep,' i.e., the trees stand in ranks like layers of feathers, 'fledge' meaning to cover with feathers. A simple change to 'pine-trees which' would have made the

quotation accurate and it would have fit grammatically, as well. She misquotes the line the same way in a chapter called 'What the Hermits Saw' in *Italian Backgrounds*.

3 The Hon. Robert Curzon, *A Visit to Monasteries in the Levant* (London: Murray, 1849; New York: George P. Putnam & Co., 1852). Lord Curzon was considered to be one of the leading nineteenth-century authorities on Mount Athos, and his book was reprinted several times, both in England and America. Robert Bridges described it as 'A Gentleman's Book.'

4 Annie Allnut Brassey wrote *Sunshine and Storm in the East: or Cruises to Cyprus and Constantinople* (New York: Henry Holt and Co., 1880). Brassey describes Captain Mansell as the 'well-known hydrographer to the Navy' who had, at that time, lived on the island of Euripo for seven years. She also recounts a story, which seems unlikely, that 'a few years ago' two English ladies had landed on Mount Athos from a yacht, undiscovered, 'as most of the men here wear petticoats and the women trousers, and the monks have not a chance of much experience in such matters, they did not discover the sacrilege that had been committed for some time' (48). She was also the author of *Around the World in the Yacht Sunbeam*.

ITALIAN VILLAS
AND THEIR GARDENS*

Villas Near Rome

I
CAPRAROLA AND LANTE

The great cardinals did not all build their villas within sight of St Peter's. One of them, Alexander Farnese, chose a site above the mountain village of Caprarola, which looks forth over the Etrurian plain strewn with its ancient cities—Nepi, Orte and Città Castellana—to Soracte, rising solitary in the middle distance, and the encircling line of snow-touched Apennines.

There is nothing in all Italy like Caprarola. Burckhardt calls it 'perhaps the highest example of restrained majesty which secular architecture has achieved'; and Herr Gurlitt makes the interesting suggestion that Vignola, in building it, broke away from the traditional palace-architecture of Italy and sought his

---

* 'Villas Near Rome' was first published in *The Century*, 67 (Apr. 1904); 860–874 and is Chapter IV of *Italian Villas and Their Gardens*. 'Villas of Venetia,' the last of the series and Chapter VII of the book, was also published in *The Century*, 68 (Oct. 1904), 884–894.

inspiration in France. 'Caprarola,' he says, 'shows the northern castle in the most modern form it had then attained... We have to do here with one of the fortified residences rarely seen save in the north, but doubtless necessary in a neighbourhood exposed to the ever-increasing dangers of brigandage. Italy, indeed, built castles and fortified works, but the fortress-palace, equally adapted to peace and war, was almost unknown.'

The numerous illustrated publications on Caprarola make it unnecessary to describe its complex architecture in detail. It is sufficient to say that its five bastions are surrounded by a deep moat, across which a light bridge at the back of the palace leads to the lower garden. To pass from the threatening façade to the widespread beauty of pleached walks,[1] fountains and grottoes, brings vividly before one the curious contrasts of Italian country life in the transition period of the sixteenth century. Outside, one pictures the cardinal's soldiers and *bravi* lounging on the great platform above the village; while within, one has a vision of noble ladies and their cavaliers sitting under rose-arbours or strolling between espaliered lemon-trees, discussing a Greek manuscript or a Roman bronze, or listening to the last sonnet of the cardinal's court poet.

The lower garden of Caprarola is a mere wreck of overgrown box-parterres and crumbling wall and balustrade. Plaster statues in all stages of decay stand in the niches or cumber the paths; fruit-trees have been planted in the flower-beds, and the maiden-hair withers in grottoes where the water no longer flows. The architectural detail of the fountains and arches is sumptuous and beautiful, but the outline of the general plan is not easy to trace; and one must pass out of this enclosure and climb through hanging oak-woods to a higher level to gain an idea of what the gardens once were.

Beyond the woods a broad *tapis vert* leads to a level space with a circular fountain sunk in turf. Partly surrounding this is an architectural composition of rusticated arcades, between which a *château d'eau* descends the hillside from a grotto surmounted by two mighty river-gods, and forming the central motive of a majestic double stairway of rusticated stonework. This leads up to the highest terrace, which is crowned by Vignola's exquisite casino, surely the most beautiful garden-house in Italy.[2] The motive of the arcades and stairway, though fine in itself, may be criticized as too massive and important to be in keeping with the delicate little building above; but once on the upper terrace, the lack of proportion is no longer seen and all the surroundings are harmonious. The composition is simple: around the casino, with its light arcades raised on a broad flight of steps, stretches a level box-garden with fountains, enclosed in a low

101

wall surmounted by the famous Canephoræ seen in every picture of Caprarola—huge sylvan figures half emerging from their stone sheaths, some fierce or solemn, some full of rustic laughter. The audacity of placing that row of fantastic terminal divinities against reaches of illimitable air girdled in mountains gives an indescribable touch of poetry to the upper garden of Caprarola. There is a quality of inevitableness about it—one feels of it, as of certain great verse, that it could not have been otherwise, that, in Vasari's happy phrase, it was *born, not built*.[3]

Not more than twelve miles from Caprarola lies the other famous villa attributed to Vignola, and which one wishes he may indeed have built, if only to show how a great artist can vary his resources in adapting himself to a new theme. The Villa Lante, at Bagnaia, near Viterbo, appears to have been the work not of one cardinal, but of four. Raphael Riario, Cardinal Bishop of Viterbo, began it toward the end of the fifteenth century, and the work, carried on by his successors in the see, Cardinals Ridolfi and Gambara, was finally completed in 1588 by Cardinal Montalto, nephew of Sixtus V, who bought the estate from the bishops of Viterbo and bequeathed it to the Holy See. Percier and Fontaine[4] believe that several architects collaborated in the work, but its unity of composition shows that the general scheme must have originated in one mind, and Herr Gurlitt thinks there is nothing to disprove that Vignola was its author.

Lante, like Caprarola, has been exhaustively sketched and photographed, but so perfect is it, so far does it surpass, in beauty, in preservation, and in the quality of garden-magic, all the other great pleasure-houses of Italy, that the student of garden-craft may always find fresh inspiration in its study. If Caprarola is 'a garden to look out from,' Lante is one 'to look into,' not in the sense that it is enclosed, for its terraces command a wide horizon; but the pleasant landscape surrounding it is merely accessory to the gardens, a last touch of loveliness where all is lovely.

The designer of Lante understood this, and perceived that, the surroundings being unobtrusive, he might elaborate the foreground. The flower-garden occupies a level space in front of the twin pavilions; for instead of one villa there are two at Lante, absolutely identical, and connected by a *rampe douce* which ascends between them to an upper terrace. This peculiar arrangement is probably due to the fact that Cardinal Montalto, who built the second pavilion, found there was no other way of providing more house-room without disturbing the plan of the grounds. The design of the flower-garden is intricate and beautiful, and its box-bordered parterres surround one of the most famous and beautiful fountains in Italy. The abundance of water at Lante enabled the designer to produce a great variety of effects in what Germans call the 'water-art,' and nowhere was his invention happier than in planning this central fountain. It stands in a square tank or basin, surrounded by a balustrade, and crossed by four little bridges which lead to a circular balustraded walk, enclosing an inner basin from the centre of which rises the fountain. Bridges also cross from the circular walk to the platform on which the fountain is built, so that one may stand under the arch of the water-jets, and look across the garden through a mist of spray.

Lante, doubly happy in its site, is as rich in shade as in water, and the second terrace, behind the pavilions, is planted with ancient plane-trees. Above this terrace rise three others, all wooded with plane and ilex, and down the centre, from the woods above, rushes the cascade which feeds the basin in the flower-garden. The terraces, with their balustrades and obelisks and double flights of steps, form a stately setting to this central *château d'eau*, through which the water gushes by mossy steps and channels to a splendid central composition of superimposed basins flanked by recumbent river-gods.

All the garden-architecture at Lante merits special study. The twin pavilions seem plain and insignificant after the brilliant elevations of the great Roman villas, but regarded as part of the garden-scheme, and not as dominating it, they fall into their proper place, and are seen to be good examples of the severe but pure style of the early cinque-cento. Specially interesting also is the treatment of the retaining-wall which faces the entrance to the grounds; and the great gates of the flower-gardens, and the fountains and garden-houses on the upper terraces, are all happy instances of Renaissance garden-art untouched by *barocchismo*.

At Lante, also, one sees one of the earliest examples of the inclusion of the woodland in the garden-scheme. All the sixteenth-century villas had small groves adjacent to the house, and the shade of the natural woodland was used, if possible, as a backing to the gardens; but at the Villa Lante it is boldly worked into the general scheme, the terraces and garden-architecture are skillfully blent with it, and its recesses are pierced by grass alleys leading to clearings where pools surrounded by stone seats slumber under the spreading branches.

The harmonizing of wood and garden is one of the characteristic features of the villas at Frascati; but as these are mostly later in date than the Lante grounds, priority of invention may be claimed for the designer of the latter. It was undoubtedly from the Italian park of the Renaissance that Le Nôtre[5] learned the use of the woodland as an adjunct to the garden; but in France these parks had for the most part to be planted, whereas in Italy the garden-architect could use the natural woodland, which was usually hilly, and the effects thus produced were far more varied and interesting than those possible in the flat artificial parks of France.

II
VILLA D'ESTE

Of the three great villas built by cardinals beyond the immediate outskirts of Rome, the third and the most famous is the Villa d'Este at Tivoli.

Begun before 1540 by the Cardinal Bishop of Cordova, the villa became the property of Cardinal Ippolito d'Este, son of Alfonso I of Ferrara, who carried on its embellishment at the cost of over a million Roman scudi. Thence it passed successively to two other cardinals of the house of Este, who continued its adornment, and finally, in the seventeenth century, was inherited by the ducal house of Modena.

The villa, an unfinished barrack-like building, stands on a piazza at one end of the town of Tivoli, above gardens which descend the steep hillside to the gorge of the Anio.[6] These gardens have excited so much admiration that little thought has been given to the house, though it is sufficiently interesting to merit attention. It is said to have been built by

106

Pirro Ligorio,[7] and surprising as it seems that this huge featureless pile should have been designed by the creator of the Casino del Papa, yet one observes that the rooms are decorated with the same fantastic pebble-work used in such profusion at the Villa Pia. In extenuation of the ugliness of the Villa d'Este it should, moreover, be remembered that its long facade is incomplete, save for the splendid central portico; and also that, while the Villa Pia was intended as shelter for a summer afternoon, the great palace at Tivoli was planned to house a cardinal and his guests, including, it is said, 'a suite of two hundred and fifty gentlemen of the noblest blood of Italy.' When one pictures such a throng, with their innumerable retainers, it is easy to understand why the Villa d'Este had to be expanded out of all likeness to an ordinary country house.

The plan is ingenious and interesting. From the village square only a high blank wall is visible. Through a door in this wall one passes into a frescoed corridor which leads to a court enclosed in an open arcade, with fountains in rusticated niches. From a corner of the court a fine intramural stairway descends to what is, on the garden side, the *piano nobile* of the villa. On this side, looking over the gardens, is a long enfilade of rooms, gaily frescoed by the Zuccheri and their school; and behind the rooms runs a vaulted corridor built against the side of the hill, and lighted by bull's-eyes in its roof. This corridor has lost its frescoes, but preserves a line of niches decorated in coloured pebbles and stucco-work, with gaily painted stucco caryatids supporting the arches; and as each niche contains a semicircular fountain, the whole length of the corridor must once have rippled with running water.

The central room opens on the great two-storied portico or loggia, whence one descends by an outer stairway to a terrace running the length of the building, and terminated at one end by an ornamental wall, at the other by an open loggia overlooking the Campagna.[8] From this upper terrace, with its dense wall of box and laurel, one looks down on the towering cypresses and ilexes of the lower gardens. The grounds are not large, but the impression produced is full of a tragic grandeur. The villa towers above so high and bare, the descent from terrace to terrace is so long and steep, there are such depths of mystery in the infinite green distances and in the cypress-shaded pools of the lower garden, that one has a sense of awe rather than of pleasure in descending from one level to another of darkly rustling green. But it is the omnipresent rush of water which gives the Este gardens their peculiar character. From the Anio, drawn up the hillside at incalculable cost and labour, a thousand rills gush downward, terrace by terrace, channelling the stone rails of the balusters, leaping from step to step, dripping into mossy conchs, flashing in spray from the horns of sea-gods and the jaws of mythical monsters, or forcing themselves in irrepressible overflow down the ivy-matted banks. The whole length of the second terrace is edged by a deep stone channel, into which the stream drips by countless outlets over a quivering fringe of maidenhair. Every side path or flight of steps is accompanied by its sparkling rill, every niche in the retaining-walls has its water-pouring nymph or gushing urn; the solemn depths of green reverberate with the tumult of innumerable streams. 'The Anio,' as Herr Tuckermann says, 'throbs through the whole organism of the garden like its inmost vital principle.'[9]

The gardens of the Villa d'Este were probably begun by Pirro Ligorio, and, as Herr Gurlitt thinks,[10] continued later by Giacomo della Porta. It will doubtless never be known how much Ligorio owed to the taste of Orazio Olivieri, the famous hydraulic engineer, who raised the Anio to the hilltop and organized its distribution through the grounds. But it is apparent that the whole composition was planned about the central fact of the rushing Anio: that the gardens were to be, as it were, an organ on which the water played. The results is extraordinarily romantic and beautiful, and the versatility with which the stream is used, the varying effects won from it, bear witness to the imaginative feeling of the designer.

When all has been said in praise of the poetry and charm of the Este gardens, it must be owned that from the architect's standpoint they are less satisfying than those of the other great cinque-cento villas. The plan is worthy of all praise, but the details are too complicated, and the ornament is either trivial or cumbrous. So inferior is the architecture to that of the Lante gardens and Caprarola that Burckhardt was probably right in attributing much of it to the seventeenth century. Here for the first time one feels the heavy touch of the baroque. The fantastic mosaic and stucco temple containing the water-organ above the great cascade, the arches of triumph, the celebrated 'grotto of Arethusa,' the often-sketched fountain on the second terrace, all seem pitiably tawdry when compared with the garden-architecture of Raphael or Vignola. Some of the details of the composition are absolutely puerile—such as the toy model of an ancient city, thought to be old Rome, and perhaps suggested by the miniature 'Valley of Canopus' in the neighbouring Villa of Hadrian; and there are endless complications of detail, where the earlier masters would have felt the need of breadth and simplicity. Above all, there is a want of harmony between the landscape and its treatment. The baroque garden-architecture of Italy is not without charm, and even a touch of the grotesque has its attraction in the flat gardens of Lombardy or the sunny

Euganeans; but the cypress-groves of the Villa d'Este are too solemn, and the Roman landscape is too august, to suffer the nearness of the trivial.

III
FRASCATI

The most famous group of villas in the Roman country-side lies on the hill above Frascati. Here, in the middle of the sixteenth century, Flaminio Ponzio built the palace of Mondragone for Cardinal Scipione Borghese.* Aloft among hanging ilex-woods rises the mighty pile on its projecting basement. This fortress-like ground floor, with high-placed grated windows, is common to all the earlier villas on the brigand-haunted slopes of Frascati. An avenue of ancient ilexes (now cruelly cut down) leads up through the park to the villa, which is preceded by a great walled courtyard, with fountains in the usual rusticated niches. To the right of this court is another, flanked by the splendid loggia of vignola, with the Borghese eagles and dragons alternating in its sculptured spandrels, and a

---

* The villa was begun by Martino Lunghi the Elder, in 1567, for the Cardinal Marco d'Altemps, enlarged by Pope Gregory VII, and completed by Paul V and his nephew, Cardinal Scipione Borghese. See Gustav Ebe, 'Die Spätrenaissance.'

vaulted ceiling adorned with *stucchi*—one of the most splendid pieces of garden-architecture in Italy.

At the other end of this inner court, which was formerly a flower-garden, Giovanni Fontana, whose name is identified with the fountains of Frascati, constructed a *théâtre d'eau*, raised above the court, and approached by a double ramp elaborately inlaid in mosaic. This ornate composition, with a series of mosaic niches simulating arcaded galleries in perspective, is now in ruins, and the most impressive thing about Mondragone is the naked majesty of its great terrace, unadorned save by a central fountain and two tall twisted columns, and looking out over the wooded slopes of the park to Frascati, the Campagna, and the sea.

On a neighbouring height lies the more famous Villa Aldobrandini, built for the cardinal of that name by Giacomo della Porta in 1598, and said by Evelyn,[11] who saw it fifty years later, 'to surpass the most delicious places ... for its situation, elegance, plentiful water, groves, ascents and prospects.'

The house itself does not bear comparison with such buildings as the Villa Medici or the Villa Pamphily. In style it shows the first stage of the baroque, before that school had found its formula. Like all the hill-built villas of Frascati, it is a story lower at the back than in front; and the roof of this lower story forms at each end a terrace level with the first-floor windows. These terraces are adorned with two curious turrets, resting on baroque basements and crowned by swallow-tailed crenellations—a fantastic reversion to mediævalism, more suggestive of 'Strawberry Hill Gothic' than of the Italian seventeenth century.

Orazio Olivieri and Giovanni Fontana are said to have collaborated with Giacomo della Porta in designing the princely gardens of the villa. Below the house a series of splendid stone terraces lead to a long *tapis vert*, with an ilex avenue down its centre, which descends to the much-admired grille of stone and wrought-iron enclosing the grounds at the foot of the hill. Behind the villa, in a semicircle cut out of the hillside, is Fontana's famous water-theatre, of which Evelyn gives a picturesque description: 'Just behind the Palace ... rises a high hill or mountain all overclad with tall wood, and so formed by nature as if it had been cut out by art, from the summit of which falls a cascade ... precipitating into a large theatre of water. Under this is an artificial grot wherein are curious rocks, hydraulic organs, and all sorts of singing birds, moving and chirping by force of the water, with several other pageants and surprising inventions. In the centre of one of these rooms rises a copper ball that continually dances about three feet above the pavement, by virtue of a wind conveyed secretly to a hole beneath it; with many other devices for wetting the unwary spectators ... In one of these theatres of water is an Atlas spouting, ... and another monster makes a terrible roaring with a horn; but, above all, the representation of a storm is most natural, with such fury of rain, wind and thunder as one would imagine oneself in some extreme tempest.'

Atlas and the monster are silent, and the tempest has ceased to roar; but the architecture of the great water-theatre remains intact. It has been much extolled by so good a critic as Herr Gurlitt, yet compared with Vignola's loggia at Mondragone or the terrace of the Orti Farnesiani, it is a heavy and uninspired production. It suffers also from too great a proximity to the villa, and from being out of scale with the latter's modest elevation: there is a distinct lack of harmony between the two façades. But even Evelyn could not say too much in praise of the glorious descent of the cascade from the hilltop. It was in the guidance of rushing water that the Roman garden-architects of the seventeenth century showed their poetic feeling and endless versatility; and the architecture of the upper garden at the Aldobrandini merits all the admiration which has been wasted on its pompous theatre.

Another example of a *théâtre d'eau*, less showy but far more beautiful, is to be seen at the neighbouring Villa Conti (now Torlonia).

Of the formal gardens of this villa there remain only the vast terraced stairways which now lead to an ilex-grove level with the first story of the villa. This grove is intersected by mossy alleys, leading to circular clearings where fountains overflow their wide stone basins, and benches are ranged about in the deep shade. The central alley, on the axis of the villa, leads through the wood to a great grassy semicircle at the foot of an ilex-clad hill. The base of the hillside is faced with a long arcade of twenty niches, divided by pilasters, and each containing a fountain. In the centre is a great baroque pile of rock-work, from which the spray tosses into a semicircular basin, which also receives the cascade descending from the hilltop. This cascade is the most beautiful example of fountain-architecture in Frascati. It falls by a series of inclined stone ledges into four oval basins, each a little wider than the one above it. On each side, stone steps which follow the curves of the basins lead to a grassy plateau above, with a balustraded terrace overhanging the rush of the cascade. The upper plateau is enclosed in ilexes, and in its centre is one of the most beautiful fountains in Italy—a large basin surrounded by a richly sculptured balustrade. The plan of this fountain is an interesting example of the variety which the Italian garden-architects gave to the outline of their basins. Even in the smaller gardens the plan of these basins is varied with taste and originality; and the small wall-fountains are also worthy of careful study.

Among the villas of Frascati there are two, less famous than the foregoing, but even more full of a romantic charm. One is the Villa Muti, a mile or two beyond the town, on the way to Grotta Ferrata. From the gate three ancient ilex avenues lead to the villa, the central ones being on the axis of the lowest garden. The ground rises gradually toward the house, and the space between the ilex avenues was probably once planted in formal *boschi*, as fragments of statuary are still seen among the trees. The house, set against the hillside, with the usual fortress-like basement, is two stories lower toward the *basse-cour* than toward the gardens. The avenue to the left of the entrance leads to a small garden, probably once a court, in front of the villa, whence one looks down over a mighty retaining-wall at the *basse-cour* on the left. On the right, divided from the court by a low wall surmounted by vases, lies the most beautiful box-garden in Italy, laid out in an elaborate geometrical design, and enclosed on three sides by high clipped walls of box and laurel, and on the fourth by a retaining-wall which sustains an upper garden. Nothing can surpass the hushed and tranquil beauty of the scene. There are no flowers or bright colours— only the contrasted tints of box and ilex and laurel, and the vivid green of the moss spreading over damp paths and ancient stonework.

In the upper garden, which is of the same length but narrower, the box-parterres are repeated. This garden, at the end nearest the villa, has a narrow raised terrace, with an elaborate architectural retaining-wall, containing a central fountain in stucco-work. Steps flanked by statues lead up to this fountain, and thence one passes by another flight of steps to the third, or upper, garden, which is level with the back of the villa. This third garden, the largest of the three, was once also laid out in formal parterres and *bosquets* set with statues, and though it has now been remodelled in the landscape style, its old plan may still be traced. Before it was destroyed the three terraces of the Villa Muti must have formed the most enchanting garden in Frascati, and their plan and architectural details are worthy of careful study, for they belong to the rare class of small Italian gardens where grandeur was less sought for than charm and sylvan seclusion, and where the Latin passion for the monumental was subordinated to a desire for moderation and simplicity.

The Villa Falconieri, on the hillside below Mondragone, is remarkable for the wealth of its garden-architecture. The grounds are entered by two splendid stone gateways, the upper one being on an axis with the villa. A grass avenue leads from this gate to an arch of triumph, a rusticated elevation with niches and statues, surmounted by the inscription 'Horatius Falconieris,' and giving access to the inner grounds. Hence a straight avenue runs between formal ilex-groves to the court before the house. On the right, above the *bosco*, is a lofty wall of rock, picturesquely overgrown by shrubs and creepers, with busts and other fragments of antique sculpture set here and there on its projecting ledges. This natural cliff sustains an upper plateau, where there is an oblong artificial water (called 'the lake') enclosed in rock-work and surrounded by a grove of mighty cypresses. From this shady solitude the wooded slopes of the lower park are reached by a double staircase so simple and majestic in design that it harmonizes perfectly with the sylvan wildness which characterizes the landscape. This staircase should be studied as an example of the way in which the Italian garden-architects could lay aside exuberance and whimsicality when their work was intended to blend with some broad or solemn effect of nature.

The grounds of the Villa Falconieri were laid out by Cardinal Ruffini in the first half of the sixteenth century, but the villa was not built till 1648. It is one of the most charming creations of Borromini,[12] that brilliant artist in whom baroque architecture found its happiest expression; and the Villa Falconieri makes one regret that he did not oftener exercise his fancy in the construction of such pleasure-houses.

The elevation follows the tradition of the Roman *villa suburbana*. The centre of the ground floor is an arcaded loggia, the roof of which forms a terrace to the recessed story above; while the central motive of this first story was another semicircular recess, adorned with stucco ornament and surmounted by a broken pediment. The attic story is set still farther back, so that its balustraded roof-line forms a background for the richly decorated façade, and the building, though large, thus preserves the airy look and lightness of proportion which had come to be regarded as suited to the suburban pleasure-house.

To the right of the villa, the composition is prolonged by a gateway with coupled columns surmounted by stone dogs, and leading from the forecourt to the adjoining *basse-cour*. About the latter are grouped a number of low farm-buildings, to which a touch of the baroque gives picturesqueness. In the charm of its elevation, and in the happy juxtaposition of garden-walls and outbuildings, the Villa Falconieri forms the most harmonious and successful example of garden-architecture in Frascati.

The elevation which most resembles it is that of the Villa Lancellotti. Here the house, which is probably nearly a century earlier, shows the same happy use of the open loggia, which in this case forms the central feature of the first story, above a stately pedimented doorway.

The loggia is surmounted by a kind of square-headed gable crowned by a balustrade with statues, and the facade on each side of this central composition is almost Tuscan in its severity. Before the house lies a beautiful box-garden of intricate design, enclosed in high walls of ilex, with the inevitable *théâtre d'eau* at its farther end. This is a semicircular composition, with statues in niches between rusticated pilasters, and a central grotto whence a fountain pours into a wide balustraded basin; the whole being surmounted by another balustrade, with a statue set on each pier. It is harmonious and dignified in design, but unfortunately a fresh coating of brown and yellow paint has destroyed that exquisite *patina* by means of which the climate of Italy effects the gradual blending of nature and architecture.

Villas of Venetia

Writers on Italian architecture have hitherto paid little attention to the villa-architecture of Venetia. It is only within the last few years that English and American critics have deigned to recognize any architectural school in Italy later than that of Vignola and Palladio,[13] and even these two great masters of the sixteenth century have been held up as examples of degeneracy to a generation bred in the Ruskinian code of art ethics. In France, though the influence of

Violett-le-Duc was nearly as hostile as Ruskin's to any true understanding of Italian art, the Latin instinct for form has asserted itself in a revived study of the classic tradition; but French writers on architecture have hitherto confined themselves chiefly to the investigation of their national styles.

It is only in Germany that Italian architecture from Palladio to Juvara[14] has received careful and sympathetic study. Burckhardt pointed the way in his 'Cicerone' and in 'The Architecture of the Renaissance in Italy'; Herr Gustav Ebe followed with an interesting book on the late Renaissance throughout Europe; and Herr Gurlitt has produced the most masterly work yet written on the subject, his 'History of the Baroque Style in Italy.' These authors, however, having to work in a new and extensive field, have necessarily been obliged to restrict themselves to its most important divisions. Burckhardt's invaluable 'Renaissance Architecture,' though full of critical insight, is rather a collection of memoranda than a history of the subject; and even Herr Gurlitt, though he goes into much greater detail, cannot forsake the highroad for the by-paths, and has consequently had to pass by many minor ramifications of his subject. This is especially to be regretted in regard to the villa-architecture of Venetia, the interest and individuality of which he fully appreciates. He points out that the later Venetian styles

121

spring from two sources, the schools of Palladio and of Sansovino.[15] The former, greatly as his work was extolled, never had the full sympathy of the Venetians. His art was too pure and severe for a race whose taste had been formed on the fantastic mingling of Gothic and Byzantine and on the glowing decorations of the greatest school of colourists the world has known. It was from the warm and picturesque art of Sansovino and Longhena[16] that the Italian baroque naturally developed; and though the authority of Palladio made itself felt in the official architecture of Venetia, its minor constructions, especially the villas and small private houses, seldom show any trace of his influence save in the grouping of their windows. So little is known of the Venetian villa-builders that this word as to their general tendencies must replace the exact information which still remains to be gathered.

Many delightful examples of the Venetian *maison de plaisance* are still to be found in the neighborhood of Padua and Treviso, along the Brenta, and in the country between the Euganeans and the Monti Berici. Unfortunately, in not more than one or two instances have the old gardens of these houses been preserved in their characteristic form; and, by a singular perversity of fate, it happens that the villas which have kept their gardens are not typical of the Venetian style. One of them, the castle of Cattajo, at Battaglia in the

Euganean Hills, stands in fact quite apart from any contemporary style. This extraordinary edifice, built for the Obizzi of Venice about 1550, is said to have been copied from the plans of a castle in Tartary brought home by Marco Polo. It shows, at any rate, a deliberate reversion, in mid-cinque-cento, to a kind of Gothicism which had become obsolete in northern Italy three hundred years earlier; and the mingling of this rude style with classic detail and Renaissance sculpture has produced an effect picturesque enough to justify so quaint a tradition.

Cattajo stands on the edge of the smiling Euganean country, its great fortress-like bulk built up against a wooded knoll with a little river at its base. Crossing the river by a bridge flanked by huge piers surmounted with statues, one reaches a portcullis in a massive gate-house, also adorned with statues. The portcullis opens on a long narrow court planted with a hedge of clipped euonymus; and at one end a splendid balustraded stairway *á cordon* leads up to a flagged terrace with yew-trees growing between the flags. To the left of this terrace is a huge artificial grotto, with a stucco Silenus lolling on an elephant, and other life-size animals and figures, a composition recalling the zoölogical wonders of the grotto at Castello. This Italian reversion to the grotesque, at a time when it was losing its fascination for the Northern races, might form the subject of an interesting study of race æsthetics. When the coarse and sombre fancy of mediæval Europe found expression in grinning gargoyles and baleful or buffoonish images, Italian art held serenely to the beautiful, and wove the most tragic themes into a labyrinth of lovely lines; but in the seventeenth and eighteenth centuries, when the classical graces had taken possession of northern Europe, the chimerical animals, the gnomes and goblins, the gargoyles and broomstick-riders, fled south of the Alps, and reappeared in the queer fauna of Italian grottoes and in the leering dwarfs and satyrs of the garden-walk.

From the yew-tree terrace at Cattajo an arcaded loggia gives access to the interior of the castle, which is a bewilderment of low-storied passageways and long flights of steps hewn in the rock against which the castle is built. From a vaulted tunnel of stone one passes abruptly into a suite of lofty apartments decorated with seventeenth-century frescoes and opening on a balustraded terrace guarded by marble divinities; or, taking another turn, one finds one's self in a sham Gothic chapel or in a mediæval *chemin de ronde* on the crenelated walls. This fantastic medley of styles, in conjunction with the unusual site of the castle, has produced several picturesque bits of garden, wedged between the walls and the hillside, or on the terraces overhanging the river; but from the architectural point of view, the most interesting thing about Cattajo is the original treatment of the great stairway in the court.

Six or seven miles from Battaglia, in a narrow and fertile valley of the Euganeans, lies one of the most beautiful pleasure-grounds in Italy. This is the garden of the villa at Val San Zibio. On approaching it, one sees, across a grassy common, a stately and ornate arch of triumph with a rusticated façade and a broken pediment enriched with statues. This arch, which looks as though it were the principal entrance-gate, appears to have been placed in the high boundary-wall merely in order to afford from the highway a vista of the *château d'eau* which is the chief feature of the gardens. The practice of breaking the wall to give a view of some special point in the park or garden was very common in France, but is seldom seen in Italy, though there is a fine instance of it in the open grille below the Villa Aldobrandini at Frascati.

The house at Val San Zibio is built with its back to the highroad, and is an unpretentious structure of the seventeenth century, not unlike the Villa de' Gori at Siena, though the Palladian grouping of its central windows shows the nearness of Venice. It looks on a terrace enclosed by a balustrade, whence a broad flight of steps descends to the gently sloping gardens. They are remarkable for their long pleached alleys of beech, their wide *tapis verts* fountains, marble benches and statues charmingly placed in niches of clipped verdure. In one direction is a little lake, in another a 'mount' crowned by a statue, while a long alley leads to a well-preserved maze with a raised platform in its centre. These labyrinths are now rarely found in Italian gardens, and were probably never as popular south of the Alps as in Holland and England. The long *château d'eau*, with its couchant Nereids and conch-blowing Tritons, descends a gentle slope instead of a steep hill, and on each side high beech-hedges enclose tall groves of deciduous trees. These hedges are characteristic of the north Italian gardens, where the plane, beech and elm replace the 'perennial greens' of the south; and there is one specially charming point at Val San Zibio, where four grass-alleys walled with clipped beeches converge on a stone basin sunk in the turf, with four marble putti seated on the curb, dangling their feet in the water. An added touch of quaintness is given to the gardens by the fact that the old water-works are still in action, so that the unwary visitor, assailed by fierce jets of spray darting up at him from the terrace steps, the cracks in the flagstones, and all manner of unexpected ambushes, may form some idea of the aquatic surprises which afforded his ancestors such inexhaustible amusement.

There are few gardens in Italy comparable with Val San Zibio; but in Padua there is one of

126

another sort which has kept something of the same ancient savor. This is the famous Botanic Garden, founded in 1545, and said to be the oldest in Italy. The accompanying plan, though roughly sketched from memory, will give some idea of its arrangement. Outside is a grove of exotic trees, which surrounds a large circular space enclosed in a beautiful old brick wall surmounted by a marble balustrade and adorned alternately with busts and statues. The wall is broken by four gateways, one forming the principal entrance from the grove, the other three opening on semicircles in which statues are set against a background of foliage. In the garden itself the beds for 'simples' are enclosed in low iron railings, within which they are again subdivided by stone edgings, each subdivision containing a different species of plant.

Padua, in spite of its flat surroundings, is one of the most picturesque cities of upper Italy; and the seeker after gardens will find many charming bits along the narrow canals, or by the sluggish river skirting the city walls. Indeed, one might almost include in a study of gardens the beautiful Prato della Valle, the public square before the church of Sant' Antonio,[17] with its encircling canal crossed by marble bridges, its range of baroque statues of 'worthies,' and its central expanse of turf and trees. There is no other example in Italy of a square laid out in this park-like way, and the

Figure 1   The Botanic Garden in Padua

Prato de Valle would form an admirable model for the treatment of open spaces in a modern city.

A few miles from Padua, at Ponte di Brenta, begins the long line of villas which follows the course of the river of its outlet at Fusina. Dante speaks in the 'Inferno' of the villas and castles on the Brenta, and it continued the favourite villeggiatura of the Venetian nobility till the middle of the nineteenth century. There dwelt the Signor Pococurante, whom Candide visited on his travels;[18] and of flesh-and-blood celebrities many might be cited, from the famous Procuratore Pisani to Byron, who in 1819 carried off the Guiccioli to his villa at La Mira on the Brenta.[19]

The houses still remain almost line for line as they were drawn in Gianfrancesco Costa's admirable etchings, 'Le Delizie del Fiume Brenta,' published in 1750; but unfortunately almost all the old gardens have disappeared. One, however, has been preserved, and as it is the one most often celebrated by travellers and poets of the eighteenth century, it may be regarded as a good example of a stately Venetian garden. This is the great villa built at Strà, in 1736, for Alvise Pisani, procurator of St Mark's, by the architects Prati and Frigimelica. In size and elegance it far surpasses any other house on the Brenta. The prevailing note of the other villas is one of simplicity and amenity. They stand near each other, either on the roadside or divided from it by a low wall bordered with statues and a short strip of garden, also thickly peopled with nymphs, satyrs, shepherdesses, and the grotesque and comic figures of the Commedia dell'Arte; unassuming *villini* for the most part, suggesting a life of suburban neighbourliness and sociability. But the Villa Pisani is a palace. Its majestic façade, with pillared central *corps de bâtiment* and far-reaching wings, stands on the highway bordering the Brenta; behind are the remains of the old formal gardens, and on each side, the park extends along the road, from which it is divided by a high wall and several imposing gateways. The palace is built about two inner courts, and its innumerable rooms are frescoed by the principal Italian decorative painters of the day, while the great central saloon has one of Tiepolo's most riotously splendid ceilings.[20] Fortunately for the preservation of these treasures, Strá, after being the property of Eugène Beauharnais, was acquired by the Italian government, and is now a 'villa nazionale,' well kept up and open to the public.

In the etching of Costa, an elaborate formal garden with *parterres de broderie* is seen to extend from the back of the villa to the beautifully composed stables which face it. This garden has unfortunately been replaced by a level meadow, flanked on both sides by *boschi*, with long straight walks piercing the dense green leafage of elm, beech and lime. Here and there fragments of garden-architecture have survived the evident attempt to convert the grounds into a *jardin anglais* of the sentimental type. There is still a maze, with a fanciful little central tower ascended by winding stairs; there is a little wooded 'mount,' with a moat about it, and a crowning temple; and there are various charming garden-pavilions, orangeries, gardeners' houses, and similar small constructions, all built in the airy and romantic style of which the Italian villa-

130

architect had not yet lost the secret. Architecturally, however, the stables are perhaps the most interesting buildings at Strà. Their classical central façade is flanked by two curving wings, forming charmingly proportioned lemon-houses, and in the stables themselves the stalls are sumptuously divided by columns of red marble, each surmounted by the gilded effigy of a horse.

From Strà to Fusina the shores of the Brenta are lined with charming pleasure-houses, varying in size from the dignified villa to the little garden-pavilion, and all full of interest and instruction to the student of villa-architecture; but unhappily no traces of their old gardens remain, save the statues which once peopled the parterres and surmounted the walls. Several of the villas are attributed to Palladio, but only one is really typical of his style: the melancholy Malcontenta, built by the Foscari, and now standing ruinous and deserted in a marshy field beside the river.

The Malcontenta has all the chief characteristics of Palladio's manner: the high basement, the projecting pillared portico, the general air of classical correctness, which seems a little cold beside the bright and graceful villa-architecture of Venetia. Burckhardt, with his usual discernment, remarks in this connection that it was a fault of Palladio's to substitute for the recessed loggia of the Roman villa a projecting portico, thus

131

sacrificing one of the most characteristic and original features of the Italian country house to a not particularly appropriate adaptation of the Greek temple porch.

But Palladio was a great artist, and if he was great in his civic architecture rather than in his country houses, if his stately genius lent itself rather to the grouping of large masses than to the construction of pretty toys, yet his most famous villa is a distinct and original contribution to the chief examples of the Italian pleasure-house. The Villa Capra, better known as the Rotonda, which stands on a hill above Vicenza, has been criticized for having four fronts instead of one front, two sides and a back. It is, in fact, a square building with a projecting Ionic portico on each face—a plan open to the charge of monotony, but partly justified in this case by the fact that the house is built on the summit of a knoll from which there are four views, all equally pleasing, and each as it were entitled to the distinction of having a loggia to itself. Still, it is certain that neither in the Rotonda nor in his other villas did Palladio hit on a style half as appropriate or pleasing as the typical manner of the Roman villa-architects, with its happy mingling of freedom and classicalism, its wonderful adaptation to climate and habits of life, its capricious grace of detail, and its harmony with the garden-architecture which was designed to surround it.

The Villa Capra has not preserved its old gardens, and at the Villa Giacomelli, at Maser, Palladio's other famous country house, the grounds have been so modernized and stripped of all their characteristic features that it is difficult to judge of their original design; but one feels that all Palladio's rural architecture lacked that touch of fancy of freedom which, in the Roman school, facilitated the transition of manner from the house to the garden-pavilion, and from the pavilion to the half-rustic grotto and the woodland temple.

The Villa Valmarana, also at Vicenza, on the Monte Berico, not far from the Rotonda, has something of the intimate charm lacking in the latter. The low and simply designed house is notable only for the charming frescoes with which Tiepolo adorned its rooms; but the beautiful loggia in the garden is attributed to Palladio, and this, together with the old beech-alleys, the charming frescoed fountain, the garden-wall crowned by Venetian grotesques, forms a composition of exceptional picturesqueness.

The beautiful country-side between Vicenza and Verona is strewn with old villas, many of which would doubtless repay study; but there are no gardens of note in this part of Veneto, except the famous Giusti gardens at Verona, probably better known to sight-seers than any others in northern Italy. In spite of all their charm, however, the dusky massing of their old cypresses, and their winding walks along the cliff-side, the Giusti gardens preserve few traces of their original design, and are therefore not especially important to the student of Italian garden-architecture. More interesting in this connection is the Villa Cuzzano, about seven miles from Verona, a beautiful old house standing above a terrace-garden planted with an elaborate *parterre de broderie*. Behind the villa is a spacious court bounded by a line of low buildings with a central chapel. The interior of the house has been little changed, and is an interesting example of north Italian villa planning and decoration. The passion of the Italian architects for composition and continuity of design is seen in the careful placing of the chapel, which is exactly on an axis with the central saloon of the villa, so that, standing in the chapel, one looks across the court, through this lofty saloon, and out on the beautiful hilly landscape beyond. It was by such means that the villa-architects obtained, with simple materials and in a limited space, impressions of distance, and sensations of the unexpected, for which one looks in vain in the haphazard and slipshod designs of the present day.

REFERENCES

1 'Pleached' walks or alleys have branches of trees interwoven or braided across the top to provide shade.

2 In the list of architects and landscape gardeners provided at the end of the book, Wharton describes Giacomo Barozzi da Vignola (1507–1573) of Modena as 'one of the greatest architects of the sixteenth century.' He was one of the architects of St Peter's, and also built the villa Lante and the Farnese Palace at Piacenza.

3 Giorgio Vasari of Arezzo (1511–1574), an architect, painter, and critic, built the court of the Uffizi in Florence. He is usually remembered for his *Lives of the Most Eminent Painters, Sculptors, and Architects* (1550).

4 Charles Percier (1764–1838), French architect, collaborated with Pierre Fontaine (1762–1853), architect of the Paris Opera and the Louvre.

5 André le Nôtre (1613–1700), French landscape gardener, designed the gardens at Chantilly and Versailles.

6 The River Anio, below Tivoli.

7 Pirro Ligorio (1493–1580) of Naples, an architect, made additions to the Vatican and designed the Villa d'Este.

8 The Campagna di Roma is a plain, the territory of Old Latium, surrounding Rome. Flocks of grazing sheep and the

ruins of Roman aqueducts and tombs give the landscape a particular charm that appealed to Wharton, Henry James, and other writers.

9 W. C. Tuckermann was the author of *Die Gartenkunst der Italienischen Renaissance-Zeit* (1884).

10 Cornelius Gurlitt was a German art historian whose *Geschichte des Barockstils in Italien* (1887) influenced Wharton's appreciation of the art and architecture of the Baroque.

11 John Evelyn (1620–1706) was an English government official and diarist. His *Diary* (1644) is listed by Wharton as one of the English books on which she relied.

12 Francesco Borromini (1599–1667) was, in Wharton's words, 'next to Bernini, the most original and brilliant exponent of *baroque* architecture in Italy' (IV 254, 'Architects and Landscape-Gardeners Mentioned'). Some of his most noted work is in the Villa Falconieri at Frascati.

13 Andrea Palladio (1508–1580), a native of Vicenza, was an architect who, in Wharton's words, 'turned the development of Italian Renaissance architecture in the direction of pure classicalism' (IV 260, 'Architects and Landscape-Gardeners Mentioned'). Among his works are the church of San Giorgio Maggiore, Venice, and the Villa Malcontenta, near Fusina on the Brenta.

14 Filippo Juvara (1685–1735) was a major Italian architect of the eighteenth century; he studied with Carlo Fontana, architect of St Peter's. His major works are near Turin.

15 Jacopo Tatti Sansovino (1487–1570), of Florence, designed the Library of San Marco in Venice.

16 Baldassare Longhena (1604–1682), of Venice, designed the churches of Santa Maria della Salute, Santa Maria ai Scalzi, and the Ospedaletto.

17 The 'church of Sant' Antonio,' which had also appeared in *The Century* article, was replaced in the Fall 1905 reprinting by the 'church of Santa Giustina,' apparently at Wharton's request. In the Beinecke Library copy of the first edition (November 1904), 'Sant' Antonio' is lined through and 'Santa Giustina' is written in Wharton's hand in the margin. The 1910 printing (Library of Virginia) has 'Santa Giustina.' Other printings (Century 1907, 1920; Da Capo 1976, 1988) presumably reflected this change, although it has not been possible to verify each one. Why Wharton wanted the alteration is uncertain unless, in her memory, she had confused the two churches, each of which has many domes. Both Santa Giustina, a sixteenth-century classical building, and Sant' Antonio, a thirteenth-century pilgrimage church dedicated to St Anthony, are near the Prato

della Valle, although Santa Giustina is closer to it. Neither is far from the 'encircling canal' ornamented with statues.

18 The hero of Voltaire's philosophical novel *Candide* (or *Optimism*; 1759) visited Signor Pococurante on the Brenta.

19 Countess Teresa Guiccioli, an Italian noblewoman, had a long-lasting liaison with the poet Lord Byron. Although married to a much older man, she became his mistress in 1819; the attachment endured throughout Byron's life. He was in Italy from 1816–1822 and died of malaria in Greece in 1824.

20 Giovanni Battista Tiepolo (1696–1770) was a painter of the Venetian school much admired by Wharton. In addition to the ceiling at Strà, he painted the ceilings of the Villa Valmarana at Vicenza and the Church of Santa Maria del Rosario at Venice, as well as the ceiling of the Church of the Scalzi (unfortunately bombed by the Austrians in 1915). His most famous paintings are in the royal palace at Würzburg and the royal palace at Madrid.

ITALIAN BACKGROUNDS*

A Midsummer Week's Dream: August in Italy

... Un paysage choisi
Que vont charmant masques et bergamasques.[1]

I

For ten days we had not known what ailed us. We had fled from the August heat and crowd of the Vorderrheinthal[2] to the posting-inn below the Splügen pass; and here fortune had given us all the midsummer tourist can hope for— solitude, cool air and fine scenery. A dozen times a day we counted our mercies, but still privately felt them to be insufficient. As we walked through the larch-groves beside the Rhine, or climbed the grassy heights above the valley, we were oppressed by the didactic quality of our surroundings—by the aggressive salubrity and repose of this *bergerie de Florian*.[3] We seemed to be living in the landscape of a sanatorium prospectus. It was all pleasant enough, according to

---

* 'A Midsummer Week's Dream: August in Italy,' Chapter 2 of *Italian Backgrounds*, was first published in *Scribner's Magazine*, 32 (No. 2, Aug. 1902), 212–222. Chapter 8, 'Picturesque Milan,' (*Scribner' Magazine*, 33 [Feb. 1903].

Schopenhauer's definition of pleasure. We had none of the things we did not want; but then we did not particularly want any of the things we had. We had fancied we did till we got them; and as we had to own that they did their part in fulfilling our anticipations, we were driven to conclude that the fault was in ourselves. Then suddenly we found out what was wrong. Splügen was charming, but it was too near Italy.

One can forgive a place three thousand miles from Italy for not being Italian; but that a village on the very border should remain stolidly, immovably Swiss was a constant source of exasperation. Even the landscape had neglected its opportunities. A few miles off it became the accomplice of man's most exquisite imaginings; but here we could see in it only endless material for Swiss clocks and fodder.

The trouble began with our watching the diligences. Every evening we saw one toiling up the pass from Chiavenna, with dusty horses and perspiring passengers. How we pitied those passengers! We walked among them puffed up with all the good air in our lungs. We felt fresh and cool and enviable, and moralized on the plaintive lot of those whose scant holidays compelled them to visit Italy in August. But already the poison was at work. We pictured what our less fortunate brothers had seen till we began to wonder if, after all, they were less fortunate. At least they had *been there*; and what drawbacks could qualify that fact? Was it better to be cool and look at a water-fall, or to be hot and look at Saint Mark's? Was it better to walk on gentians or on mosaic, to smell fir-needles or incense? Was it, in short, ever well to be elsewhere when one might be in Italy?

We tried to quell the rising madness by interrogating the travellers. Was it very hot on the lakes and in Milan? 'Terribly!' they answered, and mopped their brows. 'Unimaginative idiots!' we grumbled, and forbore to question the next batch. Of course it was hot there—but what of that? Think of the compensations! To take it on the lowest plane, think of the empty hotels and railway carriages, the absence of tourists and Baedekers! Even the Italians were away, among the Apennines and in the Engadine; we should have the best part of the country to ourselves. Gradually we began to picture our sensations should we take seats in the diligence on its return journey. From that moment we were lost. We did not say much to each other, but one morning at sunrise we found a travelling-carriage at the door. No one seemed to know who had ordered it, but we noticed that our luggage was being strapped on behind. We took our seats and the driver turned his horses toward the Splügen pass. It was not the way to Switzerland.

We mounted to ice and snow. The savage landscape led us to the top of the pass and dogged us down to the miserable Italian custom-house on the other side. Then began the long descent through snow-galleries and steep pine-forests, above the lonely gorge of the Madesimo: Switzerland still in every aspect, but with a promise of Italy in the names of the dreary villages. Visible Italy began with the valley of the Lira, where, in a wild Salvator Rosa landscape,[4] the beautiful campanile of the Madonna of Gallevaggio rises above embowering walnuts. After that each successive village declared its allegiance more openly. The huddled stone houses disappeared in a wealth of pomegranates and oleanders. Vine-pergolas shaded the doorways, roses and dahlias overflowed the terraces of rough masonry, and between the walnut-groves there were melon-patches and fields of maize.

As we approached Chiavenna a thick bloom of heat lay on the motionless foliage, and the mountains hung like thunder-clouds on the horizon. There was something oppressive, menacing almost, in the still weight of the atmosphere. It seemed to have absorbed all the ardour of the sun-baked Lombard plain, of the shadeless rice and maize fields stretching away to the south of us. But the eye had ample compensation. The familiar town of Chiavenna had grown as fantastically picturesque as the background of a fresco. The old houses, with their medallioned doorways of worn marble; the courtyards bright with flowers and shaded by trellised vines; the white turbulence of the Lira, rushing between gardens, balconies and terraces set at reckless angles above the water—were all these a part of the town we had so often seen at less romantic seasons? The general impression was of an exuberance of rococo—as though the sportive statue of Saint John Nepomuc on the bridge, the grotesque figures on the balustrade of the pale-green villa near the hotel, and the stucco shrines at the street corners, had burst into a plastic efflorescence rivalling the midsummer wealth of the gardens.

We had left Switzerland with the general object of going to Italy and the specific one of exploring the Bergamasque Alps. It was the name which had attracted us, as much from its intrinsic picturesqueness as from its associations with the *commedia dell'arte* and the jolly figures of Harlequin and Brighella. I have often journeyed thus in pursuit of a name, and have seldom been unrewarded. In this ease the very aspect of the map was promising. The region included in the scattered lettering—*Bergamasker Hochthäler*—had that furrowed, serried look so encouraging to the experienced traveller. It was rich, crowded, suggestive; and the names of the villages were enchanting.

Early the next morning we set out for Colico, at the head of the Lake of Como, and thence took train for Sondrio, the chief town of the Valtelline. The lake, where we had to wait for our train, lay in unnatural loveliness beneath a breathless sky, the furrowed peaks bathed in subtle colour-gradations of which, at other seasons, the atmosphere gives no hint. At Sondrio we found all the dreariness of a modern Italian town with wide unshaded streets; but taking carriage in the afternoon for Madonna di Tirano we were soon in the land of romance again. The Valtelline, through which we drove, is one vast fruit and vegetable garden of extra-ordinary fertility. The *gran turco* (as the maize is called) grows in jungles taller than a man, and the grapes and melons have the exaggerated size and bloom of their counterfeits in a Dutch fruit-piece. The rich dulness of this foreground was relieved by the noble lines of the hills, and the air cooled by the rush of the Adda, which followed the windings of our road, and by a glimpse of snow-peaks at the head of the valley. The villages were uninteresting, but we passed a low-lying deserted church, a charming bit of seventeenth-century decay, with peeling stucco ornaments, and weeds growing from the florid vases of the pediment; and far off, on a lonely wooded height, there was a tantalizing glimpse of another church, a Renaissance building rich with encrusted marbles: one of the nameless uncatalogued treasures in which Italy still abounds.

144

Toward sunset we reached Madonna di Tirano, the great pilgrimage church of the Valtelline. With its adjoining monastery it stands alone in poplar-shaded meadows a mile or more from the town of Tirano. The marble church, a late fifteenth-century building by Battagio (the architect of the Incoronata of Lodi), has the peculiar charm of that transitional period when individuality of detail was merged, but not yet lost, in the newly-recovered sense of unity. From the columns of the porch, with their Verona-like arabesques, to the bronze Saint Michael poised like a Mercury on the cupola, the whole building combines the charm and naïveté of the earlier tradition with the dignity of a studied whole. The interior, if less homogeneous, is, in the French sense, even more 'amusing.' Owing, doubtless, to the remote situation of the church, it has escaped the unifying hand of the improver, and presents three centuries of conflicting decorative treatment, ranging from the marble chapel of the Madonna, so suggestive, in its clear-edged reliefs, of the work of Omodeo at Pavia, to the barocco carvings of the organ and the eighteenth-century *grisailles* beneath the choir-gallery.

The neighbouring monastery of Saint Michael has been turned into an inn without farther change than that of substituting tourists for monks in the whitewashed cells around the cloisters. The old building is a dusty

145

labyrinth of court-yards, loggias and pigeon-haunted upper galleries, which it needs but little imagination to people with cowled figures gliding to lauds or benediction; and the refectory where we supped is still hung with portraits of cardinals, monsignori, and lady abbesses holding little ferret-like dogs.

The next day we drove across the rich meadows to Tirano, one of those unhistoried and unconsidered Italian towns which hold in reserve for the observant eye a treasure of quiet impressions. It is difficult to name any special 'effect': the hurried sight-seer may discover only dull streets and featureless house-fronts. But the place has a fine quality of age and aloofness. The featureless houses are 'palaces,' long-fronted and escutcheoned, with glimpses of arcaded courts, and of gardens where maize and dahlias smother the broken statues and choked fountains, and where grapes ripen on the peeling stucco walls. Here and there one comes on a frivolous rococo church, subdued by time to delicious harmony with its surroundings; on a fountain in a quiet square, or a wrought-iron balcony projecting romantically from a shuttered façade; or on one or another of the hundred characteristic details which go to make up the *mise en scène* of the average Italian town. It is precisely in places like Tirano, where there are no salient beauties to fix the eye, that one appreciates the value of these details, that one realizes what may be called the negative strength of the Italian artistic sense. Where the Italian builder could not be grand, he could always abstain from being mean and trivial; and this artistic abnegation gives to many a dull little town like Tirano an architectural dignity which our great cities lack.

II

The return to secular life was made two days later, when we left our monastery and set out to drive across the Aprica pass to Edolo. Retracing for a mile or two the way toward Sondrio, we took a turn to the left and began to mount the hills through forests of beech and chestnut. With each bend of the road the views down the Valtelline toward Sondrio and Como grew wider and more beautiful. No one who has not looked out on such a prospect in the early light of an August morning can appreciate the poetic truth of Claude's interpretation of nature: we seemed to be moving through a gallery hung with his pictures.[5] There was the same expanse of billowy forest, the same silver winding of a river through infinite gradations of distance, the same aërial line of hills melting into illimitable sky.

As we neared the top of the pass the air freshened, and pines and open meadows replaced the forest. We lunched at a little hotel in a bare meadow, among a crowd of Italians enjoying the *villeggiatura* in their shrill gregarious fashion; then we began the descent to Edolo in the Val Camonica.

The scenery changed rapidly as we drove on. There was no longer any great extent of landscape, as on the other side of the pass, but a succession of small park-like views: rounded clumps of trees interspersed with mossy glades, water-falls surmounted by old mills, *campanili* rising above villages hidden in foliage. On these smooth grassy terraces, under the walnut boughs, one expected at each turn to come upon some pastoral of Giorgione's, or on one of Bonifazio's sumptuous picnics. The scenery has a studied beauty in which velvet robes and caparisoned palfreys would not be out of place, and even the villages might have been 'brushed in' by an artist skilled in effects and not afraid to improve upon reality.

It was after sunset when we reached Edolo, a dull town splendidly placed at the head of the Val Camonica, beneath the ice-peaks of the Adamello. The Oglio, a loud stream voluble of the glaciers, rushes through the drowsy streets as though impatient to be gone; and we were not sorry, the next morning, to follow its lead and continue our way down the valley.

III

The Val Camonica, which extends from the Adamello group to the head of the lake of Iseo, is a smaller and more picturesque reproduction of the Valtelline. Vines and maize again fringed our way; but the mountains were closer, the villages more frequent and more picturesque.

We had read in the invaluable guide-book of Gsell-Fels a vague allusion to an interesting church among these mountains, but we could learn nothing of it at Edolo, and only by persistent enquiries along the road did we finally hear that there *was* a church with 'sculptures' in the hill-village of Cerveno, high above the reach of carriages. We left the high-road at the point indicated, and drove in a light country carriole up the stony mule-path, between vines and orchards, till the track grew too rough for wheels; then we continued the ascent on foot. As we approached the cluster of miserable hovels which had been pointed out to us we felt sure we had been misled. Not even in Italy, the land of unsuspected treasures, could one hope to find a church with 'sculptures' in a poverty-stricken village on this remote mountain! Cerveno does not even show any signs of past prosperity. It has plainly never been more than it now is—the humblest of *paesi*, huddled away in an unvisited fold of the Alps. The peasants whom we met still insisted that the church we sought was close at hand; but the higher we mounted the lower our anticipations fell.

Then suddenly, at the end of a long stony lane, we came on an imposing doorway. The church to which it belonged stood on a higher ledge of the hill, and the door led into a vaulted ascent, with shallow flights of steps broken by platforms or landings—a small but yet impressive imitation of the Bernini staircase in the Vatican. As we mounted we found that each landing opened into a dimly-lit chapel with grated doors, through which we discerned terra-cotta groups representing the scenes of the Passion. The staircase was in fact a Sacred Way like the more famous one of Varallo; but there was distinct originality in placing the chapels on each side of the long flight of steps leading to the church, instead of scattering them on an open hill-side, according to the traditional plan common to all the other sacred mountains of northern Italy.

The dilettante will always allow for the heightening of emotion that attends any unexpected artistic 'find'; but, setting this subjective impression aside, the Via Crucis of Cerveno remains in my memory as among the best examples of its kind—excepting always the remarkable terra-cottas of San Vivaldo in Tuscany. At Cerveno, as at Varallo, the groups are marked by unusual vivacity and expressiveness. The main lines of the composition are conventional, and the chief personages—Christ and the Apostles, the Virgin and the other holy characters—are modelled on traditional types; but the minor figures, evidently taken from life, are rendered with frank realism and with extraordinary truth of expression and gesture. Just such types—the dwarf, the beggar, the hunchback, the brawny waggoner or ploughman—had met us in every village on the way to Cerveno. As in all the hill-regions where the goitre is prevalent, the most villanous [*sic*] characters in the drama are depicted with a hideous bag of flesh beneath the chin; and Signorelli could not have conceived more bestial leering cruelty than that in some of the faces which press about the dying Christ. The scenes follow the usual order of the sacred story, without marked departure from the conventional grouping; but there is unusual pathos in the Descent from the Cross, where the light from the roof of the chapel falls with tragic intensity on the face of a Magdalen full of suave Lombard beauty.

Hardly less surprising than this remarkable stairway is the church to which it leads. The walls are hung with devotional pictures set in the faded gilding of rich old frames, the altar-fronts are remarkable examples of sixteenth-century wood-carving, and the high altar is surmounted by an elaborate tabernacle, also of carved wood, painted and gilt, that in itself repays the effort of the climb to Cerveno. This tabernacle is a complicated architectural composition—like one of the fantastic designs of Fontana or Bibbiena—thronged with tiny saints and doctors, angels and *putti*, akin to the little people of the Neapolitan *presepii*:: a celestial company fluttering.

Si come schiera d'api che s'infiora[6]

around the divine group which surmounts the shrine.

This prodigality of wood-carving, surprising as it is in so remote and humble a church, is yet characteristic of the region about Brescia and Bergamo, Lamberti of Brescia, the sculptor of the famous frame of Romanino's Madonna in the church of San Francesco, was one of the greatest wood-carvers of the Italian Renaissance; and every church and chapel in the country through which we were travelling bore witness to the continued practice of the art in some graceful frame or altar-front, some saint or angel rudely but expressively modelled.

We lunched that day at Breno, a town guarded by a ruined castle on a hill, and sunset brought us to Lovere, at the head of the lake of Iseo. It was the stillest of still evenings, and the little town which Lady Mary Wortley Montagu has immortalized was reflected, with every seam and wrinkle of its mountain background, in the pearly surface of the lake. Literal-minded critics, seeking in vain along the shore for Lady Mary's villa and garden, have grumbled at the inaccuracy of her descriptions; but every lover of Italy will understand the mental process by which she

152

Figure 2   By the Port of Lovere

unconsciously created an imaginary Lovere.[7]
For though the town, at first sight, is dull and
disappointing, yet, taken with its
surroundings, it might well form the
substructure of one of those Turneresque
visions which, in Italy, are perpetually
intruding between the most conscientious
traveller and his actual surroundings. It is
indeed almost impossible to see Italy steadily
and see it whole. The onset of impressions and
memories is at times so overwhelming that
observation is lost in mere sensation.

Certainly he who, on an August morning,
sails from Lovere to Iseo, at the southern end
of the lake, is likely to find himself succumbing
to Lady Mary's hallucinations. Warned by her
example, and conscious of lacking her
extenuating gift, I hesitate to record my
impressions of the scene; or venture, at most, to
do so in the past tense, asserting (and this even
with a mental reservation) that on a certain
morning a certain number of years ago the lake
of Iseo wore such and such an aspect. But the
difficulty of rendering the aspect remains. I can
only say it was that very lake of the *carte du
Tendre* upon which, in the eighteenth-century
romances, gay parties in velvet-hung barges
used to set out for the island of Cythera. Every
village on that enchanted shore might have
been the stage of some comedy in the
Bergamasque dialect, with Harlequin in
striped cloak, and Brighella in conical hat and

wide green and white trousers, strutting up and down before the shuttered house in which Dr Graziano hides his pretty ward; every villa reflecting its awnings and bright flowers in the lake might have housed some Rosaura to whom Leandro, the Tuscan lover, warbled *rispetti* beneath the padlocked water-gate; every pink or yellow monastery on the hill-side might have sent forth its plausible friar, descendant of Macchiavelli's Fra Timoteo, to preach in the market-place, beg at the villa-door, and help Rosaura and Leandro cozen the fat dupe of a Pantaloon in black cloak and scarlet socks. The eighteenth century of Longhi, of Tiepolo and Goldoni was reflected in the lake as in some magic crystal. Did the vision dissolve as we landed at Iseo, or will some later traveller find it still lying beneath the wave like the vanished city of Ys?[8] There is no telling, in such cases, how much the eye receives and how much it contributes; and if ever the boundaries between fact and fancy waver, it may well be under the spell of the Italian midsummer madness.

IV

The sun lay heavy on Iseo; and the railway journey thence to Brescia left in our brains a golden dazzle of heat. It was refreshing, on reaching Brescia, to enter the streets of the old town, where the roofs almost meet and there is always a blessed strip of shade to walk in. The

Figure 3   Chiesa dei Miracoli—Brescia

cities in Italy are much cooler than the country.
It is in August that one understands the
wisdom of the old builders, who made the
156

streets so narrow, and built dim draughty arcades around the open squares. In Brescia the effects of light and shade thus produced were almost Oriental in their sharp-edged intensity; the rough stucco surfaces gilded with vivid sunlight bringing out the depths of contrasting shade, and the women with black veils over their heads slipping along under the mysterious balconies and porticoes like flitting fragments of the shadow.

Brescia is at all times a delightful place to linger in. Its chief possessions—the bronze Victory, and that room in the Martinengo palace where Moretto, in his happiest mood, depicted the ladies of the line under arches of trellis-work backed by views of the family villas—make it noteworthy even among Italian cities; and it has, besides, its beautiful town-hall, its picture-gallery, and the curious court-yards painted in perspective that are so characteristic of the place. But in summer there is a strong temptation to sit and think of these things rather than to go and see them. In the court-yard of the hotel, where a fountain tinkles refreshingly, and the unbleached awnings flap in the breeze of the electric fans, it is pleasant to feel that the Victory and the pictures are close at hand, like old friends waiting on one's inclination; but if one ventures forth, let it be rather to the churches than to the galleries. Only at this season can one appreciate the atmosphere of the churches:

that chill which cuts the sunshine like a knife as one steps across the dusky threshold. When we entered the cathedral its vast aisles were empty, but far off, in the dimness of the pillared choir, we heard a drone of intoning canons that freshened the air like the sound of a water-fall in a forest. Thence we wandered on to San Francesco, empty too, where, in the sun-spangled dimness, the great Romanino throned behind the high altar. The sacristan drew back the curtain before the picture, and as it was revealed to us in all its sun-bathed glory he exclaimed with sudden wonder, as though he had never seen it before: '*È stupendo! È stupendo!*' Perhaps he vaguely felt, as we did, that Romanino, to be appreciated, must be seen in just that light, a projection of the suave and radiant atmosphere in which his own creations move. Certainly no Romanino of the great public galleries arrests the imagination like the Madonna of San Francesco; and in its presence one thinks with a pang of all the beautiful objects uprooted from their native soil to adorn the herbarium of the art-collector...

V

It was on the last day of our journey that the most imperturbable member of the party, looking up from a prolonged study of the guide-books, announced that we had not seen

158

the Bergamasque Alps after all.

In the excited argument that followed, proof seemed to preponderate first on one side and then on the other; but a closer scrutiny of the map confirmed the fear that we had not actually penetrated beyond the borders of the promised land. It must be owned that at first the discovery was somewhat humiliating; but on reflection it left us overjoyed to think that we had still the Bergamasque Alps to visit. Meanwhile our pleasure had certainly been enhanced by our delusion; and we remembered with fresh admiration Goethe's profound saying—a saying which Italy inspired—

O, wie beseliget uns Menschen ein falscher Begriff![9]

Picturesque Milan

I

It is hard to say whether the stock phrase of the stock tourist—'there is so little to see in Milan'—redounds most to the derision of the speaker or to the glory of Italy. That such a judgment should be possible, even to the least instructed traveller, implies a surfeit of impressions procurable in no other land; since, to the hastiest observation, Milan could hardly seem lacking in interest when compared to any but Italian cities. From comparison with the latter, even, it suffers only on a superficial

159

estimate, for it is rich in all that makes the indigenous beauty of Italy, as opposed to the pseudo-Gothicisms, the trans-Alpine points and pinnacles, which Ruskin taught a submissive generation of art critics to regard as the typical expression of the Italian spirit. The guidebooks, long accustomed to draw their Liebig's extract[10] of art from the pages of this school of critics, have kept the tradition alive by dwelling only on the monuments which conform to perpendicular ideals, and by apologetic allusions to the 'monotony' and 'regularity' of Milan—as though endeavouring in advance to placate the traveller for its not looking like Florence or Siena!

Of late, indeed, a new school of writers, among whom Mr J. W. Anderson, and the German authors, Messrs. Ebe[11] and Gurlitt, deserve the first mention, have broken through this conspiracy of silence, and called attention to the intrinsically Italian art of the post-Renaissance period; the period which, from Michael Angelo to Juvara,[12] has been marked in sculpture and architecture (though more rarely in painting) by a series of memorable names. Signor Franchetti's admirable monograph on Bernini, and the recent volume on Tiepolo in the Knackfuss series of Künstler-Monographien have done their part in this redistribution of values; and it is now possible for the traveller to survey the course of Italian art with the impartiality needful for its due enjoyment, and to admire, for instance, the tower of the Mangia without scorning the palace of the Consulta.

II

But, it may be asked, though Milan will seem more interesting to the emancipated judgment, will it appear more picturesque? Picturesqueness is, after all, what the Italian pilgrim chiefly seeks; and the current notion of the picturesque is a purely Germanic one, connoting Gothic steeples, pepper-pot turrets, and the huddled steepness of the northern burgh.

Italy offers little, and Milan least of all, to satisfy these requirements. The Latin ideal demanded space, order, and nobility of composition. But does it follow that picturesqueness is incompatible with these? Take up one of Piranesi's etchings—those strange compositions in which he sought to seize the spirit of a city or a quarter by a mingling of its most characteristic features. Even the northern conception of the picturesque must be satisfied by the sombre wildness of these studies—here a ruined aqueduct, casting its shade across a lonely stretch of ground tufted with acanthus, there a palace colonnade through which the moonlight sweeps on a winter wind, or the recesses of some mighty Roman bath where

161

Figure 4   Court of the Palazzo Marino,
now the Municipio

cloaked figures are huddled in dark confabulation.

Canaletto's black-and-white studies give, in a lesser degree, the same impression of the grotesque and the fantastic—the underside of that *barocchismo* so long regarded as the smirk on the face of a conventional age.

But there is another, a more typically Italian picturesqueness, gay rather than sinister in its suggestions, made up of lights rather than of shadows, of colour rather than of outline, and this is the picturesqueness of Milan. The city abounds in vivid effects, in suggestive juxtapositions of different centuries and styles—in all those incidental contrasts and surprises which linger in the mind after the catalogued 'sights' have faded. Leaving behind the wide modern streets—which have the merit of having been modernized under Eugène Beauharnais rather than under King Humbert—one enters at once upon some narrow byway overhung by the grated windows of a seventeenth-century palace, or by the delicate terra-cotta apse of a *cinque-cento* church. Everywhere the forms of expression are purely Italian, with the smallest possible admixture of that Gothic element which marks the old free cities of Central Italy. The rocca Sforzesca (the old Sforza castle) and the houses about the Piazza de' Mercanti are the chief secular buildings recalling the pointed architecture of the north; and the older churches are so old that they antedate Gothic influences, and lead one back to the round-arched basilican type. But in the line of national descent what exquisite varieties the Milanese streets present! Here, for instance, is the Corinthian colonnade of San Lorenzo, the only considerable fragment of ancient

Mediolanum,[13] its last shaft abutting on a Gothic archway against which clings a flower-decked shrine. Close by, one comes on the ancient octagonal church of San Lorenzo, while a few minutes' drive leads to where the Borromeo palace looks across a quiet grassy square at the rococo front of the old family church, flanked by a fine bronze statue of the great saint and cardinal.

The Palazzo Borromeo is itself a notable factor in the picturesqueness of Milan. The entrance leads to a court-yard enclosed in an ogive arcade[14] surmounted by pointed windows in terra-cotta mouldings. The walls of this court are still frescoed with the Borromean crown, and the *Humilitas* of the haughty race; and a doorway leads into the muniment-room, where the archives of the house are still stored, and where, on the damp stone walls, Michelino da Milano has depicted the scenes of a fifteenth-century villeggiatura. Here the noble ladies of the house, in high fluted turbans and fantastic fur-trimmed gowns, may be seen treading the measures of a mediæval dance with young gallants in parti-coloured hose, or playing at various games—the *jeu de tarots*, and a kind of cricket played with a long wooden bat; while in the background rise the mountains about Lake Maggiore and the peaked outline of the Isola Bella, then a bare rock unadorned with gardens and architecture. These frescoes, the only existing works of a little-known Lombard artist, are suggestive in style of Pisanello's dry and vigorous manner, and as records of the private life of the Italian nobility in the fifteenth century they are second only to the remarkable pictures of the Schifanoia at Ferrara.

Not far from the Borromean palace, another doorway leads to a different scene: the great cloister of the Ospedale Maggiore [General Hospital], one of the most glorious monuments that man ever erected to his fellows. The old hospitals of Italy were famous not only for their architectural beauty and great extent, but for their cleanliness and order and the enlightened care which their inmates received. Northern travellers have recorded their wondering admiration of these lazarets, which seemed as stately as palaces in comparison with the miserable pest-houses north of the Alps. What must have been the astonishment of such a traveller, whether German or English, on setting foot in the principal court of the Milanese hospital, enclosed in its vast cloister enriched with traceries and medallions of terra-cotta, and surmounted by the arches of an open loggia whence the patients could look down on a peaceful expanse of grass and flowers! Even now, one wonders whether this poetizing of philanthropy, this clothing of charity in the garb of beauty, may not have had its healing uses: whether the ugliness of the modern hospital may not make it, in another sense, as unhygienic as the more picturesque buildings it has superseded? It is at least pleasant to think of the poor sick people sunning themselves in the beautiful loggia of the Ospedale Maggiore, or sitting under the magnolia-trees in the garden, while their blue-gowned and black-veiled nurses move quietly through the cloisters at the summons of the chapel-bell.

But one need not enter a court-yard or cross a threshold to appreciate the variety and colour of Milan. The streets themselves are full of charming detail—*quattro-cento* marble portals set with medallions of bushy-headed Sforzas in round caps and plaited tunics; windows framed in terra-cotta wreaths of fruit and flowers; iron balconies etching their elaborate arabesques against the stucco house-fronts; mighty doorways flanked by Atlantides, like that of Pompeo Leoni's house (the *Casa degli Omenoni*) and of the Jesuit seminary; or yellow-brown rococo churches with pyramids, broken pediments, flying angels, and vases filled with wrought-iron palm-branches. It is in summer that these streets are at their best. Then the old gardens overhanging the Naviglio—the canal which intersects Milan with a layer of Venice—repeat in its waters their marble loggias hung with the vine, and their untrained profusion of roses and camellias. Then, in the more aristocratic streets, the palace doorways yield vistas of double and triple court-yards, with creeper-clad arcades enclosing spaces of shady turf, and terminating perhaps in a fountain set in some splendid architectural composition against the inner wall of the building. In summer, too, the dark archways in the humbler quarters of the town are brightened by fruit-stalls embowered in foliage, and heaped with such melons, figs and peaches as would have driven to fresh extravagance the exuberant brush of a Flemish fruit-painter. Then again, at the turn of a street, one comes across some little church just celebrating the feast of its patron saint with a brave display of garlands and red hangings; while close by a cavernous *bottegha* has been festooned with more garlands and with bright nosegays, amid which hang the painted candles and other votive offerings designed to attract the small coin of the faithful.

III

Yet Milan is not dependent on the seasons for this midsummer magic of light and colour. For dark days it keeps its store of warmth and brightness hidden behind palace walls and in the cold dusk of church and cloister. Summer in all its throbbing heat has been imprisoned by Tiepolo in the great ceiling of the Palazzo Clerici: that revel of gods and demi-gods, and mortals of all lands and races, who advance with linked hands out of the rosy vapours of

167

dawn. Nor are loftier colour-harmonies wanting. On the walls of San Maurizio Maggiore, Luini's virgin martyrs move as in the very afterglow of legend: that hesitating light in which the fantastic becomes probable, and the boundaries between reality and vision fade; while tints of another sort, but as tender, as harmonious, float through the dusk of the sacristy of Santa Maria delle Grazie, a dim room panelled with intarsia-work, with its grated windows veiled by vine-leaves.

But nothing in Milan approaches in beauty the colour-scheme of the Portinari chapel behind the choir of Sant' Eustorgio. In Italy, even, there is nothing else exactly comparable to this masterpiece of collaboration between architect and painter. At Ravenna, the tomb of Galla Placidia and the apse of San Vitale glow with richer hues, and the lower church of Assisi is unmatched in its shifting mystery of chiar'-oscuro; but for pure light, for a clear shadowless scale of iridescent tints, what can approach the Portinari chapel? Its most striking feature is the harmony of form and colour which makes the decorative design of Michelozzo flow into and seem a part of the exquisite frescoes of Vincenzo Foppa. This harmony is not the result of any voluntary feint, any such trickery of the brush as the later decorative painters delighted in. In the Portinari chapel, architecture and painting are kept distinct in treatment, and the fusion between them is effected by unity of line and colour, and still more, perhaps, by an identity of sentiment, which keeps the whole chapel in the same mood of blitheness,—a mood which makes it difficult to remember that the chapel is the mausoleum of a martyred saint. But Saint Peter Martyr's marble sarcophagus, rich and splendid as it is, somehow fails to distract the attention from its setting. There are so many mediæval monuments like it in Italy—and there is but one Portinari chapel. From the cupola, with its scales of pale red and blue, overlapping each other like the breast-plumage of a pigeon, and terminating in a terra-cotta frieze of dancing angels, who swing between them great bells of fruit and flowers, the eye is led by insensible gradations of tint to Foppa's frescoes in the spandrils—iridescent saints and angels in a setting of pale classical architecture—and thence to another frieze of terra-cotta seraphs with rosy-red wings against a background of turquoise-green; this lower frieze resting in turn on pilasters of pale green adorned with white stucco *rilievi* of little bell-ringing angels. It is only as a part of this colour-scheme that the central sarcophagus really affects one—the ivory tint of its old marble forming a central point for the play of light, and allying itself with the sumptuous hues of Portinari's dress, in the fresco which represents the donator of the chapel kneeling before his patron saint.

The picturesqueness of Milan has overflowed on its environs, and there are several directions in which one may prolong the enjoyment of its characteristic art. The great Certosa of Pavia can, alas, no longer be included in a category of the picturesque. Secularized, catalogued, railed off from the sight-seer, who is hurried through its endless corridors on the heels of a government custodian, it still ministers to the sense of beauty, but no longer excites those subtler sensations which dwell in the atmosphere of a work of art rather than in itself. Such sensations must be sought in the other deserted Certosa at Chiaravalle. The abbey church, with its noble colonnaded cupola, is still one of the most conspicuous objects in the flat landscape about Milan; but within all is falling to ruin, and one feels the melancholy charm of a beautiful building which has been allowed to decay as naturally as a tree. The disintegrating touch of nature is less cruel than the restoring touch of man, and the half-ruined frescoes and intarsia-work of Chiaravalle retain more of their original significance than the carefully-guarded treasures of Pavia.

Less melancholy than Chiaravalle, and as yet unspoiled by the touch of official preservation, is the pilgrimage church of the Madonna of Saronno. A long avenue of plane-trees leads from the village to the sumptuous

Figure 5   The Church at Saronna

marble façade of the church, an early Renaissance building with ornamental additions of the seventeenth century. Within, it is famous for the frescoes of Luini in the choir, and of Gaudenzio Ferrari in the cupola. The Luini frescoes are full of a serene impersonal beauty. Painted in his latest phase, when he had fallen under the influence of Raphael and the 'grand manner,' they lack the intimate charm of his early works; yet the Lombard note, the Leonardesque quality, lingers here

171

and there in the side-long glance of the women, and in the yellow-haired beauty of the adolescent heads; while it finds completer expression in the exquisite single figures of Saint Catherine and Saint Apollonia.

If these stately compositions are less typical of Luini than, for instance, the frescoes of San Maurizio Maggiore, or of the Casa Pelucca (now in the Brera), Gaudenzio's cupola seems, on the contrary, to sum up in one glorious burst of expression all his fancy had ever evoked and his hand longed to embody. It seems to have been given to certain artists to attain, once at least, to this full moment of expression: to Titian, for instance, in the Bacchus and Ariadne, to Michael Angelo in the monuments of the Medici, to Giorgione in the Sylvan Concert of the Louvre. In other works they may reveal greater powers, more magnificent conceptions; but once only, perhaps, is it given to each to achieve the perfect equipoise of mind and hand; and in that moment even the lesser artists verge on greatness. Gaudenzio found his opportunity in the cupola of Saronno, and for once he rises above the charming anecdotic painter of Varallo to the brotherhood of the masters. It is as the expression of a mood that his power reveals itself—the mood of heavenly joyousness, so vividly embodied in his circle of choiring angels that form seems to pass into sound, and the dome to be filled with a burst of heavenly jubilation. With unfaltering hand he has sustained this note of joyousness. Nowhere does his invention fail or his brush lag behind it. The sunny crowding heads, the flying draperies, the fluttering scores of the music, are stirred as by a wind of inspiration—a breeze from the celestial pastures. The walls of the choir seem to resound with one of the angel-choruses of 'Faust,' or with the last chiming lines of the 'Paradiso.' Happy the artist whose full powers find voice in such a key!

V

The reader who has followed these desultory wanderings through Milan has but touched the hem of her garment. In the Brera, the Ambrosiana, the Poldi-Pezzoli gallery, and the magnificent new Archaeological Museum, now fittingly housed in the old castle of the Sforzas, are treasures second only to those of Rome and Florence. But these are among the catalogued riches of the city. The guide-books point to them, they lie in the beaten track of sight-seeing, and it is rather in the intervals between such systematized study of the past, in the parentheses of travel, that one obtains those more intimate glimpses which help to compose the image of each city, to preserve its personality in the traveller's mind.

REFERENCES
1 The epigraph is from Paul Verlaine's 'Clair de Lune,' ll. 1–2. The full text of the two

lines is 'Votre âme est un paysage choisi/Que vont charmant masques et bergamasques,' or '[Your soul is] a choice landscape/Beguiled by masques and bergamasques' (translation by Mary Ann Caws, Graduate Center, CUNY, New York). Wharton omits the first three words in order that the epigraph might better suggest the principal purpose she and her travelling companions had, that of 'exploring the Bergamasque Alps.' Throughout the chapter, she makes explicit associations between the scenery and the *commedia dell'arte*, which originated in Bergamo.

2 The valley of the Vorderrhein (one of the headstreams later forming the Rhine River).

3 A *bergerie* is a sheep-fold or pen; 'Florian' refers to Jean Pierre Claris de Florian (1755–1794), who wrote comedies depicting bourgeois life. His novels were called 'milk soup' by Marie Antoinette, who found them insipid, as Wharton and her party found Switzerland compared with Italy.

4 Wharton was an admirer of the Italian artist Salvator Rosa (1615–1673), of the Neapolitan school, known for his landscapes and battle scenes.

5 Claude Lorrain, the professional name of Claude Gellée or Gelée (1600–1682), was a

174

French landscape painter whose studio was in Rome after 1627.

6 'Just like a swarm of bees that, at one moment, enter the flower'; Dante Alighieri, *The Divine Comedy*, 'Paradisco,' Canto XXXI, 1.7, trans. Allen Mandelbaum (Berkeley: University of California Press, 1982), p. 272. There are several errors in this line as given by Wharton: '*Si*' should be '*si*' and '*api*' should be '*ape*'; the correct line is '*si come schiera d'ape che s'infiora*.' (The same errors appeared in the article when first published in Scribner's Magazine [Vol. 32, No. 2, Aug. 1902, 212–222]).

7 The Englishwoman Lady Mary Wortley Montagu (1689–1762), an inveterate traveller and witty letter writer, described Lovere in July 1749 in a letter to her daughter, Lady Bute: 'I am now in a place the most beautifully Romantick I ever saw in my life. It is the Tunbridge of this part of the World.' She praised the 'Beauty of the Prospect' of the lake, and described evening operas three times a week and 'Diversions on the Water, where all the Town assembles every night, and never without Music' (*The Complete Letters of Lady Mary Wortley Montagu*, ed. Robert Halsband [Oxford: Clarendon Press, 1966].

8 Ys (also Is) is a legendary city off the coast of Brittany. King Gradlon (fifth century) supposedly held the only keys to the

floodgate on the dike protecting Ys. His daughter, carousing with her lover, stole them and, as a prank, flooded the city. The cathedral is said to be visible rising through the mists.

9 A line from Goethe's *Venetian Epigrams* (6), which may be translated as 'How a false concept blesses us men!' (trans. Mary Ann Caws) or 'O how a false conception can make mankind happy' (trans. L. R. Lind). The preceding line of the couplet is: '*Seh ich den Pilgrim, so kann ich mich nie der Tränen enthalten,*' or 'I can never restrain my tears when I see a pilgrim' (Roman Elegies and Venetian Epigrams; A Bilingual Text, trans., with introd., notes, and commentaries by L. R. Lind [Lawrence: University Press of Kansas, 1974], 86–87).

10 The German chemist Baron Justus von Liebig improved organic analysis and made valuable contributions to chemistry. He did not invent the 'Liebig' condenser, but popularized its use. The analogy Wharton suggests between Liebig's work and that of a guidebook writer is not, therefore, wholly valid.

11 Gustav Ebe's *Die Spätrenaissance* (1886) was a source on which Wharton also relied in *Italian Villas and Their Gardens*.

12 Filippo Juvara or Iuvara (1676?–1736), of Messina, was chief architect to the King at Turin.

13 The Roman town that became Milan was known as Mediolanum. The Church of San Lorenzo Maggiore was founded in the fourth century; the portico, with sixteen columns, is all that remains of the Roman town.

14 Arcade with pointed arches.

A MOTOR-FLIGHT THROUGH
FRANCE*

From Rouen to Fontainebleau

The Seine, two days later, by the sweetest curves, drew us on from Rouen to Les Andelys, past such bright gardens terraced above its banks, such moist poplar-fringed islands, such low green promontories deflecting its silver flow, that we continually checked the flight of the motor, pausing here, and here, and here again, to note how France understands and enjoys and lives with her rivers.

With her great past, it seems, she has partly ceased to live; for ask as we would, we could not, that morning, learn the way to King Richard's Château Gaillard on the cliff above Les Andelys. Every turn from the route de Paris seemed to lead straight into the unknown; *'mais c'est tout droit pour* Paris' was the invariable answer when we asked our way. Yet a few miles off were two of the quaintest towns of France—the Little and Great Andely—surmounted by a fortress marking an epoch in military architecture, and associated with the fortunes of one of the most romantic

---

* *A Motor-Flight Through France* was serialized in *The Atlantic Monthly*. 1906–1908.

figures in history; and we knew that if we clung to the windings of the Seine they must lead us, within a few miles, to the place we sought. And so, having with difficulty disentangled ourselves from the route de Paris, we pushed on, by quiet by-roads and unknown villages, by *manoirs* of grey stone peeping through high thickets of lilac and laburnum, and along shady river-reaches where fishermen dozed in their punts, and cattle in the meadow-grass beneath the willows—till the soft slopes broke abruptly into tall cliffs shaggy with gorse, and the easy flow of the river was forced into a sharp twist at their base. There is something fantastic in this sudden change of landscape near Les Andelys from the familiar French river-scenery to what might be one of Piero della Francesca's backgrounds of strangely fretted rock and scant black vegetation; while the Seine, roused from its progress through yielding meadows, takes a majestic bend toward the Little Andely in the bay of the cliffs, and then sweeps out below the height on which Coeur-de-Lion planted his subtly calculated bastions.

Ah—poor fluttering rag of a ruin, so thin, so time-worn, so riddled with storm and shell, that it droops on its rock like a torn banner with forgotten victories in its folds! How much more eloquently these tottering stones tell their story, how much deeper into the past they take us, than the dapper weather-tight castles—

179

Pierrefonds, Langeais, and the rest[1]—on which the arch-restorer has worked his will, reducing them to mere museum specimens, archaeological toys, from which all the growths of time have been ruthlessly stripped! The eloquence of the Château Gaillard lies indeed just there—in its telling us so discursively, so plaintively, the *whole* story of the centuries—how long it has stood, how much it has seen, how far the world has travelled since then, and to what a hoarse, cracked whisper the voice of feudalism and chivalry has dwindled ...

The town that once cowered under the protection of those fallen ramparts still groups its stout old houses about a church so grey and venerable, yet so sturdily planted on its ancient piers, that one might fancy its compassionately bidding the poor ghost of a fortress come down and take shelter beneath its vaultings. Commune and castle, they have changed places with the shifting fortunes of the centuries, the weak growth of the town outstripping the arrogant brief bloom of the fortress—Richard's 'fair daughter of one year'—which had called it arbitrarily into being. The fortress itself is now no more than one of the stage-properties of the Muse of History; but the town, poor little accidental offshoot of a military exigency, has built up a life for itself, become an abiding centre of human activities—though, by an accident in which the traveller cannot but rejoice, it still keeps, in spite of its sound masonry and air of ancient health, that almost unmodernised aspect which makes some little French burghs recall the figure of a lively centenarian, all his faculties still active, but wearing the dress of a former day.

Regaining the route de Paris, we passed once more into the normal Seine landscape, with smiling towns close-set on its shores, with lilac and wistaria pouring over high walls, with bright little cafés on sunny village squares, with flotillas of pleasure-boats moored under willow-shaded banks.

Never more vividly than in this Seine country does one feel the amenity of French manners, the long process of social adaptation which has produced so profound and general an intelligence of life. Every one we passed on our way, from the canal-boatman to the white-capped baker's lad, from the *marchande des quatre saisons* to the white dog curled philosophically under her cart, from the pastry-cook putting a fresh plate of *brioches* in his appetising window to the curé's *bonne* who had just come out to drain the lettuce on the curé's doorstep—all these persons (under which designation I specifically include the dog) took their ease or pursued their business with that cheerful activity which proceeds from an intelligent acceptance of given conditions. They each had their established niche in life, the frankly avowed interests and preoccupations of their order, their pride in the smartness of the canal-boat, the seductions of the show-window, the glaze of the *brioches*, the crispness of the lettuce. And this admirable *fitting into the pattern*, which seems almost as if it were a moral outcome of the universal French sense of form, has led the race to the happy, the momentous discovery that good manners are a short cut to one's goal, that they lubricate the wheels of life instead of obstructing them. This discovery—the result, as it strikes one, of the application of the finest of mental instruments to the muddled process of living—seems to have illuminated not only the social relation but its outward, concrete expression, producing a finish in the material setting of life, a kind of conformity in inanimate things—forming, in short, the background of the spectacle through which we pass, the canvas on which it is painted, and expressing itself no less in the trimness of each individual garden than in that insistence on civic dignity and comeliness so miraculously maintained, through every torment of political passion, every change of social conviction, by a people resolutely addressed to the intelligent enjoyment of living.

By Vernon, with its trim lime-walks *en berceau*, by Mantes with its bright gardens, and the graceful over-restored church which dominates its square, we passed on to

Versailles, forsaking the course of the Seine that we might have a glimpse of the country about Fontainebleau.

At the top of the route du Buc, which climbs by sharp windings from the Place du Château at Versailles, one comes upon the arches of the aqueduct of Buc—one of the monuments of that splendid folly which created the 'Golden House' of Louis XIV, and drew its miraculous groves and gardens from the waterless plain of Versailles. The aqueduct, forming part of the extravagant scheme of irrigation of which the Machine de Marly[2] and the great canal of Maintenon commemorate successive disastrous phases, frames, in its useless lofty openings, such charming glimpses of the country to the southwest of Versailles, that it takes its place among those abortive architectural experiments which seem, after all, to have been completely justified by time.

The landscape upon which the arches look is a high-lying region of wood and vale, with châteaux at the end of long green vistas, and old flowery villages tucked into folds of the hills. At the first turn of the road above Versailles the well-kept suburbanism of the Parisian environ gives way to the real look of the country—well-kept and smiling still, but tranquil and sweetly shaded, with big farmyards, quiet country lanes, and a quiet country look in the peasants' faces.

In passing through some parts of France one

wonders where the inhabitants of the châteaux go when they emerge from their gates—so interminably, beyond those gates, do the flat fields, divided by straight unshaded roads, reach out to every point of the compass; but here the wooded undulations of the country, the friendliness of the villages, the recurrence of big rambling farmsteads—some, apparently, the remains of fortified monastic granges—all suggest the possibility of something resembling the English rural life, with its traditional ties between park and fields.

The brief journey between Versailles and Fontainebleau offers—if one takes the longer way, by Saint Rémy-les-Chevreuse and Etampes—a succession of charming impressions, more varied than one often finds in a long day's motor-run through France; and midway one comes upon the splendid surprise of Dourdan.

Ignorance is not without its aesthetic uses; and to drop down into the modest old town without knowing—or having forgotten, if one prefers to put it so—the great castle of Philip Augustus, which, moated, dungeoned, ivy-walled, still possesses its peaceful central square—to come on this vigorous bit of mediæval arrogance, with the little houses of Dourdan still ducking their humble roofs to it in an obsequious circle—well! to taste the full flavour of such sensations, it is worth while to be of a country where the last new grain-elevator or office building is the only monument that receives homage from the surrounding architecture.

Dourdan, too, has the crowning charm of an old inn facing its *château-fort*—such an inn as Manon and des Grieux dined in on the way to Paris—where, in a large courtyard shaded by trees, one may feast on strawberries and cheese at a table enclosed in clipped shrubs, with dogs and pigeons amicably prowling for crumbs, and the host and hostess, their maid-servants, ostlers and *marmitons* breakfasting at another long table, just across the hedge. Now that the demands of the motorist are introducing modern plumbing and Maple furniture into the uttermost parts of France, these romantic old inns, where it is charming to breakfast, if precarious to sleep, are becoming as rare as the mediæval keeps with which they are, in a way, contemporaneous; and Dourdan is fortunate in still having two such perfect specimens to attract the attention of the archaeologist.

Etampes, our next considerable town, seemed by contrast rather featureless and disappointing; yet, for that very reason, so typical of the average French country town— dry, compact, unsentimental, as if avariciously hoarding a long rich past—that its one straight grey street and squat old church will hereafter always serve for the *ville de province* background in my staging of French fiction. Beyond Etampes, as one approaches

Fontainebleau, the scenery grows extremely picturesque, with bold outcroppings of blackened rock, fields of golden broom, groves of birch and pine—first hints of the fantastic sandstone scenery of the forest. And presently the long green aisles opened before us in all the freshness of spring verdure—tapering away right and left to distant *ronds-points*, to mossy stone crosses and obelisks—and leading us toward sunset to the old town in the heart of the forest.

Paris to Poitiers

Spring again, and the long white road unrolling itself southward from Paris. How could one resist the call?

We answered it on the blandest of late March mornings, all April in the air, and the Seine fringing itself with a mist of yellowish willows as we rose over it, climbing the hill to Ville d'Avray. Spring comes soberly, inaudibly as it were, in these temperate European lands, where the grass holds its green all winter, and the foliage of ivy, laurel, holly, and countless other evergreen shrubs, links the lifeless to the living months. But the mere act of climbing that southern road above the Seine meadows seemed as definite as the turning of a leaf—the passing from a black-and-white page to one illuminated. And every day now would turn a brighter page for us.

186

Goethe has a charming verse, descriptive, it is supposed, of his first meeting with Christiane Vulpius: 'Aimlessly I strayed through the wood, *having it in my mind to seek nothing.*'[3]

Such, precisely, was our state of mind on that first day's run. We were simply pushing south toward the Berry, through a more or less familiar country, and the real journey was to begin for us on the morrow, with the run from Châteauroux to Poitiers. But we reckoned without our France! It is easy enough, glancing down the long page of the Guide Continental, to slip by such names as Versailles, Rambouillet, Chartres and Valençay, in one's dash for the objective point; but there is no slipping by them in the motor, they lurk there in one's path, throwing out great loops of persuasion, arresting one's flight, complicating one's impressions, oppressing, bewildering one with the renewed, half-forgotten sense of the hoarded richness of France.

Versailles first, unfolding the pillared expanse of its north facade to vast empty perspectives of radiating avenues; then Rambouillet, low in a damp little park, with statues along green canals, and a look, this moist March weather, of being somewhat below sea-level; then Maintenon, its rich red-purple walls and delicate stone ornament reflected in the moat dividing it from the village street. Both Rambouillet and Maintenon are characteristically French in their way of keeping company with their villages. Rambouillet, indeed, is slightly screened by a tall gate, a wall and trees; but Maintenon's warm red turrets look across the moat, straight into the windows of the opposite houses, with the simple familiarity of a time when class distinctions were too fixed to need emphasising.

Our third château, Valençay—which, for comparison's sake, one may couple with the others though it lies far south of Blois— Valençay bears itself with greater aloofness, bidding the town 'keep its distance' down the hill on which the great house lifts its heavy angle-towers and flattened domes. A huge cliff-like wall, enclosing the whole southern flank of the hill, supports the terraced gardens before the château, which to the north is divided from the road by a vast *cour d'honneur* with a monumental grille and gateway. The impression is grander yet less noble.

But France is never long content to repeat her effects; and between Maintenon and Valençay she puts Chartres and Blois. Ah, these grey old cathedral towns with their narrow clean streets widening to a central *place*—at Chartres a beautiful oval, like the market-place in an eighteenth-century print— with their clipped lime-walks, high garden walls, Balzacian gables looking out on sunless lanes under the flanks of the granite giant! Save in the church itself, how frugally all the effects are produced—with how sober a use of greys and blacks, and pale high lights, as in some Van der Meer interior; yet how intense a suggestion of thrifty compact traditional life one gets from the low house-fronts, the bared barred gates, the glimpses of clean bare courts, the calm yet quick faces in the doorways! From these faces again one gets the same impression of remarkable effects produced by the discreetest means. The French physiognomy if not vividly beautiful is vividly intelligent; but the long practice of manners has so veiled its keenness with refinement as to produce a blending of vivacity and good temper nowhere else to be matched. And in looking at it one feels once more, as one so often feels in trying to estimate French architecture or the French landscape, how much of her total effect France achieves by elimination. If marked beauty be absent from the French face, how much more is marked dullness, marked brutality, the lumpishness of the clumsily made and the unfinished! As a mere piece of workmanship, of finish, the French provincial face—the peasant's face, even—often has the same kind of interest as a work of art.

One gets, after repeated visits to the 'show' towns of France, to feel these minor characteristics, the incidental graces of the foreground, almost to the exclusion of the great official spectacle in the centre of the picture; so that while the first image of Bourges or Chartres is that of a cathedral surrounded by a blur, later memories of the same places present a vividly individual town, with doorways, street-corners, faces intensely remembered, and in the centre a great cloudy Gothic splendour.

At Chartres the cloudy splendour is shot through with such effulgence of colour that its vision, evoked by memory, seems to beat with a fiery life of its own, as though red blood ran in its stone veins. It is this suffusion of heat and radiance that chiefly, to the untechnical, distinguishes it from the other great Gothic interiors. In all the rest, colour, if it exists at all, burns in scattered unquiet patches, between wastes of shadowy grey stone and the wan pallor of later painted glass; but at Chartres those quivering waves of unearthly red and blue flow into and repeat each other in rivers of light, from their source in the great western rose, down the length of the vast aisles and clerestory, till they are gathered up at last into the mystical heart of the apse.

A short afternoon's run carried us through dullish country from Chartres to Blois, which we reached at the fortunate hour when sunset burnishes the great curves of the Loire and lays a plum-coloured bloom on the slate roofs overlapping, scale-like, the slope below the castle. There are few finer *roof-views* than this from the wall at Blois: the blue sweep of gables and ridge-lines billowing up here and there into a church tower with its *clocheton* mailed in slate, or breaking to let through the glimpse of a carved façade, or the blossoming depths of a hanging garden; but perhaps only the eye subdued to tin housetops and iron chimney-pots can feel the full poetry of old roofs.

Coming back to the Berry six weeks earlier than on our last year's visit, we saw how much its wide landscape needs the relief and modelling given by the varied foliage of May. Between bare woods and scarcely budded hedges the great meadows looked bleak and monotonous; and only the village gardens hung out a visible promise of spring. But in the sheltered enclosure at Nohant, spring seemed much nearer; at hand already in clumps of snowdrops and violets loosening the soil, in young red leaves on the rose-standards, and the twitter of birds in the heavy black-fruited ivy of the grave-yard wall. A gate leads from the garden into the corner of the grave-yard where George Sand and her children lie under an ancient yew. Feudal even in burial, they are walled off from the village dead, and the tombstone of Maurice Sand, as well as the monstrous stone chest over his mother's grave, bears the name of Dudevant and asserts a claim to the barony. Strange inconsequence of human desires, that the woman who had made her pseudonym illustrious enough to have it assumed by her whole family should cling in death to the obscure name of a repudiated

191

husband; more inconsequent still that the descendant of kings, and the priestess of democracy and Fourierism,[4] should insist on a right to the petty title which was never hers, since it was never Dudevant's to give! On the whole, the grave-stones at Nohant are disillusioning; except indeed that of the wretched Solange, with its four tragic words: *La mère de Jeanne.*

But the real meaning of the place must be sought close by, behind the row of tall windows opening on the tangled mossy garden. They lead, these windows, straight into the life of George Sand: into the big cool dining-room, with its flagged floor and simple white-panelled walls, and the *salon* adjoining: the *salon*, alas, so radically remodelled in the unhappy mid-century period of wall-papers, stuffed furniture and centre table, that one seeks in vain for a trace of the original chatelaine of Nohant—that high-spirited, high-heeled old Madame Dupin who still haunts the panelled dining-room and the box-edged garden. Yet the *salon* has its special story to tell, for in George Sand's culminating time just such a long table with fringed cover and encircling arm-chairs formed the centre of French indoor life. About this elongated board sat the great woman's illustrious visitors, prolonging, as at a mental *table d'hôte*, that interminable dinner-talk which still strikes the hurried Anglo-Saxon as the typical expression of French sociability; and here the different arts of the household were practised—the painting, carving and fine needle-work which a stronger-eyed generation managed to carry on by the light of a single lamp. Here, one likes especially to fancy, Maurice Sand exercised his chisel on the famous marionettes for the little theatre, while his mother, fitting their costumes with skilful fingers, listened, silent *comme une bête*, to the dissertations of Gautier, Flaubert or Dumas. The earlier life of the house still speaks, moreover, from the walls of the drawing-room, with the voice of jealously treasured ancestral portraits—pictures of the demoiselles Verrières, of the great Marshal and the beautiful Aurora—strange memorials of a past which explains so much in the history of George Sand, even to the tempestuous face of Solange Clésinger, looking darkly across the room at her simpering unremorseful progenitors.

Our guide, a close-capped brown-and-ruddy *bonne*, led us next, by circuitous passages, to the most interesting corner of the house: the little theatre contrived with artless ingenuity out of what might have been a store-room or wine-cellar. One should rather say the little theatres, however, for the mistress of revels had managed to crowd two stages into the limited space at her disposal; one, to the left, an actual *scène*, with 'life-size' scenery for real actors, the other, facing the entrance-door, the more celebrated marionette theatre, raised a few feet from the floor, with miniature proscenium arch and curtain; just such a *Puppen-theatre* as Wilhelm Meister described to Marianne, with a prolixity which caused that amiable but flighty young woman to fall asleep.

Between the two stages about twenty spectators might have found seats behind the front row of hard wooden benches reserved for the châtelaine and her most distinguished guests. A clean emptiness now pervades this temple of the arts: an emptiness made actually pathetic by the presence, on shelves at the back of the room, of the whole troupe of marionettes, brushed, spotless, well cared for, and waiting only a touch on their wires to spring into life and populate their little stage. There they stand in wistful rows, the duenna, the Chimène, the *grande coquette*, Pantaloon, Columbine and Harlequin,[5] Neapolitan fishers, odalisques and peasants, brigands and soldiers of the guard; all carved with a certain rude vivacity, and dressed, ingeniously and thriftily, by the indefatigable fingers which drove the quill all night upstairs.

It brought one close to that strange unfathomable life, which only at Nohant grows clear, shows bottom, as it were; closer still to be told by the red-brown *bonne* that 'Monsieur Maurice' had modelled many of his humorous peasant-types on 'les *gens du pays*';

194

closest of all when she added, in answer to a question as to whether Madame Sand had really made the little frocks herself: 'Oh, yes, I remember seeing her at work on them, and helping her with it. I was twelve years old when she died.'

Here, then, was an actual bit of the Nohant tradition, before us in robust and lively middle age: one of the *berrichonnes* whom George Sand loved and celebrated, and who loved and served her in return. For a moment it brought Nohant within touch; yet the final effect of the contact, as one reflected on the vanished enthusiasms and ideas that George Sand's name revives, was the sense that the world of beliefs and ideas has seldom travelled so fast and far as in the years between 'Indiana' and to-day.

* * *

From La Châtre, just south of Nohant, we turned due west along the valley of the Creuse, through a country possessing some local fame for picturesqueness, but which struck us, in its early spring nudity, as somewhat parched and chalky-looking, without sufficient woodland to drape its angles. It makes up, however, in architectural interest for what its landscape lacks, and not many miles beyond La Châtre the otherwise featureless little town of Neuvy-Saint-Sépulcre presents one feature of unusual prominence. This is the ancient round church from which the place is named: one of those copies of the church of the Holy Sepulchre at Jerusalem with which the returning crusader dotted western Europe. Aside from their intrinsic interest, these 'sepulchre' churches have gained importance from the fact that but three or four are still extant. The most typical, that of Saint Bénigne at Dijon, has been levelled to a mere crypt, and that of Cambridge deviates from the type by reason of its octagonal dome; so that the church of Neuvy is of quite pre-eminent interest. A late Romanesque nave—itself sufficiently venerable looking to stir the imagination in its own behalf—was appended in the early thirteenth century to the circular shrine; but the latter still presents to the dull old street its unbroken cylindrical wall, built close on a thousand years ago, and surmounted, some ninety years later, by a second story with a Romanesque exterior arcade. At this stage, however, one is left to conjecture, with the aid of expert suggestion, what manner of covering the building was meant to have. The present small dome, perched on the inner drum of the upper gallery, is an expedient of the most obvious sort; and the archæologists have inferred that the thinness of this drum may have made a more adequate form of roofing impossible.

To the idle sight-seer, at any rate, the interior

of the church is much more suggestive than its bare outer shell. We were happy enough to enter it toward sunset, when dusk had gathered under the heavy encircling columns, and lights twinkled yellow on the central altar which has so regrettably replaced the 'Grotto of the Sepulchre.' It was our added good fortune that a small train of the faithful, headed by a red-cassocked verger and a priest with a benignant Massillon-like head,[6] were just making a circuit of the stations of the cross affixed to the walls of the aisle; and as we stood withdrawn, while the procession wound its way between shining altar and shadowy columns, some of the faces of the peasants seemed to carry us as far into the past as the strange symbolic masks on the capitals above their heads.

But what carries one farthest of all is perhaps the fact, well known to modern archæology, that the original church built by Constantine over the grotto-tomb of Christ was not a round temple at all, but a vast basilica with semi-circular apse. The Persians destroyed this building in the seventh century, and the Christians who undertook to restore it could do no more than round the circle of the apse, thus at least covering over the sacred tomb in the centre. So swift was the succession of demolition and reconstruction in that confused and clashing age, so vague and soon obliterated were the records of each previous rule, that when the crusaders came they found no memory of this earlier transformation, and carried back with them that model of the round temple which was henceforth to stand, throughout western Europe, as the venerated image of the primitive church of Jerusalem.

Too much lingering in this precious little building brought twilight on us soon after we joined the Creuse at Argenton; and when we left it again at Le Blanc lights were in the windows, and the rest of our run to Poitiers was a ghostly flight through a moon-washed landscape, with here and there a church tower looming in the dimness, or a heap of ruined walls rising mysteriously above the white bend of a river. We suffered a peculiar pang when a long-roofed pile towering overhead told us that we were passing the great Benedictine abbey of Saint Savin, with its matchless lining of frescoes; but a certain mental satiety urged us on to Poitiers.

Travellers accustomed to the marked silhouette of Italian cities—to their immediate proffer of the picturesque impression—often find the old French provincial towns lacking in physiognomy. Each Italian city, whether of the mountain or the plain, has an outline easily recognisable after individual details have faded, and it is, obviously, much easier to keep separate one's memories of Siena and Orvieto than of Bourges and Chartres. Perhaps, therefore, the few French towns with definite physiognomies seem the more definite from their infrequency; and Poitiers is foremost in this distinguished group.

Not that it offers the distinctive *galbe* of such bold hill-towns as Angoulême or Laon. Though a hill-town in fact, it somehow makes next to nothing of this advantage, and the late Mr Freeman was justified in grumbling at the lack of character in its sky-line. That character reveals itself, in fact, not in any picturesqueness of distant effect—in no such far-seen crown as the towers of Laon or the domes of Périgueux—but in the homogeneous interest of the old buildings within the city: the way they carry on its packed romantic history like the consecutive pages of a richly illuminated chronicle. The illustration of that history begins with the strange little 'temple' of Saint John, a baptistery of the fourth century, and accounted the earliest Christian building in France—though this applies only to the lower story (now virtually the crypt), the upper having been added some three hundred years later, when baptism by aspersion had replaced the primitive plunge. Unhappily the ancient temple has suffered the lot of the too-highly treasured relic, and fenced about, restored, and converted into a dry little museum, has lost all that colour and pathos of extreme age that make the charm of humbler monuments.

This charm, in addition to many others, still clings to the expressive west front of Notre Dame la Grande, the incomparable little

Romanesque church holding the centre of the market-place. Built of a dark grey stone which has taken on—and been suffered to retain—a bloom of golden lichen like the trace of ancient weatherworn gilding, it breaks, at the spring of its portal-arches, into a profusion of serried, overlapping sculpture, which rises tier by tier to the splendid Christ Triumphant of the crowning gable, yet never once crowds out and smothers the structural composition, as Gothic ornament, in its most exuberant phase, was wont to do. Through all its profusion of statuary and ornamental carving, the front of Notre Dame preserves that subordination to classical composition that marks the Romanesque of southern France; but between the arches, in the great spandrils of the doorways, up to the typically Poitevin scales of the beautiful arcaded angle turrets, what richness of detail, what splendid play of fancy!

After such completeness of beauty as this little church presents—for its nave and transept tower are no less admirable than the more striking front—even such other monuments as Poitiers has to offer must suffer slightly by comparison. Saint Hilaire le Grand, that notable eleventh-century church, with its triple aisles and its nave roofed by cupolas, and the lower-lying temple of Sainte Radegonde, which dates from the Merovingian queen from whom it takes its name, have both suffered such repeated alterations that neither carries the imagination back with as direct a flight as the slightly less ancient Notre Dame; and the cathedral itself, which one somehow comes to last in an enumeration of the Poitiers churches, is a singularly charmless building. Built in the twelfth century, by Queen Eleanor of Guyenne, at the interesting moment of transition from the round to the pointed arch, and completed later by a wide-sprawling Gothic front, it gropes after and fails of its effect both without and within. Yet it has one memorable possession in its thirteenth-century choir-stalls, almost alone of that date in France—tall severe seats, their backs formed by pointed arches with delicate low-relief carvings between the spandrils. There is, in especial, one small bat, with outspread web-like wings, so exquisitely fitted into its allotted space, and with such delicacy of observation shown in the modelling of its little half-human face, that it remains in memory as having the permanence of something classical, outside of dates and styles.

Having lingered over these things, and taken in by the way an impression of the confused and rambling ducal palace, with its magnificent *grande salle* completed and adorned by Jean de Berry, we began to think remorsefully of the wonders we had missed on our run from Le Blanc to Poitiers. We could not retrace the whole distance; but at least we could return to the curious little town of

201

Chauvigny, of which we had caught a tantalising glimpse above a moonlit curve of the Vienne.

We found it, by day, no less suggestive, and full of unsuspected riches. Of its two large Romanesque churches, the one in the lower town, beside the river, is notable, without, for an extremely beautiful arcaded apse, and contains within a striking fresco of the fifteenth century, in which Christ is represented followed by a throng of the faithful—kings, bishops, monks and clerks—who help to carry the cross. The other, and larger, church, planted on the summit of the abrupt escarpment which lifts the *haute ville* above the Vienne, has a strange body-guard composed of no fewer than five feudal castles, huddled so close together on the narrow top of the cliff that their outer walls almost touch. The lack, in that open country, of easily fortified points doubtless drove the bishops of Poitiers (who were also barons of Chauvigny) into this strange defensive alliance with four of their noble neighbours; and one wonders how the five-sided ménage kept the peace, when local disturbances made it needful to take to the rock.

The gashed walls and ivy-draped dungeons of the rival ruins make an extraordinarily romantic setting for the curious church of Saint Pierre, staunchly seated on an extreme ledge of the cliff, and gathering under its flank the handful of town within the fortified circuit. There is nothing in architecture so suggestive of extreme age, yet of a kind of hale durability, as these thick-set Romanesque churches, with their prudent vaulting, their solid central towers, the close firm grouping of their apsidal chapels. The Renaissance brought the classic style into such permanent relationship to modern life that eleventh-century architecture seems remoter than Greece and Rome; yet its buildings have none of the perilous frailty of the later Gothic, and one associates the idea of romance and ruin rather with the pointed arch than with the round.

Saint Pierre is a singularly good example of this stout old school, which saw the last waves of barbarian invasion break at its feet, and seems likely to see the ebb and flow of so many other tides before its stubborn walls go under. It is in their sculptures, especially, that these churches reach back to a dim and fearful world of which few clues remain to us: the mysterious baleful creatures peopling their archivolts and capitals seem to have come out of some fierce vision of Cenobite temptation, when the hermits of the desert fought with the painted devils of the tombs.

The apsidal capitals of Saint Pierre are a very menagerie of such strange demons—evil beasts grinning and mocking among the stocky saints and angels who set forth, unconcerned by such hideous propinquity, the story of the birth of

Christ. The animals are much more skillfully modelled than the angels, and at Chauvigny one slender monster, with greyhound flanks, sub-human face, and long curved tail ending in a grasping human hand, haunts the memory as an embodiment of subtle malevolence.

REFERENCES

1 Langeais is a fortress-castle on the Loire begun by Louis XI in 1465. It was restored by a later owner, Jacques Siegfried. Pierrefonds, a castle in the environs of Paris, was reconstructed by Eugène Violett-le-Duc (probably the 'arch-restorer' to whom Wharton refers) between 1859 and 1870.

2 In 1684, Louis XIV caused an immense hydraulic engine to be built in the small village of Marly to tap the waters of the Seine for the fountains and canals at Versailles. As a result, there were acute water shortages in Paris and the surrounding countryside. The Marly machine was regarded almost as the eighth wonder of the world. Françoise d'Aubigné Maintenon was the second wife of Louis XIV. While she was still the governess of his illegitimate children, the king presented her with Maintenon, a moated château between Chartres and Rambouillet, and she became the Marquise de Maintenon. The seventeenth-century aqueduct is one of the principal sights at Maintenon.

3 The German poet and novelist Johann Wolfgang von Goethe (1749–1832) married Christiane Vulpius, who had been a member of his household, in 1806.
4 Charles Fourier (1772–1837), French social philosopher, originated the idea of social utopias in small economic units, a theory that became known as Fourierism.
5 Stock characters from the *commedia dell'arte* (see Introduction).
6 Jean Baptiste (1663–1742) was bishop of Clermont; he pronounced the funeral oration for Louis XIV.

FIGHTING FRANCE:
FROM DUNKERQUE TO BELFORT*

In Argonne

I

The permission to visit a few ambulances and evacuation hospitals behind the lines gave me, at the end of February, my first sight of War.

Paris is no longer included in the military zone, either in fact or in appearance. Though it is still manifestly under the war-cloud, its air of reviving activity produces the illusion that the menace which casts that cloud is far off not only in distance but in time. Paris, a few months ago so alive to the nearness of the enemy, seems to have grown completely oblivious of that nearness; and it is startling, not more than twenty miles from the gates, to pass from such an atmosphere of workaday security to the imminent sense of War.

Going eastward, one begins to feel the change just beyond Meaux. Between that quiet episcopal city and the hill-town of Montmirail, some forty miles farther east, there are no

---

* 'In Argonne,' Chapter 2 of *Fighting France: From Dunkerque to Belfort*, was first published in *Scribner's Magazine*, 57 (June 1915), 'In Lorraine and the Vosges' *Scribner's Magazine*, 58 (Oct. 1915).

sensational evidences of the great conflict of September—only, here and there, in an unploughed field, or among the fresh brown furrows, a little mound with a wooden cross and a wreath on it. Nevertheless, one begins to perceive, by certain negative signs, that one is already in another world. On the cold February day when we turned out of Meaux and took the road to the Argonne, the change was chiefly shown by the curious absence of life in the villages through which we passed. Now and then a lonely ploughman and his team stood out against the sky, or a child and an old woman looked from a doorway; but many of the fields were fallow and most of the doorways empty. We passed a few carts driven by peasants, a stray wood-cutter in a copse, a road-mender hammering at his stones; but already the 'civilian motor' had disappeared, and all the dust-coloured cars dashing past us were marked with the Red Cross or the number of an army division. At every bridge and railway-crossing a sentinel, standing in the middle of the road with lifted rifle, stopped the motor and examined our papers. In this negative sphere there was hardly any other tangible proof of military rule; but with the descent of the first hill beyond Montmirail there came the positive feeling: *This is war!*

Along the white road rippling away eastward over the dimpled country the army motors were pouring by in endless lines, broken now and then by the dark mass of a tramping regiment or the clatter of a train of artillery. In the intervals between these waves of military traffic we had the road to ourselves, except for the flashing past of despatch-bearers on motor-cycles and of hideously hooting little motors carrying goggled officers in goat-skins and woollen helmets.

The villages along the road all seemed empty—not figuratively but literally empty. None of them has suffered from the German invasion, save by the destruction, here and there, of a single house on which some random malice has wreaked itself; but since the general flight in September all have remained abandoned, or are provisionally occupied by troops, and the rich country between Montmirail and Châlons is a desert.

The first sight of Châlons is extraordinarily exhilarating. The old town lying so pleasantly between canal and river is the Headquarters of an army—not of a corps or of a division, but of a whole army—and the network of grey provincial streets about the Romanesque towers of Notre Dame rustles with the movement of war. The square before the principal hotel—the incomparably named 'Haute Mère-Dieu'—is as vivid a sight as any scene of modern war can be. Rows of grey motor-lorries and omnibuses do not lend themselves to as happy groupings as a detachment of cavalry, and spitting and spurting motor-cycles and 'torpedo' racers are no substitute for the glitter of helmets and the curvetting of chargers;[1] but once the eye has adapted itself to the ugly lines and the neutral tints of the new warfare, the scene in the crowded clattering square becomes positively brilliant. It is a vision of one of the central functions of a great war, in all its concentrated energy, without the saddening suggestions of what, on the distant periphery, that energy is daily and hourly resulting in. Yet even here such suggestions are never long out of sight; for one cannot pass through Châlons without meeting, on their way from the station, a long line of 'éclopés'—the unwounded but battered, shattered, frost-bitten, deafened and half-paralyzed wreckage of the awful struggle. These poor wretches, in their thousands, are daily shipped back from the front to rest and be restored; and it is a grim sight to watch them limping by, and to meet the dazed stare of eyes that have seen what one dare not picture.

If one could think away the 'éclopés' in the streets and the wounded in the hospitals, Châlons would be an invigorating spectacle. When we drove up to the hotel even the grey motors and the sober uniforms seemed to sparkle under the cold sky. The continual coming and going of alert and busy messengers, the riding up of officers (for some still ride!), the arrival of much-decorated military personages in luxurious motors, the hurrying to and fro of orderlies, the perpetual depleting and refilling of the long rows of grey vans across the square, the movements of Red Cross ambulances and the passing of detachments for the front, all these are sights that the pacific stranger could forever gape at. And in the hotel, what a clatter of swords, what a piling up of fur coats and haversacks, what a grouping of bronzed energetic heads about the packed tables in the restaurant! It is not easy for civilians to get to Châlons, and almost every table is occupied by officers and soldiers—for, once off duty, there seems to be no rank distinction in this happy democratic army, and the simple private, if he chooses to treat himself to the excellent fare of the Haute Mère-Dieu, has as good a right to it as his colonel.

The scene in the restaurant is inexhaustibly interesting. The mere attempt to puzzle out the different uniforms is absorbing. A week's experience near the front convinces me that no two uniforms in the French army are alike either in colour or in cut. Within the last two years the question of colour has greatly preoccupied the French military authorities, who have been seeking an invisible blue; and the range of their experiments is proved by the extraordinary variety of shades of blue, ranging from a sort of greyish robin's-egg to the darkest navy, in which the army is clothed. The result attained is the conviction that no blue is really inconspicuous, and that some of the harsh new slaty tints are no less striking than the deeper shades they have superseded. But to this scale of experimental blues, other colours must be added: the poppy-red of the Spahis' tunics,[2] and various other less familiar colours—grey, and a certain greenish khaki— the use of which is due to the fact that the cloth supply has given out and that all available materials are employed. As for the differences in cut, the uniforms vary from the old tight tunic to the loose belted jacket copied from the English, and the emblems of the various arms and ranks embroidered on these diversified habits add a new element of perplexity. The aviator's wings, the motorist's wheel, and many of the newer symbols, are easily recognizable—but there are all the other arms, and the doctors and the stretcher-bearers, the sappers[3] and miners, and heaven knows how many more ramifications of this great host which is really all the nation.

The main interest of the scene, however, is that it shows almost as many types as uniforms, and that almost all the types are so good. One begins to understand (if one has failed to before) why the French say of themselves: '*La France est une nation guerrière*'.[4] War is the greatest of paradoxes: the most senseless and disheartening of human retrogressions, and yet the stimulant of qualities of soul which, in every race, can seemingly find no other means of renewal. Everything depends, therefore, on the category of impulses that war excites in a people. Looking at the faces at Châlons, one sees at once in which sense the French are 'une nation guerrière.' It is not too much to say that war has given beauty to faces that were interesting, humorous, acute, malicious, a hundred vivid and expressive things, but last and least of all beautiful. Almost all the faces about these crowded tables—young or old, plain or handsome, distinguished or average—have the same look of quiet authority: it is as though all 'nervosity,' fussiness, little personal oddities, meannesses and vulgarities, had been burnt away in a great flame of self-dedication. It is a wonderful example of the rapidity with which purpose models the human countenance. More than half of these men were probably doing dull or useless or unimportant things till the first of last August; now each one of them, however small his job, is sharing in a great task, and knows it, and has been made over by knowing it.

Our road on leaving Châlons continued to run northeastward toward the hills of the Argonne.

We passed through more deserted villages, with soldiers lounging in the doors where old women should have sat with their distaffs, soldiers watering their horses in the village pond, soldiers cooking over gypsy fires in the

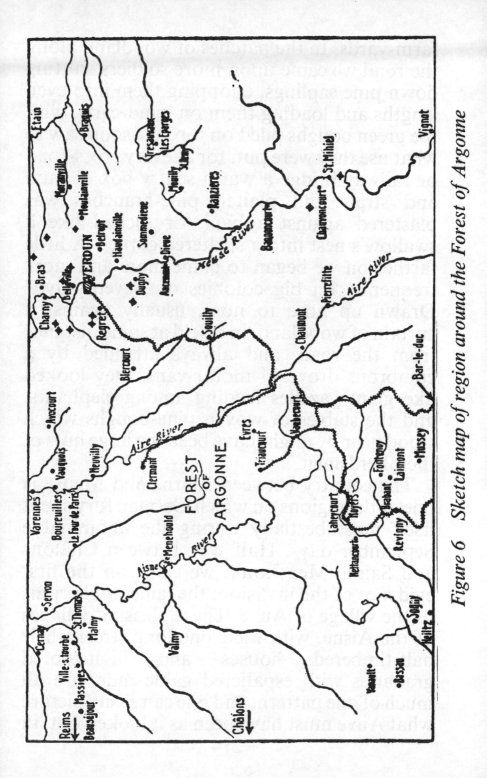

Figure 6   Sketch map of region around the Forest of Argonne

farm-yards. In the patches of woodland along the road we came upon more soldiers, cutting down pine saplings, chopping them into even lengths and loading them on hand-carts, with the green boughs piled on top. We soon saw to what use they were put, for at every cross-road or railway bridge a warm sentry-box of mud and straw and plaited pine-branches was plastered against a bank or tucked like a swallow's nest into a sheltered corner. A little farther on we began to come more and more frequently on big colonies of 'Seventy-five.' Drawn up nose to nose, usually against a curtain of woodland, in a field at some distance from the road, and always attended by a cumbrous drove of motor-vans, they looked like giant gazelles feeding among elephants; and the stables of woven pine-boughs which stood near by might have been the huge huts of their herdsmen.

The country between Marne and Meuse is one of the regions on which German fury spent itself most bestially during the abominable September days. Half way between Châlons and Sainte Menehould we came on the first evidence of the invasion: the lamentable ruins of the village of Auve. These pleasant villages of the Aisne, with their one long street, their half-timbered houses and high-roofed granaries with espaliered gable-ends, are all much of one pattern, and one can easily picture what Auve must have been as it looked out, in the blue September weather, above the ripening pears of its gardens to the crops in the valley and the large landscape beyond. Now it is a mere waste of rubble and cinders, not one threshold distinguishable from another. We saw many other ruined villages after Auve, but this was the first, and perhaps for that reason one had there, most hauntingly, the vision of all the separate terrors, anguishes, uprootings and rendings apart involved in the destruction of the obscurest of human communities. The photographs on the walls, the twigs of withered box above the crucifixes, the old wedding-dresses in brass-clamped trunks, the bundles of letters laboriously written and as painfully deciphered, all the thousand and one bits of the past that give meaning and continuity to the present—of all that accumulated warmth nothing was left but a brick-heap and some twisted stove-pipes!

As we ran on toward Sainte Menehould the names on our map showed us that, just beyond the parallel range of hills six or seven miles to the north, the two armies lay interlocked. But we heard no cannon yet, and the first visible evidence of the nearness of the struggle was the encounter, at a bend of the road, of a long line of grey-coated figures tramping toward us between the bayonets of their captors. They were a sturdy lot, this fresh 'bag' from the hills, of a fine fighting age, and much less famished and war-worn than one could have wished.

Their broad blond faces were meaningless, guarded, but neither defiant nor unhappy: they seemed none too sorry for their fate.

Our pass from the General Head-quarters carried us to Sainte Menehould on the edge of the Argonne, where we had to apply to the Head-quarters of the division for a farther extension. The Staff are lodged in a house considerably the worse for German occupancy, where offices have been improvised by means of wooden hoardings, and where, sitting in a bare passage on a frayed damask sofa surmounted by theatrical posters and faced by a bed with a plum-coloured counterpane, we listened for a while to the jingle of telephones, the rat-tat of typewriters, the steady hum of dictation and the coming and going of hurried despatch-bearers and orderlies. The extension to the permit was presently delivered with the courteous request that we should push on to Verdun as fast as possible, as civilian motors were not wanted on the road that afternoon; and this request, coupled with the evident stir of activity at Head-quarters, gave us the impression that there must be a good deal happening beyond the low line of hills to the north. How much there was we were soon to know.

We left Sainte Menehould at about eleven, and before twelve o'clock we were nearing a large village on a ridge from which the land swept away to right and left in ample reaches.

The first glimpse of the outlying houses showed nothing unusual; but presently the main street turned and dipped downward, and below and beyond us lay a long stretch of ruins: the calcined remains of Clermont-en-Argonne, destroyed by the Germans on the 4th of September. The free and lofty situation of the little town—for it was really a good deal more than a village—makes its present state the more lamentable. One can see it from so far off, and through the torn traceries of its ruined church the eye travels over so lovely a stretch of country! No doubt its beauty enriched the joy of wrecking it.

At the farther end of what was once the main street another small knot of houses has survived. Chief among them is the Hospice for old men, where Sister Gabrielle Rosnet, when the authorities of Clermont took to their heels, stayed behind to defend her charges, and where, ever since, she has nursed an undiminishing stream of wounded from the eastern front. We found Sœur Rosnet, with her Sisters, preparing the midday meal of her patients in the little kitchen of the Hospice: the kitchen which is also her dining-room and private office. She insisted on our finding time to share the *filet* and fried potatoes that were just being taken off the stove, and while we lunched she told us the story of the invasion—of the Hospice doors broken down 'à coups de crosse' and the grey officers bursting in with revolvers, and finding her there before them, in the big vaulted vestibule, 'alone with my old men and my Sisters.' Sœur Gabrielle Rasher is a small round active woman, with a shrewd and ruddy face of the type that looks out calmly from the dark background of certain Flemish pictures. Her blue eyes are full of warmth and humour, and she puts as much gaiety as wrath into her tale. She does not spare epithets in talking of 'ces satanés Allemands'—these Sisters and nurses of the front have seen sights to dry up the last drop of sentimental pity—but through all the horror of those fierce September days, with Clermont blazing about her and the helpless remnant of its inhabitants under the perpetual threat of massacre, she retained her sense of the little inevitable absurdities of life, such as her not knowing how to address the officer in command 'because he was so tall that I couldn't see up to his shoulder-straps.'—'*Et ils étaient tous comme ça*,'[5] she added, a sort of reluctant admiration in her eyes.

A subordinate 'good Sister' had just cleared the table and poured out our coffee when a woman came in to say, in a matter-of-fact tone, that there was hard fighting going on across the valley. She added calmly, as she dipped our plates into a tub, that an obus had just fallen a mile or two off, and that if we liked we could see the fighting from a garden over the way. It did not take us long to reach that garden! Sœur

Gabrielle showed the way, bouncing up the stairs of a house across the street, and flying at her heels we came out on a grassy terrace full of soldiers.

The cannon were booming without a pause, and seemingly so near that it was bewildering to look out across empty fields at a hillside that seemed like any other. But luckily somebody had a field-glass, and with its help a little corner of the battle of Vauquois was suddenly brought close to us—the rush of French infantry up the slopes, the feathery drift of French gun-smoke lower down, and, high up, on the wooded crest along the sky, the red lightnings and white puffs of the German artillery. Rap, rap, rap, went the answering guns, as the troops swept up and disappeared into the fire-tongued wood; and we stood there dumbfounded at the accident of having stumbled on this visible episode of the great subterranean struggle.

Though Sœur Rosnet had seen too many such sights to be much moved, she was all of a lively curiosity, and stood beside us, squarely planted in the mud, holding the field-glass to her eyes, or passing it laughingly about among the soldiers. But as we turned to go she said: 'They've sent us word to be ready for another four hundred to-night'; and the twinkle died out of her good eyes.

Her expectations were to be dreadfully surpassed; for, as we learned a fortnight later

219

from a three column *communiqué*, the scene we had assisted at was no less than the first act of the successful assault on the high-perched village of Vauquois, a point of the first importance to the Germans, since it masked their operations to the north of Varennes and commanded the railway by which, since September, they have been revictualling and reinforcing their army in the Argonne. Vauquois had been taken by them at the end of September and, thanks to its strong position on a rocky spur, had been almost impregnably fortified; but the attack we looked on at from the garden of Clermont, on Sunday, February 28th, carried the victorious French troops to the top of the ridge, and made them masters of a part of the village. Driven from it again that night, they were to retake it after a five days' struggle of exceptional violence and prodigal heroism, and are now securely established there in a position described as 'of vital importance to the operations.' 'But what it cost!' Sœur Gabrielle said, when we saw her again a few days later.

II

The time had come to remember our promise and hurry away from Clermont; but a few miles farther our attention was arrested by the sight of the Red Cross over a village house. The house was little more than a hovel, the village—Blercourt it was called—a mere hamlet of scattered cottages and cow-stables: a place so easily overlooked that it seemed likely our supplies might be needed there.

An orderly went to find the *médecin-chef,* and we waded after him through the mud to one after another of the cottages in which, with admirable ingenuity, he had managed to create out of next to nothing the indispensable requirements of a second-line ambulance: sterilizing and disinfecting appliances, a bandage-room, a pharmacy, a well-filled wood-shed, and a clean kitchen in which 'tisanes' were brewing over a cheerful fire. A detachment of cavalry was quartered in the village, which the trampling of hoofs had turned into a great morass, and as we picked our way from cottage to cottage in the doctor's wake he told us of the expedients to which he had been put to secure even the few hovels into which his patients were crowded. It was a complaint we were often to hear repeated along this line of the front, where troops and wounded are packed in thousands into villages meant to house four or five hundred; and we admired the skill and devotion with which he had dealt with the difficulty, and managed to lodge his patients decently.

We came back to the high-road, and he asked us if we should like to see the church. It was about three o'clock, and in the low porch the curé was ringing the bell for vespers. We pushed open the inner doors and went in. The church was without aisles, and down the nave stood four rows of wooden cots with brown blankets. In almost every one lay a soldier—the doctor's 'worst cases'—few of them wounded, the greater number stricken with fever, bronchitis, frost-bite, pleurisy, or some other form of trench-sickness too severe to permit of their being carried farther from the front. One or two heads turned on the pillows as we entered, but for the most part the men did not move.

The curé, meanwhile, passing around to the sacristy, had come out before the altar in his vestments, followed by a little white acolyte. A handful of women, probably the only 'civil' inhabitants left, and some of the soldiers we had seen about the village, had entered the church and stood together between the rows of cots; and the service began. It was a sunless afternoon, and the picture was all in monastic shades of black and white and ashen grey: the sick under their earth-coloured blankets, their livid faces against the pillows, the black dresses of the women (they seemed all to be in mourning) and the silver haze floating out from the little acolyte's censer. The only light in the scene—the candle-gleams on the altar, and their reflection in the embroideries of the curé's chasuble—were like a faint streak of sunset on the winter dusk.

For a while the long Latin cadences sounded on through the church; but presently the curé took up in French the Canticle of the Sacred Heart, composed during the war of 1870, and the little congregation joined their trembling voices in the refrain:

'Sauvez, sauvez la France,
Ne l'abandonnez pas!'[6]

The reiterated appeal rose in a sob above the rows of bodies in the nave: '*Sauvez, sauvez la France,*' the women wailed it near the altar, the soldiers took it up from the door in stronger tones; but the bodies in the cots never stirred, and more and more, as the day faded, the church looked like a quiet grave-yard in a battle-field.

After we had left Sainte Menehould the sense of the nearness and all-pervadingness of the war became even more vivid. Every road branching away to our left was a finger touching a red wound: Varennes, le Four de Paris, le Bois de la Grurie, were not more than eight or ten miles to the north. Along our own road the stream of motor-vans and the trains of ammunition grew longer and more frequent. Once we passed a long line of 'Seventy-fives' going single file up a hillside, farther on we watched a big detachment of artillery galloping across a stretch of open country. The movement of supplies was continuous, and every village through which we passed swarmed with soldiers busy loading or unloading the big vans, or clustered about the commissariat motors while hams and quarters of beef were handed out. As we approached Verdun the cannonade had grown louder again; and when we reached the walls of the town and passed under the iron teeth of the portcullis we felt ourselves in one of the last outposts of a mighty line of defense. The desolation of Verdun is as impressive as the feverish activity of Châlons. The civil population was evacuated in September, and only a small percentage have returned. Nine-tenths of the shops are closed, and as the troops are nearly all in the trenches there is hardly any movement in the streets.

The first duty of the traveller who has successfully passed the challenge of the sentinel at the gates is to climb the steep hill to the citadel at the top of the town. Here the military authorities inspect one's papers, and deliver a 'permis de séjour' which must be verified by the police before lodgings can be obtained. We found the principal hotel much less crowded than the Haute Mère-Dieu at Châlons, though many of the officers of the garrison mess there. The whole atmosphere of the place was different: silent, concentrated, passive. To the chance observer, Verdun appears to live only in its hospitals; and of these there are fourteen within the walls alone. As darkness fell, the streets became completely deserted, and the cannonade seemed to grow nearer and more incessant. That first night the hush was so intense that every reverberation from the dark hills beyond the walls brought out in the mind its separate vision of destruction; and then, just as the strained imagination could bear no more, the thunder ceased. A moment later, in a court below my windows, a pigeon began to coo; and all night long the two sounds strangely alternated ...

On entering the gates, the first sight to attract us had been a colony of roughly-built bungalows scattered over the miry slopes of a little park adjoining the railway station, and surmounted by the sign: 'Evacuation Hospital No. 6.' The next morning we went to visit it. A part of the station buildings has been adapted to hospital use, and among them a great roofless hall, which the surgeon in charge has covered in with canvas and divided down its length into a double row of tents. Each tent contains two wooden cots, scrupulously clean and raised high above the floor; and the immense ward is warmed by a row of stoves down the central passage. In the bungalows across the road are beds for the patients who are to be kept for a time before being transferred to the hospitals in the town. In one bungalow an operating-room has been installed, in another are the bathing arrangements for the newcomers from the trenches. Every possible device for the relief of the wounded has been carefully thought out and intelligently applied by the surgeon in charge and the *infirmière major* who indefatigably seconds him. Evacuation Hospital No. 6 sprang up in an hour, almost, on the dreadful August day when four thousand wounded lay on stretchers between the railway station and the gate of the little park across the way; and it has gradually grown into the model of what such a hospital may become in skilful and devoted hands.

Verdun has other excellent hospitals for the care of the severely wounded who cannot be sent farther from the front. Among them St Nicolas, in a big airy building on the Meuse, is an example of a great French Military Hospital at its best; but I visited few others, for the main object of my journey was to get to some of the second-line ambulances beyond the town. The first we went to was in a small village to the north of Verdun, not far from the enemy's lines at Cosenvoye, and was fairly representative of all the others. The dreary muddy village was crammed with troops, and the ambulance had been installed at haphazard in such houses as the military authorities could spare. The arrangements were primitive but clean, and even the dentist had set up his apparatus in one of the rooms. The men lay on mattresses or in wooden cots, and the rooms were heated by stoves. The great need, here as everywhere, was for blankets and clean underclothing; for the wounded are brought in from the front encrusted with frozen mud, and usually without having washed or changed for weeks. There are no women nurses in these second-line ambulances, but all the army doctors we saw seemed intelligent, and anxious to do the best they could for their men in conditions of unusual hardship. The principal obstacle in their way is the over-crowded state of the villages. Thousands of soldiers are camped in all of them, in hygienic conditions that would be bad enough for men in health; and there is also a great need for light diet, since the hospital commissariat of the front apparently supplies no invalid foods, and men burning with fever have to be fed on meat and vegetables.

In the afternoon we started out again in a snow-storm, over a desolate rolling country to the south of Verdun. The wind blew fiercely across the whitened slopes, and no one was in sight but the sentries marching up and down the railway lines, and an occasional cavalryman patrolling the lonely road. Nothing can exceed the mournfulness of this depopulated land: we might have been wandering over the wilds of Poland. We ran some twenty miles down the steel-grey Meuse to a village about four miles west of Les Eparges, the spot where, for weeks past, a desperate struggle had been going on. There must have been a lull in the fighting that day, for the cannon had ceased; but the scene at the

227

point where we left the motor gave us the sense of being on the very edge of the conflict. The long straggling village lay on the river, and the trampling of cavalry and the hauling of guns had turned the land about it into a mud-flat. Before the primitive cottage where the doctor's office had been installed were the motors of the surgeon and the medical inspector who had accompanied us. Near by stood the usual flock of grey motor-vans, and all about was the coming and going of cavalry remounts, the riding up of officers, the unloading of supplies, the incessant activity of mud-splashed sergeants and men.

The main ambulance was in a grange, of which the two stories had been partitioned off into wards. Under the cobwebby rafters the men lay in rows on clean pallets, and big stoves made the rooms dry and warm. But the great superiority of this ambulance was its nearness to a canal-boat which had been fitted up with hot douches. The boat was spotlessly clean, and each cabin was shut off by a gay curtain of red-flowered chintz. Those curtains must do almost as much as the hot water to make over the *morale* of the men: they were the most comforting sight of the day.

Farther north, and on the other bank of the Meuse, lies another large village which has been turned into a colony of éclopés. Fifteen hundred sick or exhausted men are housed there—and there are no hot douches or chintz curtains to cheer them! We were taken first to the church, a large featureless building at the head of the street. In the doorway our passage was obstructed by a mountain of damp straw which a gang of hostler-soldiers were pitch-forking out of the aisles. The interior of the church was dim and suffocating. Between the pillars hung screens of plaited straw, forming little enclosures in each of which about a dozen sick men lay on more straw, without mattresses or blankets. No beds, no tables, no chairs, no washing appliances—in their muddy clothes, as they come from the front, they are bedded down on the stone floor like cattle till they are well enough to go back to their job. It was a pitiful contrast to the little church at Blercourt, with the altar lights twinkling above the clean beds; and one wondered if, even so near the front, it had to be. 'The African village, we call it,' one of our companions said with a laugh: but the African village has blue sky over it, and a clear stream runs between its mud huts.

We had been told at Sainte Menehould that, for military reasons, we must follow a more southerly direction on our return to Châlons; and when we left Verdun we took the road to Bar-le-Duc. It runs southwest over beautiful broken country, untouched by war except for the fact that its villages, like all the others in this region, are either deserted or occupied by troops. As we left Verdun behind us the sound of the cannon grew fainter and died out, and we had the feeling that we were gradually passing beyond the flaming boundaries into a more normal world; but suddenly, at a cross-road, a sign-post snatched us back to war: *St Mihiel*, 18 *Kilomètres*. St Mihiel, the danger-spot of the region, the weak joint in the armour! There it lay, up that harmless-looking bye-road, not much more than ten miles away—a ten minutes' dash would have brought us into the thick of the grey coats and spiked helmets! The shadow of that sign-post followed us for miles, darkening the landscape like the shadow from a racing storm-cloud.

Bar-le-Duc seemed unaware of the cloud. The charming old town was in its normal state of provincial apathy: few soldiers were about, and here at last civilian life again predominated. After a few days on the edge of the war, in that intermediate region under its solemn spell, there is something strangely lowering to the mood in the first sight of a busy unconscious community. One looks instinctively, in the eyes of the passers by, for a reflection of that other vision, and feels diminished by contact with people going so indifferently about their business.

A little way beyond Bar-le-Duc we came on another phase of the war-vision, for our route lay exactly in the track of the August invasion, and between Bar-le-Duc and Vitry-le-François the highroad is lined with ruined towns. The first we came to was Laimont, a large village wiped out as if a cyclone had beheaded it; then comes Revigny, a town of over two thousand inhabitants, less completely levelled because its houses were more solidly built, but a spectacle of more tragic desolation, with its wide streets winding between scorched and contorted fragments of masonry, bits of shop-fronts, handsome doorways, the colonnaded court of a public building. A few miles farther lies the most piteous of the group: the village of Heiltz-le-Maurupt, once pleasantly set in gardens and orchards, now an ugly waste like the others, and with a little church so stripped and wounded and dishonoured that it lies there by the roadside like a human victim.

In this part of the country, which is one of many cross-roads, we began to have unexpected difficulty in finding our way, for the names and distances on the mile-stones have all been effaced, the sign-posts thrown down and the enamelled plaques on the houses at the entrance to the villages removed. One report has it that this precaution was taken by the inhabitants at the approach of the invading army, another that the Germans themselves demolished the sign-posts and plastered over the mile-stones in order to paint on them misleading and encouraging distances. The result is extremely bewildering, for, all the villages being either in ruins or uninhabited, there is no one to question but the soldiers one meets, and their answer is almost invariably:

'We don't know—we don't belong here.' One is in luck if one comes across a sentinel who knows the name of the village he is guarding.

It was the strangest of sensations to find ourselves in a chartless wilderness within sixty or seventy miles of Paris, and to wander, as we did, for hours across a high heathery waste, with wide blue distances to north and south, and in all the scene not a landmark by means of which we could make a guess at our whereabouts. One of our haphazard turns at last brought us into a muddy bye-road with long lines of 'Seventy-fives' ranged along its banks like grey ant-eaters in some monstrous menagerie. A little farther on we came to a bemired village swarming with artillery and cavalry, and found ourselves in the thick of an encampment just on the move. It seems improbable that we were meant to be there, for our arrival caused such surprise that no sentry remembered to challenge us, and obsequiously saluting *sous-officiers* instantly cleared a way for the motor. So, by a happy accident, we caught one more war-picture, all of vehement movement, as we passed out of the zone of war.

We were still very distinctly in it on returning to Châlons, which, if it had seemed packed on our previous visit, was now quivering and cracking with fresh crowds. The stir about the fountain, in the square before the Haute Mère-Dieu, was more melodramatic than ever. Every one was in a hurry, every one booted and mud-splashed, and spurred or sworded or despatch-bagged, or somehow labelled as a member of the huge military beehive. The privilege of telephoning and telegraphing being denied to civilians in the war-zone, it was ominous to arrive at night-fall on such a crowded scene, and we were not surprised to be told that there was not a room left at the Haute Mère-Dieu, and that even the sofas in the reading-room had been let for the night. At every other inn in the town we met with the same answer; and finally we decided to ask permission to go on as far as Epernay, about twelve miles off. At Head-quarters we were told that our request could not be granted. No motors are allowed to circulate after night-fall in the zone of war, and the officer charged with the distribution of motor-permits pointed out that, even if an exception were made in our favour, we should probably be turned back by the first sentinel we met, only to find ourselves unable to re-enter Châlons without another permit! This alternative was so alarming that we began to think ourselves relatively lucky to be on the right side of the gates; and we went back to the Haute Mère-Dieu to squeeze into a crowded corner of the restaurant for dinner. The hope that some one might have suddenly left the hotel in the interval was not realized; but after dinner we learned from the landlady that she had certain rooms permanently reserved for the use of the Staff, and that, as these rooms had not yet been called for that evening, we might possibly be allowed to occupy them for the night.

At Châlons the Head-quarters are in the Prefecture, a coldly handsome building of the eighteenth century, and there, in a majestic stone vestibule, beneath the gilded ramp of a great festal staircase, we waited in anxious suspense, among the orderlies and *estafettes*, while our unusual request was considered. The result of the deliberation was an expression of regret: nothing could be done for us, as officers might at any moment arrive from the General Head-quarters and require the rooms. It was then past nine o'clock, and bitterly cold—and we began to wonder. Finally the polite officer who had been charged to dismiss us, moved to compassion at our plight, offered to give us a *laissez-passer* back to Paris. But Paris was about a hundred and twenty-five miles off, the night was dark, the cold was piercing—and at every cross-road and railway crossing a sentinel would have to be convinced of our right to go farther. We remembered the warning given us earlier in the evening, and, declining the offer, went out again into the cold. And just then chance took pity on us. In the restaurant we had run across a friend attached to the Staff, and now, meeting him again in the depth of our difficulty, we were told of lodgings to be found near by. He could not take us there, for it was past the hour when he had a right to be out, or we either, for that matter, since curfew sounds at nine at Châlons. But he told us how to find our way through the maze of little unlit streets about the Cathedral; standing there beside the motor, in the icy darkness of the deserted square, and whispering hastily, as he turned to leave us: 'You ought not to be out so late; but the word tonight is *Jéna*. When you give it to the chauffeur, be sure no sentinel overhears you.' With that he was up the wide steps, the glass doors had closed on him, and I stood there in the pitch-black night, suddenly unable to believe that I was I, or Châlons Châlons, or that a young man who in Paris drops in to dine with me and talk over new books and plays, had been whispering a password in my ear to carry me unchallenged to a house a few streets away! The sense of unreality produced by that one word was so overwhelming that for a blissful moment the whole fabric of what I had been experiencing, the whole huge and oppressive and unescapable fact of the war, slipped away like a torn cobweb, and I seemed to see behind it the reassuring face of things as they used to be.

The next morning dispelled that vision. We woke to a noise of guns closer and more incessant than even the first night's cannonade at Verdun; and when we went out into the streets it seemed as if, overnight, a new army

235

had sprung out of the ground. Waylaid at one corner after another by the long tide of troops streaming out through the town to the northern suburbs, we saw in turn all the various divisions of the unfolding frieze: first the infantry and artillery, the sappers and miners, the endless trains of guns and ammunition, then the long line of grey supply-waggons, and finally the stretcher-bearers following the Red Cross ambulances. All the story of a day's warfare was written in the spectacle of that endless silent flow to the front: and we were to read it again, a few days later, in the terse announcement of 'renewed activity' about Suippes, and of the bloody strip of ground gained between Perthes and Beauséjour.

In Lorraine and the Vosges

Nancy, May 13th, 1915.
Beside me, on my writing-table, stands a bunch of peonies, the jolly round-faced pink peonies of the village garden. They were picked this afternoon in the garden of a ruined house at Gerbéviller—a house so calcined and convulsed that, for epithets dire enough to fit it, one would have to borrow from a Hebrew prophet gloating over the fall of a city of idolaters.

Since leaving Paris yesterday we have passed

through streets and streets of such murdered houses, through town after town spread out in its last writhings; and before the black holes that were homes, along the edge of the chasms that were streets, everywhere we have seen flowers and vegetables springing up in freshly raked and watered gardens. My pink peonies were not introduced to point the stale allegory of unconscious Nature veiling Man's havoc: they are put on my first page as a symbol of conscious human energy coming back to replant and rebuild the wilderness...

Last March, in the Argonne, the towns we passed through seemed quite dead; but yesterday new life was budding everywhere. We were following another track of the invasion, one of the huge tiger-scratches that the Beast flung over the land last September, between Vitry-le-François and Bar-le-Duc. Etrepy, Pargny, Sermaize-les-Bains, Andernay, are the names of this group of victims: Sermaize a pretty watering-place along wooded slopes, the others large villages fringed with farms, and all now mere scrofulous blotches on the soft spring scene. But in many we heard the sound of hammers, and saw bricklayers and masons at work. Even in the most mortally stricken there were signs of returning life: children playing among the stone heaps, and now and then a cautious older face peering out of a shed propped against the ruins. In one place an ancient tram-car had

237

been converted into a café and labelled: 'Au Restaurant des Ruines'; and everywhere between the calcined walls the carefully combed gardens aligned their radishes and lettuce-tops.

From Bar-le-Duc we turned northeast, and as we entered the forest of Commercy we began to hear again the Voice of the Front. It was the warmest and stillest of May days, and in the clearing where we stopped for luncheon the familiar boom broke with a magnified loudness on the noonday hush. In the intervals between the crashes there was not a sound but the gnats' hum in the moist sunshine and the dryad-call of the cuckoo from greener depths. At the end of the lane a few cavalrymen rode by in shabby blue, their horses' flanks glinting like ripe chestnuts. They stopped to chat and accept some cigarettes, and when they had trotted off again the gnat, the cuckoo and the cannon took up their trio...

The town of Commercy looked so undisturbed that the cannonade rocking it might have been some unheeded echo of the hills. These frontier towns inured to the clash of war go about their business with what one might call stolidity if there were not finer, and truer, names for it. In Commercy, to be sure, there is little business to go about just now save that connected with the military occupation; but the peaceful look of the sunny sleepy streets made one doubt if the fighting line was

238

really less than five miles away ... Yet the French, with an odd perversion of race-vanity, still persist in speaking of themselves as a 'nervous and impressionable' people!

*   *   *

This afternoon, on the road to Gerbéviller, we were again in the track of the September invasion. Over all the slopes now cool with spring foliage the battle rocked backward and forward during those burning autumn days; and every mile of the struggle has left its ghastly traces. The fields are full of wooden crosses which the ploughshare makes a circuit to avoid; many of the villages have been partly wrecked, and here and there an isolated ruin marks the nucleus of a fiercer struggle. But the landscape, in its first sweet leafiness, is so alive with ploughing and sowing and all the natural tasks of spring, that the war scars seem like traces of a long-past woe; and it was not till a bend of the road brought us in sight of Gerbéviller that we breathed again the choking air of present horror.

Gerbéviller, stretched out at ease on its slopes above the Meurthe, must have been a happy place to live in. The streets slanted up between scattered houses in gardens to the great Louis XIV château above the town and the church that balanced it. So much one can reconstruct from the first glimpse across the valley; but when one enters the town all perspective is lost in chaos. Gerbéviller has taken to herself the title of 'the martyr town'; an honour to which many sister victims might dispute her claim! But as a sensational image of havoc it seems improbable that any can surpass her. Her ruins seem to have been simultaneously vomited up from the depths and hurled down from the skies, as though she had perished in some monstrous clash of earthquake and tornado; and it fills one with a cold despair to know that this double destruction was no accident of nature but a piously planned and methodically executed human deed. From the opposite heights the poor little garden-girt town was shelled like a steel fortress; then, when the Germans entered, a fire was built in every house, and at the nicely-timed right moment one of the explosive tabloids which the fearless Teuton carries about for his land-*Lusitanias* was tossed on each hearth. It was all so well done that one wonders—almost apologetically for German thoroughness—that any of the human rats escaped from their holes; but some did, and were neatly spitted on lurking bayonets.

One old woman, hearing her son's death-cry, rashly looked out of her door. A bullet instantly laid her low among her phloxes and lilies; and there, in her little garden, her dead body was dishonoured. It seemed singularly appropriate, in such a scene, to read above a blackened doorway the sign: 'Monuments Funèbres,' and to observe that the house the doorway once belonged to had formed the angle of a lane called 'La Ruelle des Orphelines.'

At one end of the main street of Gerbéviller there once stood a charming house, of the sober old Lorraine pattern, with low door, deep roof and ample gables: it was in the garden of this house that my pink peonies were picked for me by its owner, Mr Liégeay, a former Mayor of Gerbéviller, who witnessed all the horrors of the invasion.

Mr Liégeay is now living in a neighbour's cellar, his own being fully occupied by the débris of his charming house. He told us the story of the three days of the German occupation; how he and his wife and niece, and the niece's babies, took to their cellar while the Germans set the house on fire, and how, peering through a door into the stable-yard, they saw that the soldiers suspected they were within and were trying to get at them. Luckily the incendiaries had heaped wood and straw all round the outside of the house, and the blaze was so hot that they could not reach the door. Between the arch of the doorway and the door itself was a half-moon opening; and Mr Liégeay and his family, during three days and three nights, broke up all the barrels in the cellar and threw the bits out through the opening to feed the fire in the yard.

Finally, on the third day, when they began to be afraid that the ruins of the house would fall in on them, they made a dash for safety. The house was on the edge of the town, and the women and children managed to get away into the country; but Mr Liégeay was surprised in his garden by a German soldier. He made a rush for the high wall of the adjoining cemetery, and scrambling over it slipped down between the wall and a big granite cross. The cross was covered with the hideous wire and glass wreaths dear to French mourners; and with these opportune mementoes Mr Liégeay roofed himself in, lying wedged in his narrow hiding-place from three in the afternoon till night, and listening to the voices of the soldiers who were hunting for him among the grave-stones. Luckily it was their last day at Gerbéviller, and the German retreat saved his life.

Even in Gerbéviller we saw no worse scene of destruction than the particular spot in which the ex-mayor stood while he told his story. He looked about him at the heaps of blackened brick and contorted iron. 'This was my dining-room,' he said. 'There was some good old panelling on the walls, and some fine prints that had been a wedding-present to my grand-father.' He led us into another black pit. 'This was our sitting-room: you see what a view we had.' He sighed, and added philosophically: 'I suppose we were too well off. I even had an

242

electric light out there on the terrace, to read my paper by on summer evenings. Yes, we were too well off…' That was all.

Meanwhile all the town had been red with horror—flame and shot and tortures unnameable; and at the other end of the long street, a woman, a Sister of Charity, had held her own like Sœur Gabrielle at Clermont-en-Argonne, gathering her flock of old men and children about her and interposing her short stout figure between them and the fury of the Germans. We found her in her Hospice, a ruddy, indomitable woman who related with a quiet indignation more thrilling than invective the hideous details of the bloody three days; but that already belongs to the past, and at present she is much more concerned with the task of clothing and feeding Gerbéviller. For two thirds of the population have already 'come home'—that is what they call the return to this desert! 'You see,' Sœur Julie explained, 'there are the crops to sow, the gardens to tend. They had to come back. The government is building wooden shelters for them; and people will surely send us beds and linen.' (Of course they would, one felt as one listened!) 'Heavy boots, too—boots for field-labourers. We want them for women as well as men—like these.' Soeur Julie, smiling, turned up a hob-nailed sole. 'I have directed all the work on our Hospice farm myself. All the women are working in the fields—we must take the place
243

of the men.' And I seemed to see my pink peonies flowering in the very prints of her sturdy boots!

May 14th
Nancy, the most beautiful town in France, has never been as beautiful as now. Coming back to it last evening from a round of ruins one felt as if the humbler Sisters sacrificed to spare it were pleading with one not to forget them in the contemplation of its dearly-bought perfection.

The last time I looked out on the great architectural setting of the Place Stanislas was on a hot July evening, the evening of the National Fête. The square and the avenues leading to it swarmed with people, and as darkness fell the balanced lines of arches and palaces sprang out in many coloured light. Garlands of lamps looped the arcades leading into the Place de Carrière, peacock-coloured fires flared from the Arch of Triumph, long curves of radiance beat like wings over the thickets of the park, the sculptures of the fountains, the brown-and-gold foliation of Jean Damour's great gates; and under this roofing of light was the murmur of a happy crowd carelessly celebrating the tradition of half-forgotten victories.

Now, at sunset, all life ceases in Nancy and veil after veil of silence comes down on the deserted Place and its empty perspectives. Last night by nine the few lingering lights in the streets had been put out, every window was blind, and the moonless night lay over the city like a canopy of velvet. Then, from some remote point, the arc of a search-light swept the sky, laid a fugitive pallor on darkened palace-fronts, a gleam of gold on invisible gates, trembled across the black vault and vanished, leaving it still blacker. When we came out of the darkened restaurant on the corner of the square, and the iron curtain of the entrance had been hastily dropped on us, we stood in such complete night that it took a waiter's friendly hand to guide us to the curbstone. Then, as we grew used to the darkness, we saw it lying still more densely under the colonnade of the Place de la Carrière and the clipped trees beyond. The ordered masses of architecture became august, the spaces between them immense, and the black sky faintly strewn with stars seemed to overarch an enchanted city. Not a footstep sounded, not a leaf rustled, not a breath of air drew under the arches. And suddenly, through the dumb night, the sound of the cannon began.

May 14th
Luncheon with the General Staff in an old bourgeois house of a little town as sleepy as 'Cranford.' In the warm walled gardens everything was blooming at once: laburnums,

lilacs, red hawthorn, Banksia roses and all the pleasant border plants that go with box and lavender. Never before did the flowers answer the spring roll-call with such a rush! Upstairs, in the Empire bedroom which the General has turned into his study, it was amusingly incongruous to see the sturdy provincial furniture littered with war-maps, trench-plans, aeroplane photographs and all the documentation of modern war. Through the windows bees hummed, the garden rustled, and one felt, close by, behind the walls of other gardens, the untroubled continuance of a placid and orderly bourgeois life.

We started early for Mousson on the Moselle, the ruined hill-fortress that gives its name to the better-known town at its foot. Our road ran below the long range of the 'Grand Couronné,' the line of hills curving southeast from Pont-à-Mousson to St Nicolas du Port. All through this pleasant broken country the battle shook and swayed last autumn; but few signs of those days are left except the wooden crosses in the fields. No troops are visible, and the pictures of war that made the Argonne so tragic last March are replaced by peaceful rustic scenes. On the way to Mousson the road is overhung by an Italian-looking village clustered about a hill-top. It marks the exact spot at which, last August, the German invasion was finally checked and flung back; and the Muse of History points out that on this very hill has long stood a memorial shaft inscribed: *Here, in the year 362, Jovinus defeated the Teutonic hordes.*

A little way up the ascent to Mousson we left the motor behind a bit of rising ground. The road is raked by the German lines, and stray pedestrians (unless in a group) are less liable than a motor to have a shell spent on them. We climbed under a driving grey sky which swept gusts of rain across our road. In the lee of the castle we stopped to look down at the valley of the Moselle, the slate roofs of Pont-à-Mousson and the broken bridge which once linked together the two sides of the town. Nothing but the wreck of the bridge showed that we were on the edge of war. The wind was too high for firing, and we saw no reason for believing that the wood just behind the Hospice roof at our feet was seamed with German trenches and bristling with guns, or that from every slope across the valley the eye of the cannon sleeplessly glared. But there the Germans were, drawing an iron ring about three sides of the watch-tower; and as one peered through an embrasure of the ancient walls one gradually found one's self reliving the sensations of the little mediæval burgh as it looked out on some earlier circle of besiegers. The longer one looked, the more oppressive and menacing the invisibility of the foe became. '*There* they are— and *there*—and *there*.' We strained our eyes obediently, but saw only calm hillsides, dozing farms. It was as if the earth itself were the enemy, as if the hordes of evil were in the clods and grass-blades. Only one conical hill close by showed an odd artificial patterning, like the work of huge ants who had scarred it with criss-cross ridges. We were told that these were French trenches, but they looked much more like the harmless traces of a prehistoric camp.

Suddenly an officer, pointing to the west of the trenched hill said: 'Do you see that farm?' It lay just below, near the river, and so close that good eyes could easily have discerned people or animals in the farm-yard, if there had been any; but the whole place seemed to be sleeping the sleep of bucolic peace. *'They are there,'* the officer said; and the innocent vignette framed by my field-glass suddenly glared back at me like a human mask of hate. The loudest cannonade had not made 'them' seem as real as that! ...

At this point the military lines and the old political frontier everywhere overlap, and in a cleft of the wooded hills that conceal the German batteries we saw a dark grey blur on the grey horizon. It was Metz, the Promised City, lying there with its fair steeples and towers, like the mystic banner that Constantine saw upon the sky...

Through wet vineyards and orchards we scrambled down the hill to the river and entered Pont-à-Mousson. It was by mere meteorological good luck that we got there, for

248

if the winds had been asleep the guns would have been awake, and when they wake poor Pont-à-Mousson is not at home to visitors. One understood why as one stood in the riverside garden of the great Premonstratensian Monastery which is now the hospital and the general asylum of the town. Between the clipped limes and formal borders the German shells had scooped out three or four 'dreadful hollows,' in one of which, only last week, a little girl found her death; and the façade of the building is pock-marked by shot and disfigured with gaping holes. Yet in this precarious shelter Sister Theresia, of the same indomitable breed as the Sisters of Clermont and Gerbéviller, has gathered a miscellaneous flock of soldiers wounded in the trenches, civilians shattered by the bombardment, éclopés, old women and children: all the human wreckage of this storm-beaten point of the front. Sister Theresia seems in no wise disconcerted by the fact that the shells continually play over her roof. The building is immense and spreading, and when one wing is damaged she picks up her protégés and trots them off, bed and baggage, to another. '*Je promène mes malades*,'[7] she said calmly, as if boasting of the varied accommodation of an ultra-modern hospital, as she led us through vaulted and stuccoed galleries where caryatid-saints look down in plaster pomp on the rows of brown-blanketed pallets and the long tables at which haggard éclopés were enjoying their evening soup.

May 15th
I have seen the happiest being on earth: a man who has found his job.

This afternoon we motored southwest of Nancy to a little place called Ménil-sur-Belvitte. The name is not yet intimately known to history, but there are reasons why it deserves to be, and in one man's mind it already is. Ménil-sur-Belvitte is a village on the edge of the Vosges. It is badly battered, for awful fighting took place there in the first month of the war. The houses lie in a hollow, and just beyond it the ground rises and spreads into a plateau waving with wheat and backed by wooded slopes—the ideal 'battle-ground' of the history-books. And here a real above-ground battle of the old obsolete kind took place, and the French, driving the Germans back victoriously, fell by thousands in the trampled wheat.

The church of Ménil is a ruin, but the parsonage still stands—a plain little house at the end of the street; and here the curé received us, and led us into a room which he has turned into a chapel. The chapel is also a war museum, and everything in it has something to do with the battle that took place among the wheat-fields. The candelabra on the altar are made of 'Seventy-five' shells, the Virgin's halo is composed of radiating bayonets, the walls are intricately adorned with German trophies and French relics, and on the ceiling the curé has had painted a kind of zodiacal chart of the whole region, in which Ménil-sur-Belvitte's handful of houses figures as the central orb of the system, and Verdun, Nancy, Metz, and Belfort as its humble satellites. But the chapel-museum is only a surplus expression of the curé's impassioned dedication to the dead. His real work has been done on the battle-field, where row after row of graves, marked and listed as soon as the struggle was over, have been fenced about, symmetrically disposed, planted with flowers and young firs, and marked by the names and death-dates of the fallen. As he led us from one of these enclosures to another his face was lit with the flame of a gratified vocation. This particular man was made to do this particular thing: he is a born collector, classifier, and hero-worshipper. In the hall of the 'presbytère' hangs a case of carefully-mounted butterflies, the result, no doubt, of an earlier passion for collecting. His 'specimens' have changed, that is all: he has passed from butterflies to men, from the actual to the visionary Psyche.

On the way to Ménil we stopped at the village of Crévic. The Germans were there in August, but the place is untouched—except for one house. That house, a large one, standing in a park at one end of the village, was the birthplace and home of General Lyautey, one of France's best soldiers, and Germany's worst enemy in Africa. It is no exaggeration to say that last August General Lyautey, by his promptness and audacity, saved Morocco for France. The Germans know it, and hate him; and as soon as the first soldiers reached Crévic—so obscure and imperceptible a spot that even German omniscience might have missed it—the officer in command asked for General Lyautey's house, went straight to it, had all the papers, portraits, furniture and family relics piled in a bonfire in the court, and then burnt down the house. As we sat in the neglected park with the plaintive ruin before us we heard from the gardener this typical tale of German thoroughness and German chivalry. It is corroborated by the fact that not another house in Crévic was destroyed.

May 16th.
About two miles from the German frontier (*frontier* just here as well as front) an isolated hill rises out of the Lorraine meadows. East of it, a ribbon of river winds among poplars, and that ribbon is the boundary between Empire and Republic. On such a clear day as this the view from the hill is extraordinarily interesting. From its grassy top a little aeroplane cannon stares to heaven, watching the east for the danger speck; and the circumference of the hill is furrowed by a deep trench—a 'bowel,'

rather—winding invisibly from one subterranean observation post to another. In each of these earthly warrens (ingeniously wattled, roofed and iron-sheeted) stand two or three artillery officers with keen quiet faces, directing by telephone the fire of batteries nestling somewhere in the woods four or five miles away. Interesting as the place was, the men who lived there interested me far more. They obviously belonged to different classes, and had received a different social education; but their mental and moral fraternity was complete. They were all fairly young, and their faces had the look that war has given to French faces: a look of sharpened intelligence, strengthened will and sobered judgment, as if every faculty, trebly vivified, were so bent on the one end that personal problems had been pushed back to the vanishing point of the great perspective.

From this vigilant height—one of the intentest eyes open on the frontier—we went a short distance down the hillside to a village out of range of the guns, where the commanding officer gave us tea in a charming old house with a terraced garden full of flowers and puppies. Below the terrace, lost Lorraine stretched away to her blue heights, a vision of summer peace: and just above us the unsleeping hill kept watch, its signal-wires trembling night and day. It was one of the intervals of rest and sweetness when the whole horrible black business seems to press most intolerably on the nerves.

Below the village the road wound down to a forest that had formed a dark blur in our bird's-eye view of the plain. We passed into the forest and halted on the edge of a colony of queer exotic huts. On all sides they peeped through the branches, themselves so branched and sodded and leafy that they seemed like some transition form between tree and house. We were in one of the so-called 'villages nègres' of the second-line trenches, the jolly little settlements to which the troops retire after doing their shift under fire. This particular colony has been developed to an extreme degree of comfort and safety. The houses are partly underground, connected by deep winding 'bowels' over which light rustic bridges have been thrown, and so profoundly roofed with sods that as much of them as shows above ground is shell-proof. Yet they are real houses, with real doors and windows under their grass-eaves, real furniture inside, and real beds of daisies and pansies at their doors. In the Colonel's bungalow a big bunch of spring flowers bloomed on the table, and everywhere we saw the same neatness and order, the same amused pride in the look of things. The men were dining at long trestle-tables under the trees; tired, unshaven men in shabby uniforms of all cuts and almost every colour. They were off duty, relaxed, in a good humour; but every face had the look of the faces watching on the hill-top. Wherever I go among these men of the front I have the same impression: the impression that the absorbing undivided thought of the Defence of France lives in the heart and brain of each soldier as intensely as in the heart and brain of their chief.

We walked a dozen yards down the road and came to the edge of the forest. A wattled palisade bounded it, and through a gap in the palisade we looked out across a field to the roofs of a quiet village a mile away. I went out a few steps into the field and was abruptly pulled back. 'Take care—those are the trenches!' What looked like a ridge thrown up by a plough was the enemy's line; and in the quiet village French cannon watched. Suddenly, as we stood there, they woke, and at the same moment we heard the unmistakable Gr-r-r of an aeroplane and saw a Bird of Evil high up against the blue. Snap, snap, snap barked the mitrailleuse on the hill, the soldiers jumped from their wine and strained their eyes through the trees, and the Taube, finding itself the centre of much attention, turned grey tail and swished away to the concealing clouds.

May 17th.
Today we started with an intenser sense of adventure. Hitherto we had always been told beforehand where we were going and how much we were to be allowed to see; but now we

255

were being launched into the unknown. Beyond a certain point all was conjecture—we knew only that what happened after that would depend on the good-will of a Colonel of Chasseurs-à-pied whom we were to go a long way to find, up into the folds of the mountains on our southeast horizon.

We picked up a staff-officer at Head-quarters and flew on to a battered town on the edge of the hills. From there we wound up through a narrowing valley, under wooded cliffs, to a little settlement where the Colonel of the Brigade was to be found. There was a short conference between the Colonel and our staff-officer, and then we annexed a Captain of Chasseurs and spun away again. Our road lay through a town so exposed that our companion from Headquarters suggested the advisability of avoiding it; but our guide hadn't the heart to inflict such a disappointment on his new acquaintances. 'Oh, we won't stop the motor—we'll just dash through,' he said indulgently; and in the excess of his indulgence he even permitted us to dash slowly.

Oh, that poor town—when we reached it, along a road ploughed with fresh obus-holes, I didn't want to stop the motor; I wanted to hurry on and blot the picture from my memory! It was doubly sad to look at because of the fact that it wasn't *quite dead*; faint spasms of life still quivered through it. A few children played in the ravaged streets; a few pale mothers watched them from cellar doorways. 'They oughtn't to be here,' our guide explained; 'but about a hundred and fifty begged so hard to stay that the General gave them leave. The officer in command has an eye on them, and whenever he gives the signal they dive down into their burrows. He says they are perfectly obedient. It was he who asked that they might stay...'

Up and up into the hills. The vision of human pain and ruin was lost in beauty. We were among the firs, and the air was full of balm. The mossy backs gave out a scent of rain, and little waterfalls from the heights set the branches trembling over secret pools. At each turn of the road, forest, and always more forests, climbing with us as we climbed, and dropping away from us to narrow valleys that converged on slate-blue distances. At one of these turns we overtook a company of soldiers, spade on shoulder and bags of tools across their backs—'trench-workers' swinging up to the heights to which we were bound. Life must be a better thing in this crystal air than in the mud-welter of the Argonne and the fogs of the North; and these men's faces were fresh with wind and weather.

Higher still ... and presently a halt on a ridge, in another 'black village,' this time almost a town! The soldiers gathered round us as the motor stopped—throngs of chasseurs-à-pied in faded, trench-stained uniforms—for

257

few visitors climb to this point, and their pleasure at the sight of new faces was presently expressed in a large '*Vive l'Amérique!*' scrawled on the door of the car. *L'Amérique* was glad and proud to be there, and instantly conscious of breathing an air saturated with courage and the dogged determination to endure. The men were all reservists: that is to say, mostly married, and all beyond the first fighting age. For many months there has not been much active work along this front, no great adventure to rouse the blood and wing the imagination: it has just been month after month of monotonous watching and holding on. And the soldiers' faces showed it: there was no light of heady enterprise in their eyes, but the look of men who knew their job, had thought it over, and were there to hold their bit of France till the day of victory or extermination.

Meanwhile, they had made the best of the situation and turned their quarters into a forest colony that would enchant any normal boy. Their village architecture was more elaborate then any we had yet seen. In the Colonel's 'dugout' a long table decked with lilacs and tulips was spread for tea. In other cheery catacombs we found neat rows of bunks, mess-tables, sizzling sauce-pans over kitchen-fires. Everywhere were endless ingenuities in the way of camp-furniture and household decoration. Farther down the road a path between fir-boughs led to a hidden hospital, a marvel of underground compactness. While we chatted with the surgeon a soldier came in from the trenches: an elderly, bearded man, with a good average civilian face—the kind that one runs against by hundreds in any French crowd. He had a scalp-wound which had just been dressed, and was very pale. The Colonel stopped to ask a few questions, and then turning to him, said: 'Feeling rather better now?'

'Yes, sir.'

'Good. In a day or two you'll be thinking about going back to the trenches, eh?'

'*I'm going now, sir.*' It was said quite simply, and received in the same way. 'Oh, all right,' the Colonel merely rejoined; but he laid his hand on the man's shoulder as we went out.

Our next visit was to a sod-thatched hut, 'At the sign of the Ambulant Artisans,' where two or three soldiers were modelling and chiselling all kinds of trinkets from the aluminium of enemy shells. One of the ambulant artisans was just finishing a ring with beautifully modelled fauns' heads, another offered me a 'Pickelhaube' small enough for Mustard-seed's wear, but complete in every detail, and inlaid with the bronze eagle from an Imperial pfennig. There are many such ring-smiths among the privates at the front, and the severe, somewhat archaic design of their rings is a proof of the sureness of French taste; but the

259

two we visited happened to be Paris jewellers, for whom 'artisan' was really too modest a pseudonym. Officers and men were evidently proud of their work, and as they stood hammering away in their cramped smithy, a red gleam lighting up the intentness of their faces, they seemed to be beating out the cheerful rhythm of 'I too will something make, and joy in the making...'

Up the hillside, in deeper shadow, was another little structure; a wooden shed with an open gable sheltering an altar with candles and flowers. Here mass is said by one of the conscript priests of the regiment, while his congregation kneel between the fir-trunks, giving life to the old metaphor of the cathedral-forest. Near by was the grave-yard, where day by day these quiet elderly men lay their comrades, the *pères de famille* who don't go back. The care of this woodland cemetery is left entirely to the soldiers, and they have spent treasures of piety on the inscriptions and decorations of the graves. Fresh flowers are brought up from the valleys to cover them, and when some favourite comrade goes, the men scorning ephemeral tributes, club together to buy a monstrous indestructible wreath with emblazoned streamers. It was near the end of the afternoon, and many soldiers were strolling along the paths between the graves. 'It's their favourite walk at this hour,' the Colonel said. He stopped to look down on a grave smothered in beady tokens, the grave of the last pal to fall. 'He was mentioned in the Order of the Day,' the Colonel explained; and the group of soldiers standing near looked at us proudly, as if sharing their comrade's honour, and wanting to be sure that we understood the reason of their pride...

'And now,' said our Captain of Chasseurs, 'that you've seen the second-line trenches, what do you say to taking a look at the first?'

We followed him to a point higher up the hill, where we plunged into a deep ditch of red earth—the 'bowel' leading to the first lines. It climbed still higher, under the wet firs, and then, turning, dipped over the edge and began to wind in sharp loops down the other side of the ridge. Down we scrambled, single file, our chins on a level with the top of the passage, the close green covert above us. The 'bowel' went twisting down more and more sharply into a deep ravine; and presently, at a bend, we came to a fir-thatched outlook, where a soldier stood with his back to us, his eye glued to a peep-hole in the wattled wall. Another turn, and another outlook; but here it was the iron-rimmed eye of the mitrailleuse that stared across the ravine. By this time we were within a hundred yards or so of the German lines, hidden, like ours, on the other side of the narrowing hollow; and as we stole down and down, the hush and secrecy of the scene, and the sense of that imminent

261

lurking hatred only a few branch-lengths away, seemed to fill the silence with mysterious pulsation. Suddenly a sharp noise broke on them: the rap of a rifle-shot against a tree-trunk a few yards ahead.

'Ah, the sharp-shooter,' said our guide. 'No more talking, please—he's over there, in a tree somewhere, and whenever he hears voices he fires. Some day we shall spot his tree.'

We went on in silence to a point where a few soldiers were sitting on a ledge of rock in a widening of the 'bowel'. They looked as quiet as if they had been waiting for their bocks before a Boulevard café.

'Not beyond, please,' said the officer, holding me back; and I stopped.

Here we were, then, actually and literally in the first lines! The knowledge made one's heart tick a little; but, except for another shot or two from our arboreal listener, and the motionless intentness of the soldier's back at the peep-hole, there was nothing to show that we were not a dozen miles away.

Perhaps the thought occurred to our Captain of Chasseurs; for just as I was turning back he said with his friendliest twinkle: 'Do you want awfully to go a little farther? Well, then, come on'

We went past the soldiers sitting on the ledge and stole down and down, to where the trees ended at the bottom of the ravine. The sharp-shooter had stopped firing, and nothing disturbed the leafy silence but an intermittent drip of rain. We were at the end of the burrow, and the Captain signed to me that I might take a cautious peep round its corner. I looked out and saw a strip of intensely green meadow just under me, and a wooded cliff rising abruptly on its other side. That was all. The wooded cliff swarmed with 'them,' and a few steps would have carried us across the interval; yet all about us was silence, and the peace of the forest. Again, for a minute, I had the sense of an all-pervading, invisible power of evil, a saturation of the whole landscape with some hidden vitriol of hate. Then the reaction of unbelief set in, and I felt myself in a harmless ordinary glen, like a million others on an untroubled earth. We turned and began to climb again, loop by loop, up the 'bowel'—we passed the lolling soldiers, the silent mitrailleuse, we came again to the watcher at his peep-hole. He heard us, let the officer pass, and turned his head with a little sign of understanding.

'Do you want to look down?'

He moved a step away from his window. The look-out projected over the ravine, raking its depths; and here, with one's eye to the leaf-lashed hole, one saw at last ... saw, at the bottom of the harmless glen, half way between cliff and cliff, a grey uniform huddled in a dead heap. 'He's been there for days: they can't fetch him away,' said the watcher, regluing his

263

eye to the hole; and it was almost a relief to find it was after all a tangible enemy hidden over there across the meadow ...

*   *   *

The sun had set when we got back to our starting-point in the underground village. The chasseurs-à-pied were lounging along the roadside and standing in gossiping groups about the motor. It was long since they had seen faces from the other life, the life they had left nearly a year earlier and had not been allowed to go back to for a day; and under all their jokes and good-humour their farewell had a tinge of wistfulness. But one felt that this fugitive reminder of a world they had put behind them would pass like a dream, and their minds revert without effort to the one reality: the business of holding their bit of France.

It is hard to say why this sense of the French soldier's single-mindedness is so strong in all who have had even a glimpse of the front; perhaps it is gathered less from what the men say than from the look in their eyes. Even while they are accepting cigarettes and exchanging trench-jokes, the look is there; and when one comes on them unaware it is there also. In the dusk of the forest that look followed us down the mountain; and as we skirted the edge of the ravine between the armies, we felt that on the far side of that dividing line were the men who had made the war, and on the near side the men who had been made by it.

REFERENCES
1 Leaping of horses.
2 Corps of Algerian native cavalry in the French army; originally composed largely of Turkish spahis serving in the Algerian army at the time of the French conquest in 1830.
3 Military engineers.
4 'France is a warlike nation.'
5 'And they were all like that.'
6 'Save, save, France, / Do not abandon her!'
7 'I take my invalids for walks.'

FRENCH WAYS AND THEIR
MEANING*

Taste

I

French taste? Why, of course—everybody
knows all about that! It's the way the women
put on their hats, and the upholsterers drape
their curtains.

Certainly—why not?

The artistic integrity of the French has led
them to feel from the beginning that there is no
difference in kind between the curve of a
woman's hat-brim and the curve of a Rodin
marble, or between the droop of an
upholsterer's curtain and that of the branches
along a great avenue laid out by Le Nôtre.

It was the Puritan races—every one of them
non-creative in the plastic arts—who decided
that 'Art' (that is, plastic art) was something
apart from life, as dangerous to it as Plato
thought Poets in a Republic, and to be
tolerated only when it was so lofty,
unapproachable and remote from any appeal

---

* 'Taste,' Chapter III of *French Ways and Their
Meaning*, was not published serially. Chapter VI, 'Is
There a New Frenchwoman?' was first published in
The Ladies Home Journal, April 1917, 34:12.

to average humanity that it bored people to death, and they locked it up in Museums to get rid of it.

But this article is headed 'Taste,' and taste, whatever it may be, it not, after all, the same thing as art. No; it is not art—but it is the atmosphere in which art lives, and outside of which it cannot live. It is the regulating principle of all art, of the art of dress and of manners, and of living in general, as well as of sculpture or music. It is because the French have always been so innately sure of this, that, without burdening themselves with formulas, they have instinctively applied to living the same rules that they applied to artistic creation.

II

I remember being told when I was a young girl: 'If you want to interest the person you are talking to pitch your voice so that only that one person will hear your.'

That small axiom, apart from its obvious application, contains nearly all there is to say about Taste.

That a thing should be in scale—should be proportioned to its purpose—is one of the first requirements of beauty, in whatever order. No shouting where an undertone will do; and no gigantic Statue of Liberty in butter for a World's Fair, when the little Wingless Victory, tying on her sandal on the Acropolis, holds the whole horizon in the curve of her slim arm.

The essence of taste is suitability. Divest the word of its prim and priggish implications, and see how it expresses the mysterious demand of eye and mind for symmetry, harmony and order.

Suitability—fitness—is, and always has been, the very foundation of French standards. Fitness is only a contraction of fittingness; and if any of our American soldiers in France should pause to look up at the narrow niches in the portal of a French cathedral, or at the group of holy figures in the triangle or half-circle above, they are likely to be struck first of all by the way in which the attitude of each figure or group is adapted to the space it fills.

If the figure is cramped and uncomfortable—if the saint or angel seems to be in a strait-jacket or a padded cell—then the sculptor has failed, and taste is offended. It is essential that there should be perfect harmony between the natural attitude of the figure and the space it lives in—that a square saint should not be put in a round hole. Range through plastic art, from Chaldæa to France, and you will see how this principle of adaptation has always ruled composition.

III

It is the sense of its universal applicability that makes taste so living an influence in France. French people 'have taste' as naturally as they breathe: it is not regarded as an accomplishment, like playing the flute.

The universal existence of taste, and of the standard it creates—it insists on—explains many of the things that strike Americans on first arriving in France.

It is the reason, for instance, why the French have beautiful stone quays along the great rivers on which their cities are built, and why noble monuments of architecture, and gardens and terraces, have been built along these quays. The French have always felt and reverenced the beauty of their rivers, and known the values, artistic and hygienic, of a beautiful and well-kept river-front in the heart of a crowded city.

When industrialism began its work of disfigurement in the great cities of the world, long reaches of the Thames were seized upon by the factory-builder, and London has only by a recent effort saved a short stretch of her river-front; even so, from the Embankment, whether at Westminster or Chelsea, one looks across at ugliness, untidiness and squalor.

When industrialism came to the wise old Latin cities—Paris, Lyons, Bordeaux, Florence—their river banks were already firmly and beautifully built up, and the factory chimneys had to find a footing in the outskirts. Any American with eyes to see, who compares the architectural use to which Paris has put the Seine with the wasteful degradation of the unrivalled twin river-fronts of New York, may draw his own conclusions as to the sheer material advantage of taste in the creation of a great city.

Perhaps the most curious instance of taste-blindness in dealing with such an opportunity is to be found in Boston, where Beacon Street calmly turned its wealth back to the bay, and fringed with clothes-lines the shores that might have made of Boston one of the most beautifully situated cities in the world. In this case, industry did not encroach or slums degrade. The Boston aristocracy appropriated the shore of the bay for its own residential uses, but apparently failed to notice that the bay was there.

Taste, also—the recognition of a standard—explains the existence of such really national institutions as the French Academy, and the French national theatre, the Théâtre Français. The history of the former, in particular, throws a light on much that is most distinctively French in the French character.

It would be difficult for any one walking along the Quai Malaquais, and not totally blind to architectural beauty, not to be charmed by the harmony of proportion and beauty of composition of a certain building with curved wings and a small central dome that looks across the Seine at the gardens of the Louvre and the spires of Saint Germain l'Auxerrois.

That building, all elegance, measure and balance, from its graceful cupola to the stately stone vases surmounting the lateral colonades—that building is the old 'Collège des Quatre Nations,' the Institute of France, and the home of the French Academy.

In 1635, at a time when France was still struggling with the heavy inheritance of feudalism, a bad man and great statesman, the mighty Cardinal Richelieu paused in his long fight with the rebellious vassals of the crown to create a standard of French speech: 'To establish the rules of the language, and make French not only elegant, but capable of dealing with the arts and sciences.'

Think of the significance of such an act at such a moment! France was a swelter of political and religious dissension; everything in the monarchy, and the monarchy itself, was in a state of instability. Austria and Spain menaced it from without, the great vassals tore it asunder from within. During the Great Assizes of Auvergne some of the most powerful of these nobles were tried, punished and stripped of their monstrous privileges; and the record of their misdeeds reads like a tale of Sicilian brigandage and Corsican vendetta.

Gradually the iron hand of Richelieu drew order—a grim pitiless order—out of this uninhabitable chaos. But it was in the very thick of the conflict that he seemed to feel the need of creating, then and there, some fixed principle of civilised life, some kind of ark in which thought and taste and 'civility' could take shelter. It was as if, in the general

271

upheaval, he wished to give stability to the things which humanise and unite society. And he chose 'taste'—taste in speech, in culture, in manners,—as the fusing principle of his new Academy.

The traditional point of view of its founder has been faithfully observed for nearly three hundred years by the so-called 'Forty Immortals,' the Academicians who throne under the famous cupola. The Academy has never shrunk into a mere retreat for lettered pedantry: as M. Saillens says in his admirable little book, 'Facts about France': 'The great object of Richelieu was national unity,' and 'The Forty do not believe that they can keep the language under discipline by merely publishing a Dictionary now and then (the first edition came out in 1694). They believe that a standard must be set, and that it is for them to set it. Therefore the Academy does not simply call to its ranks famous or careful writers, but soldiers as well, bishops, scientists, men of the world, men of social rank so as to maintain from generation to generation a national conservatory of good manners and good speech.'

For this reason, though Frenchmen have always laughed at their Academy, they have always respected it, and aspired to the distinction of membership. Even the rebellious spirits who satirise it in their youth usually become, in maturity, almost too eager for its recognition; and, though the fact of being an Academician gives social importance, it would be absurd to pretend that such men as Pasteur, Henri Poincaré, Marshal Joffre, sought the distinction for that reason, or that France would have thought it worthy of their seeking if the institution had not preserved its original significance.

That significance was simply the safe-guarding of what the French call *les choses de l'esprit;* which cannot quite be translated 'things of the spirits,' and yet means more nearly that than anything else. And Richelieu and the original members of the Academy had recognised from the first day that language was the chosen vessel in which the finer life of a nation must be preserved.

It is not uncommon nowadays, especially in America, to sneer at any deliberate attempts to stabilise language. To test such criticisms it is useful to reduce them to their last consequence—which is almost always absurdity. It is not difficult to discover what becomes of a language left to itself, without accepted standards or restrictions; instances may be found among any savage tribes without fixed standards of speech. Their language speedily ceases to be one, and deteriorates into a muddle of unstable dialects. Or, if an instance nearer home is needed, the lover of English need only note what that rich language has shrunk to on the lips, and in the literature, of the heterogeneous hundred millions of American citizens who, without uniformity of tradition or recognised guidance, are being suffered to work their many wills upon it.

But at this point it may be objected that, after all, England herself has never had an Academy, nor could ever conceivably have had one, and that whatever the English of America has become, the English of England is still the language of her great tradition, with perfectly defined standards of taste and propriety.

England is England, as France is France: the one feels the need of defining what the other finds it simpler to take for granted. England has never had a written Constitution; yet her constitutional government has long been the model of free nations. England's standards are all implicit. She does not feel the French need of formulating and tabulating. Her Academy is not built with hands, but it is just as powerful, and just as visible to those who have eyes to see; and the name of the English Academy is Usage.

IV

I said just now: 'If any of our American soldiers look up at the niches in the portal of a French cathedral they are likely to be struck first of all by' such and such things.

In our new army all the arts and professions are represented, and if the soldier in question happens to be a sculptor, an architect, or an art critic, he will certainly note what I have pointed out; but if he is not a trained observer, the chances are that he will not even look up.

The difference is that in France almost every one has the seeing eye, just as almost every one has the hearing ear. It is not a platitude, though it may be a truism, to say that the French are a race of artists: it is the key that unlocks every door of their complex pyschology [sic], and consequently the key that must be oftenest in the explorer's hand.

The gift of the seeing eye is, obviously, a first requisite where taste is to prevail. And the question is, how is the seeing eye to be obtained? What is the operation for taste-blindness? Or is there any; and are not some races—the artistically non-creative—born as irremediably blind as Kentucky cave-fishes?

The answer might be *yes*, in the case of the wholly non-creative races. But the men of English blood are creative artists too; theirs is the incomparable gift of poetic expression. And any race gifted with one form of artistic originality is always acutely appreciative of other cognate forms of expression. There has never been a race more capable then the English of appreciating the great plastic creators, Greece, Italy and France. This gift of the critical sense in those arts wherein the race does not excel in original expression seems an inevitable by-product of its own special endowment. In such races taste-blindness is purely accidental and the operation that cures it is the long slow old-fashioned one of education. There is no other.

The artist races are naturally less dependent on education: to a certain degree their instinct takes the place of acquired discrimination. But they set a greater store on it than any other races because they appreciate more than the others all that, even to themselves, education reveals and develops.

It is just because the French are naturally endowed with taste that they attach such importance to cultivation, and that French standards of education are so infinitely higher and more severe than those existing in Anglo-Saxon countries. We are too much inclined to think that we have disposed of the matter when we say that, in our conception of life, education should be formative and not instructive. The point is, the French might return, what are we to be formed for? And, in any case, they would not recognise the antithesis, since they believe that, to form one must instruct: instruct the eye, the ear, the brain, every one of those marvelous organs of sense so often left dormant by our Anglo-Saxon training.

It used to be thought that if savages appeared unimpressed by the wonders of occidental art or industry it was because their natural *hauteur* would not let them betray surprise to the intruder. That romantic illusion has been dispelled by modern investigation, and the traveller now knows that the savage is unimpressed because *he does not see* the new things presented to him. It takes the most complex assemblage of associations, visual and mental, to enable us to discover what a picture represents: the savage placed before such familiar examples of the graphic art as 'The Infant Samuel' or 'His Master's Voice' would not *see* the infant or the fox-terrier, much less guess what they were supposed to be doing.

As long as America believes in short-cuts to knowledge, in any possibility of buying taste in tabloids, she will never come into her real inheritance of English culture. A gentleman travelling in the Middle West met a charming girl who was a 'college graduate.' He asked her what line of study she had selected, and she replied that she had learnt music one year, and languages the next, and that last year she had 'learnt art.'

It is the pernicious habit of regarding the arts as something that can be bottled, pickled and absorbed in twelve months (thanks to 'courses,' summaries and abridgments) that prevents that development of a real artistic sensibility in our eager and richly endowed race. Patience, deliberateness, reverence: these are the fundamental elements of taste. The French have always cultivated them, and it is as much to them as to the eagle-flights of genius that France owes her long artistic supremacy.

From the Middle Ages to the Revolution all

the French trade-guilds had their travelling members, the 'Compagnons du Tour de France.' Not for greed of gold, but simply from the ambition to excel in their own craft, these 'companions,' their trade once learned, took their staves in hand, and wandered on foot over France, going from one to another of the cities where the best teachers of their special trades were to be found, and serving an apprenticeship in each till they learned enough to surpass their masters. The 'tour de France' was France's old way of acquiring 'Efficiency'; and even now she does not believe it can be found in newspaper nostrums.

The New Frenchwoman

There is no new Frenchwoman; but the real Frenchwoman is new to America, and it may be of interest to American women to learn something of what she is really like.

In saying that the real Frenchwoman is new to America I do not intend to draw the old familiar contrast between the so-called 'real Frenchwoman' and the Frenchwoman of fiction and the stage. Americans have been told a good many thousand times in the last four years that the real Frenchwoman is totally different from the person depicted under that name by French novelists and dramatists; but in truth every literature, in its main lines, reflects the chief characteristics of the people for whom, and about whom, it is written—and none more so then French literature, the freest and frankest of all.

The statement that the real Frenchwoman is new to America simply means that America has never before taken the trouble to look at her and try to understand her. She has always been there, waiting to be understood, and a little tired, perhaps, of being either caricatured or idealised. It would be easy enough to palm her off as a 'new' Frenchwoman because the war has caused her to live a new life and do unfamiliar jobs; but one need only look at the illustrated papers to see what she looks like as a tram-conductor, a taxi-driver or a munition-maker. It is certain, even now, that all these new experiences are going to modify her character, and to enlarge her view of life; but that is not the point with which these papers are concerned. The first thing for the American woman to do is to learn to know *the Frenchwoman* as she has always been; to try to find out what she is, and why she is what she is. After that it will be easy to see why the war has developed in her certain qualities rather than others, and what its after-effects on her are likely to be.

First of all, she is in nearly all respects, as different as possible from the average American woman. That proposition is fairly evident, though not always easy to explain. Is it because she dresses better, or knows more

279

about cooking, or is more 'coquettish,' or more 'feminine' or more excitable, or more emotional, or more immoral? All these reasons have been often suggested, but none of them seems to furnish a complete answer. Millions of American women are, to the best of their ability (which is not small), coquettish, feminine, emotional, and all the rest of it; a good many dress as well as Frenchwomen; some even know a little about cooking—and the real reason is quite different, and not nearly as flattering to our national vanity. It is simply that, like the men of her race, the Frenchwoman is *grown up*.

Compared with the women of France the average American woman is still in the kindergarten. The world she lives in is exactly like the most improved and advanced and scientifically equipped Montessori-method baby-school. At first sight it may seem preposterous to compare the American woman's independent and resonant activities—her 'boards' and clubs and sororities, her public investigation of everything under the heavens from 'the social evil' to baking-powder, and from 'physical culture' to the newest esoteric religion—to compare such free and busy and seemingly influential lives with the artless exercises of an infant class. But what is the fundamental principle of the Montessori system? It is the development of the child's individuality,

280

unrestricted by the traditional nursery discipline: a Montessori school is a baby world where, shut up together in the most improved hygienic surroundings, a number of infants noisily develop their individuality.

The reason why American women are not really 'grown up' in comparison with the women of the most highly civilised countries— such as France—is that all their semblance of freedom, activity and authority bears not much more likeness to real living than the exercises of the Montessori infant. Real living, in any but the most elementary sense of the word, is a deep and complex and slowly developed thing, the outcome of an old and rich social experience. It cannot be 'got up' like gymnastics, or a proficiency in foreign languages; it has its roots in the fundamental things, and above all in close and constant and interesting and important relations between men and women.

It is because American women are each other's only audience, and to a great extent each other's only companions, that they seem, compared to women who play an intellectual and social part in the lives of men, like children in a baby-school. They are 'developing their individuality,' but developing it in the void, without the checks, the stimulus, and the discipline that comes of contact with the stronger masculine individuality. And it is not only because the man is the stronger and the

281

closer to reality that his influence is necessary to develop woman to real womanhood; it is because the two sexes complete each other mentally as well as physiologically that no modern civilisation has been really rich or deep, or stimulating to other civilisations, which has not been based on the recognised interaction of influences between men and women.

There are several ways in which the Frenchwoman's relations with men may be called more important than those of her American sister. In the first place, in the commercial class, the Frenchwoman is always her husband's business partner. The lives of the French bourgeois couple are based on the primary necessity of getting enough money to live on, and of giving their children educational and material advantages. In small businesses the woman is always her husband's bookkeeper or clerk, or both; above all, she is his business adviser. France, as you know, is held up to all other countries as a model of thrift, of wise and prudent saving and spending. No other country in the world has such immense financial vitality, such powers of recuperation from national calamity. After the Franco-Prussian war of 1870, when France, beaten to earth, her armies lost, half her territory occupied, and with all Europe holding aloof, and not a single ally to defend her interest—when France was called on by her conquerors to pay an indemnity of five thousand million francs in order to free her territory of the enemy, she raised the sum, and paid it off, *eighteen months sooner than the date agreed upon:* to the rage and disappointment of Germany, and the amazement and admiration of the rest of the world.

Every economist knows that if France was able to make that incredible effort it was because, all over the country, millions of Frenchwomen, laborers' wives, farmers' wives, small shopkeepers' wives, wives of big manufacturers and commission-merchants and bankers, were to all intents and purposes their husbands' business-partners, and had had a direct interest in saving and investing the millions and millions piled up to pay France's ransom in her day of need. At every stage in French history, in war, in politics, in literature, in art and in religion, women have played a splendid and a decisive part; but none more splendid or more decisive than the obscure part played by the millions of wives and mothers whose thrift and prudence silently built up her salvation in 1872.

When it is said that the Frenchwoman of the middle class is her husband's business partner the statement must not be taken in too literal a sense. The French wife has less legal independence than the American or English wife, and is subject to a good many legal disqualifications from which women have freed themselves in other countries. That is the technical situation; but what is the practical fact? That the Frenchwoman has gone straight through these theoretical restrictions to the heart of reality, and become her husband's associate, because, for her children's sake if not for her own, her heart is in his job, and because he has long since learned that the best business partner a man can have is one who has the same interests at stake as himself.

It is not only because she saves him a salesman's salary, or a book-keeper'[s] salary, or both, that the French tradesman associates his wife with his business; it is because he has the sense to see that no hired assistant will have so keen a perception of his interests, that none will receive his customers so pleasantly, and that none will so patiently and willingly work over hours when it is necessary to do so. There is no drudgery in this kind of partnership, because it is voluntary, and because each partner is stimulated by exactly the same aspirations. And it is this practical, personal and daily participation in her husband's job that makes the Frenchwoman more grown up then others. She has a more interesting and more living life, and therefore she develops more quickly.

It may be objected that money-making is not the most interesting thing in life, and that the 'higher ideals' seem to have little place in this conception of feminine efficiency. The answer

284

to such a criticism is to be found by considering once more the difference between the French and the American views as to the main object of money-making—a point to which any study of the two races inevitably leads one back.

Americans are too prone to consider money-making as interesting in itself: they regard the fact that a man has made money as something intrinsically meritorious. But money-making in interesting only in proportion as its object is interesting. If a man piles up millions in order to pile them up, having already all he needs to live humanly and decently, his occupation is neither interesting in itself, nor conducive to any sort of real social development in the money-maker or in those about him. No life is more sterile than one into which nothing enters to balance such an output of energy. To see how different is the French view of the object of money-making one must put one's self in the place of the average French household. For the immense majority of the French it is a far more modest ambition, and consists simply in the effort to earn one's living and put by enough for sickness, old age, and a good start in life for the children.

This conception of 'business' may seem a tame one to Americans; but its advantages are worth considering. In the first place, it has the immense superiority of leaving time for living, time for men and women both. The average French business man at the end of his life may not have made as much money as the American; but meanwhile he has had, every day, something the American has not had: Time. Time, in the middle of the day, to sit down to an excellent luncheon, to eat it quietly with his family, and to read his paper afterward; time to go off on Sundays and holidays on long pleasant country rambles; time, almost any day, to feel fresh and free enough for an evening at the theatre, after a dinner as good and leisurely as his luncheon. And there is one thing certain: the great mass of men and women grow up and reach real maturity only through their contact with the material realities of living, with business, with industry, with all the great bread-winning activities; but the growth and the maturing take place *in the intervals between these activities:* and in lives where there are no such intervals there will be no real growth.

That is why the 'slow' French business methods so irritating to the American business man produce, in the long run, results which he is often the first to marvel at and admire. Every intelligent American who has seen something of France and French life has had a first moment of bewilderment on trying to explain the seeming contradiction between the slow, fumbling, timid French business methods and the rounded completeness of French civilisation. How is it that a country which seems to have almost everything to learn in the way of 'up-to-date' business has almost everything to teach, not only in the way of art and literature, and all the graces of life, but also in the way of municipal order, state administration, agriculture, forestry, engineering, and the whole harmonious running of the vast national machine? The answer is the last the American business man is likely to think of until he has had time to study France somewhat closely: it is that France is what she is because every Frenchman and every Frenchwoman takes time to live, and has an extraordinarily clear and sound sense of what constitutes *real living*.

We are too ready to estimate business successes by their individual results: a point of view revealed in our national awe of large fortunes. That is an immature and even childish way of estimating success. In terms of civilisation it is the total and ultimate result of a nation's business effort that matters, not the fact of Mr Smith's being able to build a marble villa in place of his wooden cottage. If the collective life which results from our individual money-making is not richer, more interesting and more stimulating than that of countries where the individual effort is less intense, then it looks as if there were something wrong about our method.

This parenthesis may seem to have wandered rather far from the Frenchwoman who heads the chapter; but in reality she is at its very heart. For if Frenchmen care too much about other things to care as much as we do about making money, the chief reason is largely because their relations with women are more interesting. The Frenchwoman rules French life, and she rules it under a triple crown, as a business woman, as a mother, and above all as an artist. To explain the sense in which the last word is used it is necessary to go back to the contention that the greatness of France lies in her sense of the beauty and importance of living. As life is an art in France, so woman is an artist. She does not teach man, but she inspires him. As the Frenchwoman of the bread-winning class influences her husband, and inspires in him a respect for her judgment and her wishes, so the Frenchwoman of the rich and educated class is admired and held in regard for other qualities. But in this class of society her influence naturally extends much farther. The more civilised a society is, the wider is the range of each woman's influence over men, and of each man's influence over women. Intelligent and cultivated people of either sex will never limit themselves to communing with their own households. Men and women equally, when they have the range of interests that real cultivation gives, need the stimulus of different points of view, the refreshment of new ideas as well as of new faces. The long hypocrisy which Puritan England handed on to America concerning the danger of frank and free social relations between men and women has done more than anything else to retard real civilisation in America.

Real civilisation means an education that extends to the whole of life, in contradistinction to that of school or college: it means an education that forms speech, forms manners, forms taste, forms ideals, and above all forms judgment. This is the kind of civilisation of which France has always been the foremost model: it is because she possesses its secret that she has led the world so long not only in art and taste and elegance, but in ideas and in ideals. For it must never be forgotten that if the fashion of our note-paper and the cut of our dresses come from France, so do the conceptions of liberty and justice on which our republican institutions are based. No nation can have grown-up ideas till it has a ruling caste of grown-up men and women; and it is possible to have a ruling caste of grown-up men and women only in a civilisation where the power of each sex is balanced by that of the other.

It may seem strange to draw precisely this comparison between France, the country of all the old sex-conventions, and America, which is supposedly the country of the greatest sex-freedom; and the American reader may ask: 'But where is there so much freedom of intercourse between men and women as in

America?' The misconception arises from the confusion between two words, and two states of being that are fundamentally different. In America there is complete freedom of intercourse between boys and girls, but not between men and women; and there is a general notion that, in essentials, a girl and a woman are the same thing. It is true, in essentials, that a boy and a man are very much the same thing; but a girl and a woman—a married woman—are totally different beings. Marriage, union with a man, completes and transforms a woman's character, her point of view, her sense of the relative importance of things, far more thoroughly than a boy's nature is changed by the same experience. A girl is only a sketch; a married woman is the finished picture. And it is only the married woman who counts as a social factor.

Now it is precisely at the moment when her experience is rounded by marriage, motherhood, and the responsibilities, cares and interests of her own household, that the average American woman is, so to speak, 'withdrawn from circulation.' It is true that this does not apply to the small minority of wealthy and fashionable women who lead an artificial cosmopolitan life, and therefore represent no particular national tendency. It is not to them that the country looks for the development of its social civilisation, but to the average woman who is sufficiently free from bread-winning cares to act as an incentive to other women and as an influence upon men. In America this woman, in the immense majority of cases, has roamed through life in absolute freedom of communion with young men until the day when the rounding-out of her own experience by marriage puts her in a position to become a social influence; and from that day she is cut off from men's society in all but the most formal and intermittent ways. On her wedding-day she ceases, in any open, frank and recognised manner, to be an influence in the lives of the men of the community to which she belongs.

In France, the case is just the contrary. France, hitherto, has kept young girls under restrictions at which Americans have often smiled, and which have certainly, in some respects, been a bar to their growth. The doing away of these restrictions will be one of the few benefits of the war: the French young girl, even in the most exclusive and most tradition-loving society, will never again be the prisoner she has been in the past. But this is relatively unimportant, for the French have always recognised that, as a social factor, a woman does not count till she is married; and in the well-to-do classes girls marry extremely young, and the married woman has always had extraordinary social freedom. The famous French 'Salon,' the best school of talk and of ideas that the modern world has known, was based on the belief that the most stimulating conversation in the world is that between intelligent men and women who see each other often enough to be on terms of frank and easy friendship. The great wave of intellectual and social liberation that preceded the French revolution and prepared the way, not for its horrors but for its benefits, originated in the drawing-rooms of French wives and mothers, who received every day the most thoughtful and the most brilliant men of the time, who shared their talk, and often directed it. Think what an asset to the mental life of any country such a group of women forms! And in France they were not then, and they are not now, limited to the small class of the wealthy and fashionable. In France, as soon as a woman has a personality, social circumstances permit her to make it felt. What does it matter if she had spent her girlhood in seclusion, provided she is free to emerge from it at the moment when she is fitted to become a real factor in social life?

It may, of course, be asked at this point, how the French freedom of intercourse between married men and women affects domestic life, and the happiness of a woman's husband and children. It is hard to say what kind of census could be devised to ascertain the relative percentage of happy marriages in the countries where different social systems prevail. Until such a census can be taken, it is, at any rate, rash to assert that the French system is less favourable to domestic happiness than the Anglo-Saxon. At any rate, it acts as a greater incentive to the husband, since it rests with him to keep his wife's admiration and affection by making himself so agreeable to her, and by taking so much trouble to appear at an advantage in the presence of her men friends, that no rival shall supplant him. It would not occur to any Frenchman of the cultivated class to object to his wife's friendship with other men, and the mere fact that he has the influence of other men to compete with is likely to conduce to considerate treatment of his wife, and courteous relations in the household.

It must also be remembered that a man who comes home to a wife who has been talking with intelligent men will probably find her companionship more stimulating than if she has spent all her time with other women. No matter how intelligent women are individually, they tend, collectively, to narrow down their interests, and take a feminine, or even a female, rather than a broadly human view of things. The woman whose mind is attuned to men's minds has a much larger view of the world, and attaches much less importance to trifles, because men, being usually brought by circumstances into closer contact with reality, insensibly communicate their breadth of view to women. A 'man's woman' is never fussy and seldom spiteful, because she breathes too free an air, and is having too good a time.

If, then, being 'grown up' consists in having a larger and more liberal experience of life, in being less concerned with trifles, and less afraid of strong feelings, passions and risks, then the French woman is distinctly more grown up than her American sister; and she is so because she plays a much larger and more interesting part in men's lives.

It may, of course, also be asked whether the fact of playing this part—which implies all the dangers implied by taking the open seas instead of staying in port—whether such a fact is conducive to the eventual welfare of woman and of society. Well—the answer today is: *France!* Look at her as she has stood before the world for the last four years and a half, uncomplaining, undiscouraged, undaunted, holding up the banner of liberty: liberty of speech, liberty of thought, liberty of conscience, all the liberties that we of the western world have been taught to revere as the only things worth living for—look at her, as the world has beheld her since August, 1914, fearless, tearless, indestructible, in face of the most ruthless and formidable enemy the world has ever known, determined to fight on to the end for the principles she has always lived for. Such she is to-day; such are the millions of men who have spent their best years in her trenches, and the millions of brave, uncomplaining, self-denying mothers and wives and sisters who sent them forth smiling, who waited for them patiently and courageously, or who are mourning them silently and unflinchingly, and not one of whom, at the end of the most awful struggle in history, is ever heard to say that the cost has been too great or the trial too bitter to be borne.

No one who has seen Frenchwomen since the war can doubt that their great influence on French life, French thought, French imagination and French sensibility, is one of the strongest elements in the attitude that France holds before the world to-day.

IN MOROCCO*

Harems and Ceremonies

I
THE CROWD IN THE STREET

To occidental travellers the most vivid impression produced by a first contact with the Near East is the surprise of being in a country where the human element increases instead of diminishing the delight of the eye.

After all, then, the intimate harmony between nature and architecture and the human body that is revealed in Greek art was not an artist's counsel of perfection but an honest rendering of reality: there were, there still are, privileged scenes where the fall of a green-grocer's draperies or a milkman's cloak or a beggar's rags are part of the composition, distinctly related to it in line and colour, and where the natural unstudied attitudes of the human body are correspondingly harmonious, however humdrum the acts it is engaged in. The discovery, to the traveller returning from the East, robs the romantic scenes of western

---

* 'Harems and Ceremonies,' Chapter V of *In Morocco*, was published in the *Yale Review*, IX (Oct. 1919).

296

Europe of half their charm: in the Piazza of San Marco, in the market-place of Siena, where at least the robes of the Procurators or the gay tights of Pinturicchio's striplings[1] once justified man's presence among his works, one can see, at first, only the outrage inflicted on beauty by the 'plentiful strutting manikins' of the modern world.

Moroccan crowds are always a feast to the eye. The instinct of skilful drapery, the sense of colour (subdued by custom, but breaking out in subtle glimpses under the universal ashy tints) make the humblest assemblage of donkey-men and water-carriers an ever-renewed delight. But it is only on rare occasions, and in the court ceremonies to which so few foreigners have had access, that the hidden sumptuousness of the native life is revealed. Even then, the term sumptuousness may seem ill-chosen, since the nomadic nature of African life persists in spite of palaces and chamberlains and all the elaborate ritual of the Makhzen, and the most pompous rites are likely to end in a dusty gallop of wild tribesmen, and the most princely processions to tail off in a string of half-naked urchins riding bareback on donkeys.

As in all Oriental countries, the contact between prince and beggar, vizier and serf is disconcertingly free and familiar, and one must see the highest court officials kissing the hem of the Sultan's robe, and hear authentic tales of slaves give by one merchant to another at the end of a convivial evening, to be reminded that nothing is as democratic in appearance as a society of which the whole structure hangs on the whim of one man.

II
AÏD-EL-KEBIR

In the verandah of the Residence of Rabat I stood looking out between posts festooned with gentian-blue ipomeas at the first shimmer of light on black cypresses and white tobacco-flowers, on the scattered roofs of the new town, and the plain stretching away to the Sultan's palace above the sea.

We had been told, late the night before, that the Sultan would allow Madame Lyautey, with the three ladies of her party, to be present at the great religious rite of the Aïd-el-Kebir (the Sacrifice of the Sheep). The honour was an unprecedented one, a favour probably conceded only at the last moment: for as a rule no women are admitted to these ceremonies. It was an opportunity not to be missed; and all through the short stifling night I had lain awake wondering if I should be ready early enough. Presently the motors assembled, and we set out with the French officers in attendance on the Governor's wife.

The Sultan's palace, a large modern building on the familiar Arab lines, lies in a treeless and gardenless waste enclosed by high walls and close above the blue Atlantic. We motored past the gates, where the Sultan's Black Guard was drawn up, and out to the *msalla**, a sort of common adjacent to all the Sultan's residences where public ceremonies are usually performed. The sun was already beating down on the great plain thronged with horse-men and with the native population of Rabat on mule-back and foot. Within an open space in the centre of the crowd a canvas palissade dyed with a bold black pattern surrounded the Sultan's tents. The Black Guard, in scarlet tunics and white and green turbans, were drawn up on the edge of the open space, keeping the spectators at a distance; but under the guidance of our companions we penetrated to the edge of the crowd.

The palissade was open on one side, and within it we could see moving about among the snowy-robed officials a group of men in straight narrow gowns of green, peach-blossom, lilac and pink; they were the Sultan's musicians, whose coloured dresses always flower out conspicuously among the white draperies of all the other court attendants.

---

* The *msalla* is used for the performance of religious ceremonies when the crowd is too great to be contained in the court of the mosque. [Note by E. W]

In the tent nearest the opening, against a background of embroidered hangings, a circle of majestic turbaned old men squatted placidly on Rabat rugs. Presently the circle broke up, there was an agitated coming and going, and some one said: 'The Sultan has gone to the tent at the back of the enclosure to kill the sheep.'

A sense of the impending solemnity ran through the crowd. The mysterious rumour which is the Voice of the Bazaar rose about us like the wind in a palm-oasis; the Black Guard fired a salute from an adjoining hillock; the clouds of red dust flung up by wheeling horsemen thickened and then parted, and a white-robed rider sprang out from the tent of the Sacrifice with something red and dripping across his saddle-bow, and galloped away toward Rabat through the shouting. A little shiver ran over the group of occidental spectators, who knew that the dripping red thing was a sheep with its throat so skilfully slit that, if the omen were favourable, it would live on through the long race to Rabat and gasp out its agonized life on the tiles of the Mosque.

The Sacrifice of the Sheep, one of the four great Moslem rites, is simply the annual propitiatory offering made by every Mahometan head of a family, and by the Sultan as such. It is based not on a Koranic injunction, but on the 'Souna' or record of the

300

Prophet's 'custom' or usages, which forms an authoritative precedent in Moslem ritual. So far goes the Moslem exegesis. In reality, of course, the Moslem blood-sacrifice comes, by way of the Semitic ritual, from far beyond and behind it; and the belief that the Sultan's prosperity for the coming year depends on the animal's protracted agony seems to relate the ceremony to the dark magic so deeply rooted in the mysterious tribes peopling North Africa long ages before the first Phoenician prows had rounded its coast.

Between the Black Guard and the tents, five or six horses were being led up and down by muscular grooms in snowy tunics. They were handsome animals, as Moroccan horses go, and each of a different colour; and on the bay horse was a red saddle embroidered in gold, on the piebald a saddle of peach-colour and silver, on the chestnut, grass-green encrusted with seed-pearls, on the white mare purple housings, and orange velvet on the grey. The Sultan's band had struck up a shrill hammering and twanging, the salute of the Black Guard continued at intervals, and the caparisoned steeds began to rear and snort and drag back from the cruel Arab bits with their exquisite *niello* incrustations. Some one whispered that these were His Majesty's horses—and that it was never known till he appeared which one he would mount.

Presently the crowd about the tents
301

thickened, and when it divided again there emerged from it a grey horse bearing a motionless figure swathed in blinding white. Marching at the horse's bridle, lean brown grooms in white tunics rhythmically waved long strips of white linen to keep off the flies from the Imperial Presence; and beside the motionless rider, in a line with his horse's flank, rode the Imperial Parasol-bearer, who held above the sovereign's head a great sunshade of bright green velvet. Slowly the grey horse advanced a few yards before the tent; behind rode the court dignitaries, followed by the musicians, who looked, in their bright scant caftans, like the slender music-making angels of a Florentine fresco.

The Sultan, pausing beneath his velvet dome, waited to receive the homage of the assembled tribes. An official, riding forward, drew bridle and called out a name. Instantly there came storming across the plain a wild cavalcade of tribesmen, with rifles slung across their shoulders, pistols and cutlasses in their belts, and twists of camel's-hair bound about their turbans. Within a few feet of the Sultan they drew in, their leader uttered a cry and sprang forward, bending to the saddle-bow, and with a great shout the tribe galloped by, each man bowed over his horse's neck as he flew past the hieratic figure on the grey horse.

Again and again this ceremony was

repeated, the Sultan advancing a few feet as each new group thundered toward him. There were more than ten thousand horsemen and chieftains from the Atlas and the wilderness, and as the ceremony continued the dust-clouds grew denser and more fiery-golden, till at last the forward-surging lines showed through them like blurred images in a tarnished mirror.

As the Sultan advanced we followed, abreast of him and facing the oncoming squadrons. The contrast between his motionless figure and the wild waves of cavalry beating against it typified the strange soul of Islam, with its impetuosity forever culminating in impassiveness. The sun hung high, a brazen ball in a white sky, darting down metallic shafts on the dust-enveloped plain and the serene white figure under its umbrella. The fat man with a soft round beard-fringed face, wrapped in spirals of pure white, one plump hand on his embroidered bridle, his yellow-slippered feet thrust heel-down in big velvet-lined stirrups, became, through sheer immobility, a symbol, a mystery, a God. The human flux beat against him, dissolved, ebbed away, another spear-crested wave swept up behind it and dissolved in turn; and he sat on, hour after hour, under the white-hot sky, unconscious of the heat, the dust, the tumult, embodying to the wild factious precipitate hordes a long tradition of serene aloofness.

303

III
The Imperial Mirador

As the last riders galloped up to do homage we were summoned to our motors and driven rapidly to the palace. The Sultan had sent word to Mme. Lyautey that the ladies of the Imperial harem would entertain her and her guests while his Majesty received the Resident General, and we had to hasten back in order not to miss the next act of the spectacle.

We walked across a long court lined with the Black Guard, passed under a gateway, and were met by a shabbily dressed negress. Traversing a hot dazzle of polychrome tiles we reached another archway guarded by the chief eunuch, a towering black with the enamelled eyes of a basalt bust. The eunuch delivered us to other negresses, and we entered a labyrinth of inner passages and patios, all murmuring and dripping with water. Passing down long corridors where slaves in dim greyish garments flattened themselves against the walls, we caught glimpses of great dark rooms, laundries, pantries, bakeries, kitchens, where savoury things were brewing and stewing, and where more negresses, abandoning their pots and pans, came to peep at us from the threshold. In one corner, on a bench against a wall hung with matting, grey parrots in tall cages were being fed by a slave.

A narrow staircase mounted to a landing where a princess out of an Arab fairy-tale awaited us. Stepping softly on her embroidered slippers she led us to the next landing, where another golden-slippered being smiled out on us, little girl this one, blushing and dimpling under a jewelled diadem and pearl-woven braids. On a third landing a third damsel appeared, and encircled by the three graces we mounted to the tall *mirador* in the central tower from which we were to look down at the coming ceremony. One by one, our little guides, kicking off their golden shoes, which a slave laid neatly outside the door, led us on soft bare feet into the upper chamber of the harem.

It was a large room, enclosed on all sides by a balcony glazed with panes of brightly-coloured glass. On a gaudy modern Rabat carpet stood gilt armchairs of florid design and a table bearing a commercial bronze of the 'art goods' variety. Divans with muslin-covered cushions were ranged against the walls and down an adjoining gallery-like apartment which was otherwise furnished only with clocks. The passion for clocks and other mechanical contrivances is common to all unmechanical races, and every chief's palace in North Africa contains a collection of time-pieces which might be called striking if so many had not ceased to go. But those in the Sultan's harem of Rabat are remarkable for the fact that, while designed on current European models, they are proportioned in size to the Imperial dignity, so that a Dutch 'grandfather' becomes a wardrobe, and the box-clock of the European mantel-piece a cupboard that has to be set on the floor. At the end of this avenue of time-pieces a European double-bed with a bright silk quilt covered with Nottingham lace stood majestically on a carpeted platform.

But for the enchanting glimpses of sea and plain through the lattices of the gallery, the apartment of the Sultan's ladies falls far short of occidental ideas of elegance. But there was hardly time to think of this, for the door of the *mirador* was always opening to let in another fairy-tale figure, till at last we were surrounded by a dozen houris, laughing, babbling, taking us by the hand, and putting shy questions while they looked at us with caressing eyes. They were all (our interpretess whispered) the Sultan's 'favourites,' round-faced apricot-tinted girls in their teens, with high cheek-bones, full red lips, surprised brown eyes between curved-up Asiatic lids, and little brown hands fluttering out like birds from their brocaded sleeves.

In honour of the ceremony, and of Mme. Lyautey's visit, they had put on their finest clothes, and their freedom of movement was somewhat hampered by their narrow sumptuous gowns, with over-draperies of gold and silver brocade and pale rosy gauze held in by corset-like sashes of gold tissue of Fez, and the heavy silken cords that looped their voluminous sleeves. Above their foreheads the hair was shaven like that of an Italian fourteenth-century beauty, and only a black line as narrow as a pencilled eyebrow showed through the twist of gauze fastened by a jewelled clasp above the real eye-brows. Over the forehead-jewel rose the complicated structure of the headdress. Ropes of black wool were plaited through the hair, forming, at the back, a double loop that stood out above the nape like the twin handles of a vase, the upper veiled in airy shot gauzes and fastened with jewelled bands and ornaments. On each side of the red cheeks other braids were looped over the ears hung with broad earrings of filigree set with rough pearls and emeralds, or gold hoops and pendants of coral; and an unexpected tulle ruff, like that of a Watteau shepherdess, framed the round chin above a torrent of necklaces, necklaces of amber, coral, baroque pearls, hung with mysterious barbaric amulets and fetiches. At the young things moved about us on soft hennaed feet the light played on shifting gleams of gold and silver, blue and violet and apple-green, all harmonized and bemisted by clouds of pink and sky-blue; and through the changing group capered a little black picaninny in a caftan of silver-shot purple with a sash of raspberry red.

But presently there was a flutter in the aviary. A fresh pair of *babouches* clicked on the landing, and a young girl, less brilliantly dressed and less brilliant of face than the others, came in on bare painted feet. Her movements were shy and hesitating, her large lips pale, her eye-brows less vividly dark, her head less jewelled. But all the little humming-birds gathered about her with respectful rustlings as she advanced toward us leaning on one of the young girls, and holding out her ringed hand to Mme. Lyautey's curtsy. It was the young Princess, the Sultan's legitimate daughter. She examined us with sad eyes, spoke a few compliments through the interpretess, and seated herself in silence, letting the others sparkle and chatter.

Conversation with the shy Princess was flagging when one of the favourites beckoned us to the balcony. We were told we might push open the painted panes a few inches, but as we did so the butterfly group drew back lest they should be seen looking out on the forbidden world.

Salutes were crashing out again from the direction of the *msalla*: puffs of smoke floated over the slopes like thistle-down. Farther off, a pall of red vapour veiled the gallop of the last horsemen wheeling away toward Rabat. The vapour subsided, and moving out of it we discerned a slow procession. First rode a detachment of the Black Guard, mounted on black horses, and, comically fierce in their British scarlet and Meccan green, a uniform invented at the beginning of the nineteenth century by a retired English army officer. After the Guard came the standard-bearers and the great dignitaries, then the Sultan, still aloof, immovable, as if rapt in the contemplation of his mystic office. More court officials followed, then the bright-gowned musicians on foot, then a confused irrepressible crowd of pilgrims, beggars, saints, mountebanks, and the other small folk of the Bazaar, ending in a line of boys jamming their naked heels into the ribs of world-weary donkeys.

The Sultan rode into the court below us, and Vizier and chamberlains, snowy-white against the scarlet line of the Guards, hurried forward to kiss his draperies, his shoes, his stirrup. Descending from his velvet saddle, still entranced, he paced across the tiles between a double line of white servitors bowing to the ground. White pigeons circled over him like petals loosed from a great orchard, and he disappeared with his retinue under the shadowy arcade of the audience chamber at the back of the court.

At this point one of the favourites called us in from the *mirador*. The door had just opened to admit an elderly woman preceded by a respectful group of girls. From the newcomer's round ruddy face, her short round body, the round hands emerging from her round wrists, an inexplicable majesty emanated; and though she too was less richly arrayed than the favourites she carried her headdress of striped gauze like a crown.

This impressive old lady was the Sultan's mother. As she held out her plump wrinkled hand to Mme. Lyautey and spoke a few words through the interpretess one felt that at last a painted window of the *mirador* had been broken, and a thought let into the vacuum of the harem. What thought, it would have taken deep insight into the processes of the Arab mind to discover; but its honesty was manifest in the old Empress's voice and smile. Here at last was a woman beyond the trivial dissimulations, the childish cunning, the idle cruelties of the harem. It was not a surprise to be told that she was her son's most trusted adviser, and the chief authority in the palace. If such a woman deceived and intrigued it would be for great purposes and for ends she believed in: the depth of her soul had air and daylight in it, and she would never willingly shut them out.

The Empress Mother chatted for a while with Mme. Lyautey, asking about the Resident General's health, enquiring for news of the war, and saying, with an emotion perceptible even through the unintelligible words: 'All is well with Morocco as long as all is well with France.' Then she withdrew, and we were summoned again to the *mirador*.

This time it was to see a company of officers in brilliant uniforms advancing at a trot across the plain from Rabat. At sight of the figure that headed them, so slim, erect and young on his splendid chestnut, with a pale blue tunic barred

310

by the wide orange ribbon of the Cherifian Order,[2] salutes pealed forth again from the slope above the palace and the Black Guard presented arms. A moment later General Lyautey and his staff were riding in at the gates below us. On the threshold of the inner court they dismounted, and moving to the other side of our balcony we followed the next stage of the ceremony. The Sultan was still seated in the audience chamber. The court officials still stood drawn up in a snow-white line against the snow-white walls. The great dignitaries advanced across the tiles to greet the General; then they fell aside, and he went forward alone, followed at a little distance by his staff. A third of the way across the court he paused, in accordance with the Moroccan court ceremonial, and bowed in the direction of the arcaded room; a few steps farther he bowed again, and a third time on the threshold of the room. Then French uniforms and Moroccan draperies closed in about him, and all vanished into the shadows of the audience hall.

Our audience too seemed to be over. We had exhausted the limited small talk of the harem, had learned from the young beauties that, though they were forbidden to look on at the ceremony, the dancers and singers would come to entertain them presently, and had begun to take leave when a negress hurried in to say that his Majesty begged Mme. Lyautey and her friends to await his arrival. This was the crowning incident of our visit, and I wondered with what Byzantine ritual the Anointed One fresh from the exercise of his priestly functions would be received among his women.

The door opened, and without any announcement or other preliminary flourish a fat man with a pleasant face, his djellabah stretched over a portly front, walked in holding a little boy by the hand. Such was his Majesty the Sultan Moulay Youssef, despoiled of sacramental burnouses and turban, and shuffling along on bare yellow-slippered feet with the gait of a stout elderly gentleman who has taken off his boots in the passage preparatory to a domestic evening.

The little Prince, one of his two legitimate sons, was dressed with equal simplicity, for silken garments are worn in Morocco only by musicians, boy-dancers and other hermaphrodite fry. With his ceremonial raiment the Sultan had put off his air of superhuman majesty, and the expression of his round pale face corresponded with the plainness of his dress. The favourites fluttered about him, respectful but by no means awestruck, and the youngest began to play with the little Prince. We could well believe the report that his was the happiest harem in Morocco, as well as the only one into which a breath of the outer world ever came.

Moulay Youssef greeted Mme. Lyautey with friendly simplicity, made the proper speeches to her companions, and then, with the air of the business-man who has forgotten to give an order before leaving his office, he walked up to a corner of the room, and while the flower-maidens ruffled about him, and through the windows we saw the last participants in the mystic rites galloping away toward the crenellated walls of Rabat, his Majesty the Priest and Emperor of the Faithful unhooked a small instrument from the wall and applied his sacred lips to the telephone.

IV
IN OLD RABAT

Before General Lyautey came to Morocco Rabat had been subjected to the indignity of European 'improvements', and one must traverse boulevards scored with tram-lines, and pass between hotel-terraces and cafés and cinema-palaces, to reach the surviving nucleus of the once beautiful native town. Then, at the turn of a commonplace street, one comes upon it suddenly. The shops and cafés cease, the jingle of trams and the trumpeting of motor-horns die out, and here, all at once, are silence and solitude, and the dignified reticence of the windowless Arab house-fronts.

We were bound for the house of a high government official, a Moroccan dignitary of the old school, who had invited us to tea, and added a message to the effect that the ladies of

313

his household would be happy to receive me.

The house we sought was some distance down the quietest of white-walled streets. Our companion knocked at a low green door, and we were admitted to a passage into which a wooden stairway descended: A brother-in-law of our host was waiting for us: in his wake we mounted the ladder-like stairs and entered a long room with a florid French carpet and a set of gilt furniture to match. There were no fretted walls, no painted cedar doors, no fountains rustling in unseen courts: the house was squeezed in between others, and such traces of old ornament as it may have possessed had vanished.

But presently we saw why its inhabitants were indifferent to such details. Our host, a handsome white-bearded old man, welcomed us in the doorway; then he led us to a raised oriel window at one end of the room, and seated us in the gilt armchairs face to face with one of the most beautiful views in Morocco.

Below us lay the white and blue terrace-roofs of the native town, with palms and minarets shooting up between them, or the shadows of a vine-trellis patterning a quiet lane. Beyond, the Atlantic sparkled, breaking into foam at the mouth of the Bou-Regreg and under the towering ramparts of the Kasbah of the Oudayas. To the right, the ruins of the great Mosque rose from their plateau over the river; and, on the farther side of the troubled flood, old Salé, white and wicked, lay like a jewel in its gardens. With such a scene beneath their eyes, the inhabitants of the house could hardly feel its lack of architectural interest.

After exchanging the usual compliments, and giving us time to enjoy the view, our host withdrew, taking with him the men of our party. A moment later he reappeared with a rosy fair-haired girl, dressed in Arab costume, but evidently of European birth. The brother-in-law explained that this young woman, who had 'studied in Algeria,' and whose mother was French, was the intimate friend of the ladies of the household, and would act as interpreter. Our host then again left us, joining the men visitors in another room, and the door opened to admit his wife and daughters-in-law.

The mistress of the house was a handsome Algerian with sad expressive eyes: the younger women were pale, fat and amiable. They all wore sober dresses, in keeping with the simplicity of the house, and but for the vacuity of their faces the group might have been that of a Professor's family in an English or American University town, decently costumed for an Arabian Nights' pageant in the college grounds. I was never more vividly reminded of the fact that human nature, from one pole to the other, falls naturally into certain categories, and that Respectability wears the same face in an oriental harem as in England or America.

My hostesses received me with the utmost amiability, we seated ourselves in the oriel facing the view, and the interchange of questions and compliments began.

Had I any children? (They asked it all at once.)

Alas, no.

'In Islam' (one of the ladies ventured) 'a woman without children is considered the most unhappy being in the world.'

I replied that in the western world also childless women were pitied. (The brother-in-law smiled incredulously.)

Knowing that European fashions are of absorbing interest to the harem I next enquired: 'What do these ladies think of our stiff tailor-dresses? Don't they find them excessively ugly?'

'Yes, they do;' (it was again the brother-in-law who replied.) 'But they suppose that in your own homes you dress less badly.'

'And have they never any desire to travel, or to visit the Bazaars, as the Turkish ladies do?'

'No, indeed. They are too busy to give such matters a thought. In *our country* women of the highest class occupy themselves with their household and their children, and the rest of their time is devoted to needlework.' (At this statement I gave the brother-in-law a smile as incredulous as his own.)

All this time the fair-haired interpretess had not been allowed by the vigilant guardian of the harem to utter a word.

I turned to her with a question.

'So your mother is French, *Mademoiselle*?'

'*Oui, Madame.*'

'From what part of France did she come?'

A bewildered pause. Finally: 'I don't know ... from Switzerland, I think,' brought out this shining example of the Higher Education. In spite of Algerian 'advantages' the poor girl could speak only a few words of her mother's tongue. She had kept the European features and complexion, but her soul was the soul of Islam. The harem had placed its powerful imprint upon her, and she looked at me with the same remote and passive eyes as the daughters of the house.

After struggling for a while longer with a conversation which the watchful brother-in-law continued to direct as he pleased, I felt my own lips stiffening into the resigned smile of the harem, and it was a relief when at last their guardian drove the pale flock away, and the handsome old gentleman who owned them reappeared on the scene, bringing back my friends, and followed by slaves and tea.

V
IN FEZ

What thoughts, what speculations, one wonders, go on under the narrow veiled brows of the little creatures destined to the high honour of marriage or concubinage in Moroccan palaces?

Some are brought down from mountains and cedar forests, from the free life of the tents where the nomad women go unveiled. Others come from harems in the turreted cities beyond the Atlas, where blue palm-groves beat all night against the stars and date-caravans journey across the desert from Timbuctoo. Some, born and bred in an airy palace among pomegranate gardens and white terraces, pass thence to one of the feudal fortresses near the snows, where for half the year the great chiefs of the south live in their clan, among fighting men and falconers and packs of *sloughis*. And still others grow up in a stifling Mellah, trip unveiled on its blue terraces overlooking the gardens of the great, and, seen one day at sunset by a fat vizier or his pale young master, are acquired for a handsome sum and transferred to the painted sepulchre of the harem.

Worst of all must be the fate of those who go from tents and cedar forests, or from some sea-blown garden above Rabat, into one of the houses of Old Fez. They are well-nigh impenetrable, these palaces of Elbali: the Fazi dignitaries do not welcome the visits of strange women. On the rare occasions when they are received, a member of the family (one of the sons, or a brother-in-law who has 'studied in Algeria') usually acts as interpreter; and

318

perhaps it is as well that no one from the outer world should come to remind these listless creatures that somewhere the gulls dance on the Atlantic and the wind murmurs through olive-yards and clatters the metallic fronds of palm-groves.

We had been invited, one day, to visit the harem of one of the chief dignitaries of the Makhzen at Fez, and these thoughts came to me as I sat among the pale women in their mouldering prison. The descent through the steep tunnelled streets gave one the sense of being lowered into the shaft of a mine. At each step the strip of sky grew narrower, and was more often obscured by the low vaulted passages into which we plunged. The noises of the Bazaar had died out, and only the sound of fountains behind garden walls and the clatter of our mules' hoofs on the stones went with us. Then fountains and gardens ceased also, the towering masonry closed in, and we entered an almost subterranean labyrinth which sun and air never reach. At length our mules turned into a *cul-de-sac* blocked by a high building. On the right was another building, one of those blind mysterious house-fronts of Fez that seem like a fragment of its ancient fortifications. Clients and servants lounged on the stone benches built into the wall; it was evidently the house of an important person. A charming youth with intelligent eyes waited on the threshold to receive us: he was one of the sons

319

of the house, the one who had 'studied in Algeria' and knew how to talk to visitors. We followed him into a small arcaded *patio* hemmed in by the high walls of the house. On the right was the usual long room with archways giving on the court. Our host, a patriarchal personage, draped in fat as in a toga, came toward us, a mountain of majestic muslins, his eyes sparkling in a swarthy silver-bearded face. He seated us on divans and lowered his voluminous person to a heap of cushions on the step leading into the court; and the son who had studied in Algeria instructed a negress to prepare the tea.

Across the *patio* was another arcade closely hung with unbleached cotton. From behind it came the sound of chatter, and now and then a bare brown child in a scant shirt would escape, and be hurriedly pulled back with soft explosions of laughter, while a black woman came out to readjust the curtains.

There were three of these negresses, splendid bronze creatures, wearing white djellabahs over bright-coloured caftans, striped scarves knotted about their large hips, and gauze turbans on their crinkled hair. Their wrists clinked with heavy silver bracelets, and big circular earrings danced in their purple ear-lobes. A languor lay on all the other inmates of the household, on the servants and hangers-on squatting in the shade under the arcade, on our monumental host and his smiling son; but the three negresses, vibrating with activity, rushed continually from the curtained chamber to the kitchen, and from the kitchen to the master's reception-room, bearing on their pinky-blue palms trays of Britannia metal with tall glasses and fresh bunches of mint, shouting orders to dozing menials, and calling to each other from opposite ends of the court; and finally the stoutest of the three, disappearing from view, reappeared suddenly on a pale green balcony overhead, where, profiled against a square of blue sky, she leaned over in a Veronese attitude and screamed down to the others like an excited parrot.

In spite of their febrile activity and tropical bird-shrieks, we waited in vain for tea; and after a while our host suggested to his son that I might like to visit the ladies of the household. As I had expected, the young man led me across the *patio*, lifted the cotton hanging and introduced me into an apartment exactly like the one we had just left. Divans covered with striped mattress-ticking stood against the white walls, and on them sat seven or eight passive-looking women over whom a number of pale children scrambled.

The eldest of the group, and evidently the mistress of the house, was an Algerian lady, probably of about fifty, with a sad and delicately-modelled face; the others were daughters, daughters-in-law and concubines. The latter word evokes to occidental ears images of sensual seduction which the Moroccan harem seldom realizes. All the ladies of this dignified official household wore the same look of somewhat melancholy respectability. In their stuffy curtained apartment they were like cellar-grown flowers, pale, heavy, fuller but frailer than the garden sort. Their dresses, rich but sober, the veils and diadems put on in honour of my visit, had a dignified dowdiness in odd contrast to the frivolity of the Imperial harem. But what chiefly struck me was the apathy of the younger women. I asked them if they had a garden, and they shook their heads wistfully, saying that there were no gardens in Old Fez. The roof was therefore their only escape: a roof overlooking acres and acres of other roofs, and closed in by the naked fortified mountains which stand about Fez like prison-walls.

After a brief exchange of compliments silence fell. Conversing through interpreters is a benumbing process, and there are few points of contact between the open-air occidental mind and beings imprisoned in a conception of sexual and domestic life based on slave-service and incessant espionage. These languid women on their muslin cushions toil not, neither do they spin. The Moroccan lady knows little of cooking, needlework or any household arts. When her child is ill she can only hang it with amulets and wail over it; the great lady of the Fazi palace is as ignorant of hygiene as the peasant-woman of the *bled*. And all these colourless eventless lives depend on the favour of one fat tyrannical man, bloated with good living and authority, himself almost as inert and sedentary as his women, and accustomed to impose his whims on them ever since he ran about the same *patio* as a little short-smocked boy.

The redeeming point in this stagnant domesticity is the tenderness of the parents for their children, and western writers have laid so much stress on this that one would suppose children could be loved only by inert and ignorant parents. It is in fact charming to see the heavy eyes of the Moroccan father light up when a brown grass-hopper baby jumps on his knee, and the unfeigned tenderness with which the childless women of the harem caress the babies of their happier rivals. But the sentimentalist moved by this display of family feeling would do well to consider the lives of these much-petted children. Ignorance, unhealthiness and a precocious sexual initiation prevail in all classes. Education consists in learning by heart endless passages of the Koran, and amusement in assisting at spectacles that would be unintelligible to western children, but that the pleasantries of the harem make perfectly comprehensible to Moroccan infancy. At eight or nine the little girls are married, at twelve the son of the house is 'given his first negress'; and thereafter, in the rich and leisured class, both sexes live till old age in an atmosphere of sensuality without seduction.

The young son of the house led me back across the court, where the negresses were still shrieking and scurrying, and passing to and fro like a stage-procession with the vain paraphernalia of a tea that never came. Our host still smiled from his cushions, resigned to Oriental delays. To distract the impatient westerners, a servant unhooked from the wall the cage of a gently-cooing dove. It was brought to us, still cooing, and looked at me with the same resigned and vacant eyes as the ladies I had just left. As it was being restored to its hook the slaves lolling about the entrance scattered respectfully at the approach of a handsome man of about thirty, with delicate features and a black beard. Crossing the court, he stooped to kiss the shoulder of our host, who introduced him as his eldest son, the husband of one or two of the little pale wives with whom I had been exchanging platitudes.

From the increasing agitation of the negresses it became evident that the ceremony of tea-making had been postponed till his arrival. A metal tray bearing a Britannia samovar and tea-pot was placed on the tiles of the court, and squatting beside it the newcomer gravely proceeded to infuse the mint. Suddenly the cotton hangings fluttered again, and a tiny child in the scantest of smocks rushed out and scampered across the court. Our venerable host, stretching out rapturous arms, caught the fugitive to his bosom, where the little boy lay like a squirrel, watching us with great sidelong eyes. He was the last-born of the patriarch, and the youngest brother of the majestic bearded gentleman engaged in tea-making. While he was still in his father's arms two more sons appeared: charming almond-eyed schoolboys returning from their Koran-class, escorted by their slaves. All the sons greeted each other affectionately, and caressed with almost feminine tenderness the dancing baby so lately added to their ranks; and finally, to crown this scene of domestic intimacy, the three negresses, their gigantic effort at last accomplished, passed about glasses of steaming mint and trays of gazelles' horns and white sugar-cakes.

VI
IN MARRAKECH

The farther one travels from the Mediterranean and Europe the closer the curtains of the women's quarters are drawn. The only harem in which we were allowed an interpreter was that of the Sultan himself; in the private harems of Fez and Rabat a French-speaking relative transmitted (or professed to transmit) our remarks; in Marrakech, the great nobleman and dignitary who kindly invited me to visit his household was deaf to our hint that

325

the presence of a lady from one of the French government schools might facilitate our intercourse.

When we drove up to his palace, one of the stateliest in Marrakech, the street was thronged with clansmen and clients. Dignified merchants in white muslin, whose grooms held white mules saddled with rose-coloured velvet, warriors from the Atlas wearing the corkscrew ringlets which are a sign of military prowess, Jewish traders in black gabardines, leather-gaitered peasant-women with chickens and cheese, and beggars rolling their blind eyes or exposing their fly-plastered sores, were gathered in Oriental promiscuity about the great man's door; while under the archway stood a group of youths and warlike-looking older men who were evidently of his own clan.

The Caïd's chamberlain, a middle-aged man of dignified appearance, advanced to meet us between bowing clients and tradesmen. He led us through cool passages lined with the intricate mosaic-work of Fez, past beggars who sat on stone benches whining out their blessings, and pale Fazi craftsmen laying a floor of delicate tiles. The Caïd is a lover of old Arab architecture. His splendid house, which is not yet finished, has been planned and decorated on the lines of the old Imperial palaces, and when a few years of sun and rain and Oriental neglect have worked their way on its cedarwood and gilding and ivory stucco it will have the same faded loveliness as the fairy palaces of Fez.

In a garden where fountains splashed and roses climbed among cypresses, the Caïd himself awaited us. This great fighter and loyal friend of France is a magnificent eagle-beaked man, brown, lean and sinewy, with vigilant eyes looking out under his carefully draped muslin turban, and negroid lips half-hidden by a close black beard.

Tea was prepared in the familiar setting; a long arcaded room with painted ceiling and richly stuccoed walls. All around were ranged the usual mattresses covered with striped ticking and piled with muslin cushions. A bedstead of brass, imitating a Louis XVI cane bed, and adorned with brass garlands and bows, throned on the usual platform; and the only other ornaments were a few clocks and bunches of wax flowers under glass. Like all Orientals, this hero of the Atlas, who spends half his life with his fighting clansmen in a mediæval stronghold among the snows, and the other half rolling in a 60 h.p. motor over smooth French roads, seems unaware of any degrees of beauty or appropriateness in objects of European design, and places against the exquisite mosaics and traceries of his Fazi craftsmen the tawdriest bric-a-brac of the cheap department-store.

While tea was being served I noticed a tiny negress, not more than six or seven years old,

327

who stood motionless in the embrasure of an archway. Like most of the Moroccan slaves, even in the greatest households, she was shabbily, almost raggedly, dressed. A dirty *gandourah* of striped muslin covered her faded caftan, and a cheap kerchief was wound above her grave and precocious little face. With preternatural vigilance she watched each movement of the Caïd, who never spoke to her, looked at her, or made her the slightest perceptible sign, but whose least wish she instantly divined, refilling his tea-cup, passing the plates of sweets, or removing our empty glasses, in obedience to some secret telegraphy on which her whole being hung.

The Caïd is a great man. He and his famous elder brother, holding the southern marches of Morocco against alien enemies and internal rebellion, played a preponderant part in the defence of the French colonies in North Africa during the long struggle of the war. Enlightened, cultivated, a friend of the arts, a scholar and diplomatist, he seems, unlike many Orientals, to have selected the best in assimilating European influences. Yet when I looked at the tiny creature watching him with those anxious joyless eyes I felt once more the abyss that slavery and the seraglio put between the most Europeanized Mahometan and the western conception of life. The Caïd's little black slaves are well-known in Morocco, and behind the sad child leaning in the archway stood all the shadowy evils of the social system that hangs like a millstone about the neck of Islam.

Presently a handsome tattered negress came across the garden to invite me to the harem. Captain de S. and his wife, who had accompanied me, were old friends of the Chief's, and it was owing to this that the jealously-guarded doors of the women's quarters were opened to Mme de S. and myself. We followed the negress to a marble-paved court where pigeons fluttered and strutted about the central fountain. From under a trellised arcade hung with linen curtains several ladies came forward. They greeted my companion with exclamations of delight; then they led us into the usual commonplace room with divans and whitewashed walls. Even in the most sumptuous Moroccan palaces little care seems to be expended on the fittings of the women's quarters: unless, indeed, the room in which visitors are received corresponds with a boarding-school 'parlour,' and the personal touch is reserved for the private apartments.

The ladies who greeted us were more richly dressed than any I had seen except the Sultan's favourites; but their faces were more distinguished, more European in outline, than those of the round-cheeked beauties of Rabat. My companions had told me that the Caïd's harem was recruited from Georgia, and that the ladies receiving us had been brought up in the relative freedom of life in Constantinople; and it was easy to read in their wistfully smiling eyes memories of a life unknown to the passive daughters of Morocco.

They appeared to make no secret of their regrets, for presently one of them, with a smile, called my attention to some faded photographs hanging over the divan. They represented groups of plump provincial-looking young women in dowdy European ball-dresses; and it required an effort of the imagination to believe that the lovely creatures in velvet caftans, with delicately tattooed temples under complicated head-dresses, and hennaed feet crossed on muslin cushions, were the same as the beaming frumps in the photographs. But to the sumptuously-clad exiles these faded photographs and ugly dresses represented freedom, happiness, and all they had forfeited when fate (probably in the shape of an opulent Hebrew couple 'travelling with their daughters') carried them from the Bosphorus to the Atlas.

As in the other harems I had visited, perfect equality seemed to prevail between the ladies, and while they chatted with Mme de S. whose few words of Arabic had loosed their tongues, I tried to guess which was the favourite, or at least the first in rank. My choice wavered between the pretty pale creature with a *ferronnière* across her temples and a tea-rose caftan veiled in blue gauze, and the nut-brown beauty in red velvet hung with pearls whose languid attitudes and long-lidded eyes were so like the Keepsake portraits of Byron's Haïdee.[3] Or was it perhaps the third, less pretty but more vivid and animated, who sat behind the tea-tray, and mimicked so expressively a soldier shouldering his rifle, and another falling dead, in her effort to ask us, 'when the dreadful war would be over'? Perhaps ... unless, indeed, it were the handsome octoroon, slightly older than the others, but even more richly dressed, so free and noble in her movements, and treated by the others with such friendly deference.

I was struck by the fact that among them all there was not a child; it was the first harem without babies that I had seen in that prolific land. Presently one of the ladies asked Mme. de S. about her children; in reply, she enquired for the Caïd's little boy, the son of his wife who had died. The ladies' faces lit up wistfully, a slave was given an order, and presently a large-eyed ghost of a child was brought into the room.

Instantly all the bracelet-laden arms were held out to the dead woman's son; and as I watched the weak little body hung with amulets and the heavy head covered with thin curls pressed against a brocaded bosom, I was reminded of one of the coral-hung child-Christs of Crivelli, standing livid and waxen on the knee of a splendidly dressed Madonna.

The poor baby on whom such hopes and ambitions hung stared at us with a solemn unamused gaze. Would all his pretty mothers, his eyes seemed to ask, succeed in bringing him to maturity in spite of the parched summers of the south and the stifling existence of the harem? It was evident that no precaution had been neglected to protect him from maleficent influences and the danger that walks by night, for his frail neck and wrists were hung with innumerable charms: Koranic verses, Soudanese incantations, and images of forgotten idols in amber and coral and horn and ambergris. Perhaps they will ward off the powers of evil and let him grow up to shoulder the burden of the great Caïds of the south.

REFERENCES

1 Pinturicchio, or Bernadino di Betto (*c.* 1454–1513), of Perugia, painted frescoes from the life of Pope Pius II in the library of the Siena Cathedral as well as frescoes in the Palazzo Petrucci, Siena.
2 'Cherifian' is an Arab title deriving from the Shareefian Dynasty.
3 In Byron's *Don Juan*, Juan is found by Haidée, a beautiful Greek girl, after he is cast ashore on one of the Cyclades.

We hope you have enjoyed this Large Print book. Other Chivers Press or Thorndike Press Large Print books are available at your library or directly from the publishers. For more information about current and forthcoming titles, please call or write, without obligation, to:

Chivers Press Limited
Windsor Bridge Road
Bath BA2 3AX
England
Tel. (01225) 335336

OR

Thorndike Press
P.O. Box 159
Thorndike, Maine 04986
USA
Tel. (800) 223–2336

All our Large Print titles are designed for easy reading, and all our books are made to last.